HIGH
STAKES

GARY PROVOST 1944-

HIGH

STAKES

Inside the New Las Vegas

T·T
TRUMAN TALLEY BOOKS/DUTTON
NEW YORK

TRUMAN TALLEY BOOKS/DUTTON

Published by the Penguin Group
Penguin Books USA Inc., 375 Hudson Street, New York, New York 10014, U.S.A.
Penguin Books Ltd, 27 Wrights Lane, London W8 5TZ, England
Penguin Books Australia Ltd, Ringwood, Victoria, Australia
Penguin Books Canada Ltd, 10 Alcorn Avenue, Toronto, Ontario, Canada M4V 3B2
Penguin Books (N.Z.) Ltd, 182–190 Wairau Road, Auckland 10, New Zealand

Penguin Books Ltd, Registered Offices:
Harmondsworth, Middlesex, England

First published by Truman Talley Books/Dutton, an imprint of Dutton Signet,
a division of Penguin Books USA Inc.
Distributed in Canada by McClelland & Stewart Inc.

First Printing, April, 1994
1   3   5   7   9   10   8   6   4   2

Copyright © Gary Provost, 1994
All rights reserved

 REGISTERED TRADEMARK—MARCA REGISTRADA

LIBRARY OF CONGRESS CATALOGING IN PUBLICATION DATA:
Provost, Gary. 1944–
High stakes : inside the new Las Vegas / Gary Provost.
p.   cm.
ISBN 0-525-93650-5
1. Circus Circus Enterprises.   2. Casinos—Nevada—Las Vegas—Case
studies.   3. Gambling—Nevada—Las Vegas. I. Title.
HV6721.L3P76 1994
338.4'7795'09793135—dc20   93–24040
CIP

Printed in the United States of America
Set in Times New Roman

Designed by Steven N. Stathakis

ALL THE WORLD IS CONFUSED, SAVE FOR ME AND FRANK STRUNK,
AND SOMETIMES I WONDER ABOUT STRUNK.

BUT I DEDICATE THIS BOOK TO HIM, ANYHOW.

Contents

HIGH
STAKES

Introduction: The Scrivener

In the spring of 1990 my friend Frank Strunk took me to Las Vegas. He lured me into a casino, my first time, his zillionth, and introduced me to the fine points of blackjack and craps. Even before my second $100 bill had been poked down into the darkness of the drop box under crap table number five at the Flamingo Hilton, I knew that I had found the missing piece in my life. I already had a fine career and a world-class wife, but I had no compelling hobby. Now I had found casino gambling, and the world suddenly was a better place.

Casino gambling is not a hobby I can recommend to everyone. It has, after all, ruined lives. But for me it is, like eating Quaker Oats, the right thing to do. Craps, blackjack, roulette, and slot machines create for me the same dramatic excitement that I get from watching a good film, reading a detective novel, or watching the Boston Celtics clobber the Detroit Pistons. But with an important difference: I can play in the game, I can act in the drama. And equally important, casino gambling screens out what Marilyn French has called "the shit and stringbeans of life." For me a casino is the ultimate escape from deadline worries, tax bills, leaky faucets, Madonna, telemarketers, junk mail, and treacherous politicians.

Why am I telling you this?

Because while legions of scandalmongers have slipped Las Vegas under the tarnished lenses of their microscopes in order to write stories of bankrupt lives, depraved hookers, Mafia-owned entertainers, and high-strung gangsters lurking in the shadows of that well-lighted town, I'm obliged to admit that I bring to this story a very different bias: I like Las Vegas. I like the flip of the card, the roll of the dice. I like the sound of guys shouting "Yo" at the crap table and the way young women shriek for joy when they drain 100 silver dollars out of a slot machine. I like catching three of a kind at a poker table. I like every one of those colored bulbs that glitter like cheap jewelry up and down Las Vegas Boulevard, and I like pretty cocktail waitresses in skimpy outfits. What's not to like? And I like the people who run Las Vegas, many of whom don't even own a handgun, never mind a submachine gun.

So the author likes casinos. I'm surely not going to write a book about something I hate, like, for example, the cauliflower industry. But it does raise suspicions. Who is this guy, you might ask, some shill for the gaming industry?

Let's be clear. It's okay for me to like casinos in general, but it would not be okay if I had a bias toward my specific subject, which, in this case, is Circus Circus Enterprises, Inc. Las Vegas is the capital of puffery, and I certainly don't want to add to the mountains of marshmallow fluff that are written daily by paid public relations people.

On the other hand, I didn't pick Circus Circus because I knew of some great scandal in the executive suite, or because its corporate story was filled with conflict and turbulence. I picked it because there's no sense in writing a book about a company that is second best or third best when the best is made available to you. If I had been lucky enough to uncover something shameful in this public corporation I'd have been delighted to write it. But it didn't work out that way, and for the most part this is a pretty complimentary look at the company, though I can tell you right now that it does have a shocking ending, which occurred after I wrote the book, and which I have noted in the Epilogue.

In any case, you have a right to know just what arrangements I've made with Circus Circus. Why did the company give me such free access to its properties and its people? Did the executives offer to pay me? Did they threaten to shoot me? We'll get to all of that soon.

Having discovered casino gambling, and being a writer, I naturally wanted to write a book about Las Vegas. The wisdom of such a career move could not be more obvious. "Look, honey," I could say to my wife, Gail, "this trip to Las Vegas is not for gambling. It's for research, research."

Specifically, I decided that I wanted to write a book about the gaming industry. (And it is the *gaming* industry, by

3

the way. They don't like it when you call it gambling.) I wanted to learn, and then describe, how the exotic and exciting gaming industry works, how a group of tough, but honest, businessmen have succeeded marvelously at something that nobody has been able to duplicate anywhere else in the world. I wanted to go into the boardrooms where the billion-dollar decisions are made, and into the "eye in the sky" where high-tech equipment and street-smart detectives combine to spot every false move, every vanishing chip. I wanted to go into the counting rooms, into the marketing department where the product is molded and pitched, into every nook and cranny of a fascinating corporation that starts each day with $15 million in cash in the till, more than any bank branch office.

I wanted to tell a story about success and failure in one of America's most glamorous, fascinating, and unique industries, and to show you how profoundly America's attitude toward gambling has changed. I wanted to do all that, then write it up for those who share my interest. Also, of course, I wanted to have an excuse to go to Las Vegas on business. And I knew from the beginning that I could best describe the gaming industry by focusing my lens on one major casino hotel.

I chose the Mirage.

The Mirage, after all, was shiny and glamorous, a glittering new toy on the Las Vegas Strip. It was an imposing white tower with an erupting (every fifteen minutes after dark) volcano out front, caged white tigers inside, and a pool of dolphins out back. Heavyweight champions' noses were bloodied at the Mirage. The salaries of movie stars were stacked on baccarat tables at the Mirage. And the Mirage's top man, Steve Wynn, was a colorful guy who starred in his own television commercials with Frank Sinatra. Las Vegas kingpins are a notoriously shy breed, but this guy was willing to dress up like a clown to bring in the bettors, so the Mirage made sense.

But the Mirage didn't work out.

For one thing, I was told that Steve Wynn didn't want to teach people how to run a casino through the pages of my book. (An objection that might draw giggles at the University of Nevada, Las Vegas, which requires a four-year curriculum to accomplish the same thing.) For another, I soon realized that the Mirage, though it would later become a truly great business success story, was not yet a lock. The place was raking in more money than any local hotel, but it also had a mega-nut to meet, and its financial performance tended to fluctuate wildly. One wrong turn in the economy and Wynn's billion-dollar playpen could head south. I sure as hell didn't want to write a book that says, "Hey guys, this is state-of-the-art management in the gaming industry," only to have my subject's stock dropping like a skydiver without a parachute when my book came out.

Scratch the Mirage.

So there I was sitting in my room at the Golden Nugget (another Steve Wynn hotel) in downtown Las Vegas, with five days left on my first research trip, and no subject for my book. I had two other casino hotels on my list: Circus Circus and the Excalibur. They were both colorful, themed hotels with brand names, and they seemed to be making buckets of money.

So I decided to call Glenn Schaeffer.

Schaeffer was the number two man at Circus Circus. His name had appeared a few months earlier in a small item I had clipped from *The Wall Street Journal.* The item was about William Bennett, top man at Circus Circus, who had announced that he would be retiring soon. Wall Street and its journal take notice of such things, for reasons which we will get to. So the *Journal* ran a little piece about Bennett and mentioned, among other things, the impending promotion of this guy Glenn Schaeffer to president. He was already chief financial officer. What caught my eye was the fact that Schaeffer was a graduate of the Iowa Writers' Workshop, arguably the most prestigious writing program in the country. Iowa is not a place you go to if you want to learn how to write annual reports. You go there to become the next John Irving, Flannery O'Connor, or John Gardner, all of whom graduated from the workshop, as did Schaeffer's friend, John Falsey, the Emmy-winning TV writer and coproducer of *Northern Exposure.* How interesting, I thought at the time, that a trained writer is running the finances of a major gaming company. I was glad to see one of my own kind making good. I figured this guy would probably help me make some contacts in Vegas, no matter which hotel I was writing about. I didn't know it, of course, but out of all the available Las Vegas names, I had homed in on the man who would probably be the most important person in the gaming industry in the 1990s. (In fact, according to some of the stock analysts I talked to later, Schaeffer already *was* the most important person in the gaming industry.)

So from the Golden Nugget I called Schaeffer and told

him I wanted to discuss the possibility of building my gaming industry book around Circus Circus. He asked me to come over that afternoon.

Most of the Las Vegas casinos can be found in one of two areas: downtown or the Strip. Imagine a banjo that is a mile long and lit up like a Roman candle. (Well, to be really honest with the imagery, we'd have to say a banjo that somebody has broken over his knee.) Downtown is the belly of the banjo. It consists of a dozen or so blocks of brash and colorful casinos with names like the Four Queens, Binion's Horseshoe, Lady Luck, and the Las Vegas Club. The broken neck of the banjo, running from downtown south for two miles to Interstate 10, is that part of Las Vegas Boulevard which is known as the Strip.

Circus Circus is on the west side of the Strip about a third of the way from downtown. It's a big birthday cake of a building, a tent-roofed pink and white big top that is home to the largest permanent circus in the world. The 120-foot-high sign out front, featuring Lucky the Clown who is to Circus Circus what Ronald McDonald is to McDonald's, cost $1 million and was once the biggest free-standing sign in the world. At first glance Circus Circus looks like a fun place where you would find a two-dollar blackjack table, but it does not seem particularly impressive in a town that has the Mirage, the Excalibur, the Las Vegas Hilton, and (twenty-five miles away) the seventy-story Hoover Dam. In fact, Circus Circus is a much bigger operation than, say, the Super Bowl, but from the front most of its size is hidden, so if you use the valet parking and walk in from the front, you are unlikely to guess that you are entering the fifth-largest hotel in the world. (The first four, the Excalibur, the Flamingo Hilton, the Mirage, and Bally's, are on the same street.)

Casinos are the black holes in the Las Vegas universe. They suck in any adult who comes within fifty feet with money in his or her pocket. The hotels are designed to funnel you into the casino as quickly as possible and from as many different directions as possible. So when I got into Circus Circus I was quickly swallowed up by the casino and, as I had a few minutes to spare, I felt obliged to place a roulette bet on red, which was the predominant color of the hotel.

Ten minutes later and twenty dollars richer, I checked out the circus midway and the arcade games on the mezzanine, then took a narrow elevator up to the Circus Circus executive offices.

I waited for Schaeffer in the receptionist's lobby. They didn't have *Newsweek* or *Mad* magazine on the coffee table so I thumbed through what they did have, a Circus Circus annual report. There I discovered something that everybody in Las Vegas, except me, already knew. Circus Circus and the Excalibur are part of the same corporation. It is called Circus Circus Enterprises, Inc., and in reading the annual report, I learned that CCE at that moment owned 7 properties, had 13,280 employees, operated 436,400 square feet of casino space, rented out 10,173 hotel rooms, and was the industry's most profitable company, and that all of these figures were tops in the industry. I also learned a lot of positive stuff about shares outstanding, total market value, stockholders' equity, and earnings per share before nonrecurring items, but that kind of stuff can be boring as hell if you don't own stock, so let's not go into it.

Most impressive to me was the fact that the corporation's latest product, the Excalibur, was the world's biggest hotel, and had operated that first year, 1990, at 100 percent occupancy. Moreover, CCE didn't fill those bedrooms by rustling its own customers. The pink birthday cake on the Strip, which had maintained the highest occupancy rate in Las Vegas for every single year since Nixon's resignation, still ran at 99 percent in 1991.

Before I put down the annual report I was struck by two things: One, Circus Circus Enterprises was clearly the big success story in the gaming industry. And two, I had come perilously close to making an utter fool of myself. Can you imagine me sitting down with the second top man in the company, coming on like a big-time writer and saying, "Well, I'm thinking of writing the book about you guys, but I have to be honest with you, I've also been talking with the Excalibur"?

For a man in his position, Glenn Schaeffer turned out to be young almost to the point of offensiveness. I guessed he was in his late twenties, though it turned out he was in his late thirties. Schaeffer's youth was troubling until I reminded myself that there were prepubescent rock stars and baseball players from third world countries who could buy half a million shares of Circus Circus stock, which was trading at 36 on that particular day, in case you're interested.

Schaeffer was a good-looking young fellow, trim and fit, it seemed, and he had an accent that I guessed was from one of those rectangular states. On the phone he had used words as if they cost him a dollar each—"Fine," "Come over," and

"Two o'clock" had been his end of the conversation—but now he seemed more friendly, though still a bit cool.

He used good strong words like "advocate" and "vociferous" right from the beginning. Clearly he was bright, and I would have laid 2 to 1 that he was one of those brainy kids who finished his math test and managed to sharpen all of his pencils and number the pages in his notebooks while you and I were still trying to remember which was the subtrahend and which was the subtracter. Anyhow, the important thing about Schaeffer's youth and his looks and his demeanor is that I could tell right away he was not a gangster. And I should know. I had just written four books in a row about murderers, a fact which I was not anxious to share with my host.

We probed for a while, me trying not to spook Schaeffer with my true-crime writing background, and him trying to figure out just what I wanted. He asked a lot of questions. He was trying to decide whether or not to ask his company's chairman for his blessing on this book.

Now, if you happen to run a company and you're not dumping deadly toxins into the local water supply, skimming profits, exploiting child laborers, or peddling shoddy merchandise, why would you not want a writer to come along and publish a book that basically says your company is better at making widgets than anybody else?

The answer can be found on bookshelves.

The literature on Las Vegas historically has been heavily weighted toward the negative. Comparatively speaking, Sodom and Gomorrah got off easy. Las Vegas, it has been written, is a city of shattered dreams, a city where mobsters still pull strings, a city where pathetic showgirls load their tits with silicone to squeeze a few extra years out of their careers before they turn to prostitution. And it is a city where toothless retirees pour their last quarters into soulless slot machines that never pay anybody. Much of the Las Vegas literature is marked by that smug anti-gambling paternalism in which the writer effectively tells the reader, Stay away, you're not smart enough to run your own life. All of this is laughable to anybody who knows anything about Las Vegas, but it isn't really so funny when your living depends on bringing people to town. So the people who run the gaming industry have been understandably press-shy. They've been burned too many times. Writers rank in their esteem somewhere below arsonists and card counters. And why not? If you owned an auto plant, and most of the writing about cars had focused on air pollution, fatal accidents, and faulty parts, would you want a book written about your company?

Schaeffer and I talked about all of this. He was, I think, concerned that I might put Circus Circus into a book that featured gangsters and naked showgirls, and maybe even an Elvis sighting or two at one of the big hotels. He probably would not have been disappointed if I had just walked away. But I think he was intrigued, too, by the possibility that I might get the story right.

"Of course," he said, and he said it a few times, "we're a public company, so you could go ahead and write a book about us whether we like it or not."

Technically, he was correct. Of course that book would require ten times as much work and would be as boring as unsalted peanut butter, but I didn't share that with him.

So, to make a long story medium in length, Schaeffer

and I agreed that I would write a book about the gaming industry and that it would be mostly about Circus Circus Enterprises, Inc. Subject to the company's approval, CCE would give me complete access to its properties and its employees. I would do several in-depth interviews with William G. Bennett, the father of the new Las Vegas, something no reporter had ever done. I would talk to marketing people, hotel managers, casino managers, dealers, and pit bosses; I would tour the eye-in-the-sky security, the properties in Reno and Laughlin, Nevada, the back offices; I would see how they count the money, guard the chips, protect the games; I would see how they get their customers and keep them; I would find out what exactly the product is and how Las Vegas in general, and Circus Circus in particular, have been able to package that product and sell it better than anybody in the history of the world.

So here's where we get to the part about my arrangement with Circus Circus. What did the company big shots want in return for all this cooperation? Did they want me to say only nice things about them? Did they want me to put the best possible face on everything? Of course they did, wouldn't you?

And what did I want in return? Did I want complimentary room and meals during my Las Vegas visits? Did I want beautiful girls sent to my room, and a sack full of green chips left at my door every morning? You bet. But I didn't ask for anything and they didn't offer. In fact, only a single string was attached to the deal. In return for all the cooperation CCE was giving me, the company wanted one thing: Everything I wrote about it must be true. I could interpret facts any way I wanted, I could choose what to include and what to leave out, I could mix my metaphors and split my infinitives, but I couldn't lie. That was the deal.

So, in the interest of disclosure, here is a list of everything I got for free from Circus Circus while I was writing this book:

January 21, 1991. My wife and I ate dinner at the Circus Circus Steak House. Emmett Michaels, director of corporate security, took care of the check. (Circus Circus claims, by the way, to have the best steaks in Las Vegas, but at least twelve other hotels make the same claim.)

January 24, 1991. I had lunch at the Skyway Restaurant at Circus Circus with Mel Larsen, executive vice president, marketing. Larsen took care of the check.

June 4, 1992. My friend Frank Strunk and I both had prime rib, the king-sized cut, at the Excalibur's Sir Galahad Restaurant, again courtesy of Emmett Michaels.

So that's about it for bribes. I got no free bedrooms. In fact, on my Las Vegas trips I didn't even stay at a CCE hotel. I stayed at my favorite Las Vegas hotel, the Rio. (And no, they didn't give me anything for free, either.)

"So okay, Gary," you're thinking, "you're not on the take. Big deal. I've never been to Las Vegas and I have no plans to go. Furthermore, I'm not even interested in the business, I just picked up this book in the bookstore because my ex-wife came in and I needed something to hide behind. Why should I care how a casino works?"

The answer, as you will see, is that if you live in the United States there's a better than even chance that casino gambling will soon touch your life.

1

The King

On the second floor of the Circus Circus Hotel in Las Vegas, hidden from the view of customers, there is a corridor of corporate offices. The offices are cool and efficient places, filled with wood and brass and leather, nothing garish, nothing glitzy, no hint at all that they are the heart of a particularly raucous and flashy business. In one surprisingly modest office, the sixty-eight-year-old chairman of CCE, William G. Bennett, sits behind a desk.

He can wear whatever he wants to wear, so there is no jacket, no necktie. Just a silky short-sleeved shirt open at the collar, dress trousers, and loafers. He wears glasses, his hair is silver, and often when he talks he places his hands lightly on the desk, leans back in his swivel chair, and stares at the

ceiling. By one hand is an ashtray and a pack of Merit cig-
arettes, by the other a glass of fruit juice. Though one can
sense in him the energy that must have electrified him over
the years, Bennett now seems like a man who is almost ready
to sit by the pool and enjoy the fruits of his career. He speaks
slowly, seems at times to be completely lost in thought. He
has, after all, announced his retirement.

On this particular day Bennett has been asked to go
back in time, to think about the event that caused him to
swerve from the path of life he was on, in a direction that
would eventually make him the most successful entrepreneur
in the history of the gaming industry.

The moment is no pleasure to recall.

Bennett was a thirty-seven-year-old highly successful
businessman in Phoenix, Arizona, when he heard the words
that would change his life.

"Barbara will be dead within a year."

The words were spoken by a doctor whom Bennett respected. Barbara, still in her thirties, was Bennett's beloved
wife. She suffered from a congenital heart problem.

This was a tragedy that would slice like a knife across
Bill Bennett's life, dividing it into two distinct halves. Before,
Bennett had lived most of his life in Arizona. After Barbara,
he would live in Nevada. Before, he operated a chain of furniture stores scattered around the Southwest. After Barbara's
death, he would change the face of an industry. Before, he
could see his marriage and his career as one long fruitful line
stretching out before him. After Barbara, William Bennett
would go broke, marry a second wife, Lynn, build a second

16

career, and do for a second time what few people did even once. He would make a fortune.

But in 1962, when he got the dreadful news, Bennett's career no longer was of any importance. The rough and tumble of business seemed suddenly trivial. Money became unimportant, except for its ability to buy a life of quality in the months that were left for Barbara Bennett.

"Time was suddenly the most precious commodity," Bennett says now. "What mattered then was that Barbara and I spend her remaining days together."

Like many women who marry very successful men, Barbara had learned that what she could afford was not always what she could have. She had always yearned to travel, and there was money to do it with, but she had rarely been able to pull Bennett away from business. She was married to a man who liked to keep his hands on the controls, who believed that the way to run a business was to show up. They could always travel later.

Now, of course, there would be no later. So Bennett, a master of grand plans, formed the most grandiose plan that he could for his wife. He would take Barbara on a cruise to distant ports. Though the clock ticked loudly, they would dine in Rome, they would dance in Spain, they would see all the world and cram as much living as they could into the year they had left.

But first he had to sell his business, and he had to sell it fast.

Bennett then had ten prosperous furniture stores, seven in Arizona and three in California. He sold chairs and couches and love seats and dining room tables, one at a time, to the families who came to his stores, and he sold truckloads of furniture to major hotel and motel customers.

"Time was more precious than gold," Bennett says now, "so the stores were priced to sell fast. I got a terrible price for them, but that's what happens when you're having a fire sale."

Bennett also unloaded his interest in two eateries that could not have been more different. One was a big Polynesian restaurant, with the mai tais and the little paper umbrellas in the drinks, the other a fried-chicken spot that might have put a scare into Colonel Sanders. "In fact," says Bennett, "we had started to expand the chicken place. We had the jump on the Kentucky Colonel, but we fouled up. Who knows, maybe I could have been the chicken king."

By the time the businesses were signed away and the lawyers paid, Bennett had booked Barbara's dream cruise around the world. But the tickets would never be used.

"The cruise was a month away," he recalls. "So we went to Mexico for a short trip. Barbara died there. It was approximately thirty days after I had sold the businesses."

Bennett, with a stepdaughter by Barbara's previous marriage and a son and daughter by his marriage to Barbara, had to begin again. Though he had sold his businesses at bargain-basement prices, he was nonetheless a wealthy man. He could let his grief run its natural course without the pressure of having to earn a living. For some months he spent his time reading, tinkering with machinery, and enjoying his lifelong hobby of building model boats. But the blood of a businessman still ran through Bennett's veins. He craved action, and he knew that he would not be truly himself until he was back in the game.

"So I got into a deal with a company in Arizona called FCA, Financial Corporation of Arizona," he says. "I got involved with a man who had made almost a hundred million dollars in his last venture. This fellow laid everything out for me and it looked to be a great opportunity. I put everything I had into this company."

Bennett leans back now and smiles at a memory that was a lot less funny at the time.

"The stock," he says, "went from thirty-seven dollars down to two dollars in a matter of two weeks. I was dead broke. I lost my beautiful home. I ended up in personal bankruptcy. It was the most embarrassing thing that ever happened to me."

Bennett realized quickly that he could no longer afford the luxury of wondering just how he would spend the rest of his life.

"Going back to work was no longer a matter of having something to do," he says. "It was a matter of making a living."

Certainly the idea of hard work did not trouble Bennett. He had burned more than a few calluses into his hands long before he was a man. As a kid, like his brother and sister, he had labored on the Arizona ranch and cotton farm where they lived. Young Bill had learned early how to anchor a post, tune a tractor engine, and thin his father's cotton with a hoe. In fact, young Bennett, who would later become a Navy pilot, was quite the mechanic, always tightening up a bolt, fixing a cotton stripper, or returning the roar of life to some small engine that seemed to be dead. At age fifteen he purchased a powerboat, the first in a lifelong series that would eventually include national prizewinners. But this first one was no great success. "It ended up," he says, "being a duck retriever."

Bill Bennett's first real paychecks came when he was a teenager working at his dad's cotton gin in Arizona.

"You went to work when it was light, and you stopped when it got dark," he says, recalling how he used to help the pressman and line up the bales of cotton for ten cents an hour, ten hours a day, six days a week.

If young Bill learned the value of hard work from those days in the cotton gin, he also learned a thing or two about business. His teacher was Allan Milton Bennett, his father.

"My father was an excellent businessman. He ran cotton gins and he grew cotton. He had it all worked out. In a good year, when there was a lot of cotton, cotton growers didn't make much money, but Dad made his money running the gin. In a bad year, when the crop was poor, the gin operators didn't do well, but Dad made his money from the higher price paid to cotton farmers."

Bennett, glancing now at CCE's president and second in command, Glenn Schaeffer, who has entered the room, says, "My father had other businesses, too, and he made it his practice to always replace himself with good people. He had this theory that a good manager would work himself out of a job. He was good at that."

So in 1964 when Bennett was once again as poor as a cotton farmer in a bad year, he was confident of two things: one, that he would work as hard as necessary to get back on top, and two, that he knew how to make money. His break would come from another man who was very good at making money: Del Webb.

The developer Del Webb, probably best known to the public in the 1940s as the man who built the Flamingo Hotel for Bugsy Siegel, and in the 1950s as part owner of the New York Yankees, had been one of Bennett's customers in the furniture business. Bennett's commercial division had sold furniture to Webb's chain of motels. Webb owned a house in Beverly Hills and one in Phoenix, where he and Bennett were members of the Phoenix Country Club.

"That's where the upper crust of Phoenix hung out," Bennett says. "I had made a lot of money at a young age, so I ran with an upscale crowd."

By the time of Bennett's bankruptcy, Webb had divested himself of his interest in the Yankees and was developing a small gaming empire which eventually would include the Sahara in Lake Tahoe, and in Las Vegas the Mint, the Sahara, and the Thunderbird. Webb offered Bennett a job.

Bennett had never been much of a gambler, but had from time to time gone to Las Vegas and played blackjack, which he still calls "twenty-one." (Actually, Bennett is correct. While most people call the Las Vegas game blackjack, it is really twenty-one. Blackjack is what you play at home when everybody gets a chance to deal.)

In 1965 Del Webb hired Bennett as a casino host at the Sahara in scenic Lake Tahoe, on the California-Nevada border, for $750 a month. There Bennett's job was to squire high rollers around town and make sure their wheels were oiled. Flights had to be met, credit had to be arranged, restaurant tables had to be reserved. High rollers are a precious and delicate commodity in the gaming business, and Webb probably slept more easily at night knowing that they had been put into the hands of a man he knew and trusted.

This was a job that required diplomacy, discretion, and great efficiency. But it was not a job that required Bill Bennett's business sense. Still, it was a beginning, and from the beginning Bennett was convinced that he had stumbled onto a way to make more money than he had ever made in his life.

"After I got my hands on some financial statements I knew I had discovered a glory hole and that I could make a lot of money in this business," he says. "I knew how to run a business. I had always made money at the businesses that I ran, and I had never made money at businesses that somebody else ran. Here these people were making money, but there was no management to speak of. I knew that this was a business in which I could do well. The only guy in northern Nevada whom I really respected was Bill Harrah. The rest of them were dummies. They didn't have the foggiest idea of how to make money."

As an example of unwise business practice, Bennett cites the pay structure at the Del Webb organization. "Webb had a salary pyramid," he says. "The pyramid was based on Webb's salary. So all of the general managers of the various hotels made seventy-five thousand dollars and a thirteen-thousand-dollar bonus, whether they made or lost money. In other words, a guy who was running one hotel and losing his shirt was getting the same compensation as a guy who was running another hotel and making a big profit. Not much incentive for success in that, is there?"

Bennett moved quickly through the ranks, first in northern Nevada and then in Las Vegas, where "Papa Webb" put him in charge of the Las Vegas Mint. By early 1970 Bennett had risen to executive vice president for all of Webb's gaming operations. He was running two casino hotels, or "stores," as he called them.

Much of what Bennett did then foreshadowed the management style that would infuse Circus Circus later. Bennett is a technical type, and even then he was a stickler for controls and instantaneous reporting of results. One of his masterstrokes at Webb was the adaptation to gaming of his system of controls and daily financial reporting from his furniture retailing business. This same highly accurate and almost up-to-the-minute system is used at CCE today.

Bennett forced himself to learn how to deal all the live games, and became an expert in the operation of slot machines. He absorbed all he could learn about the gaming industry. He had studied the methods used by Harrah's and Harvey's, the two northern Nevada operations that he considered the best managed.

"Harrah's was particularly strong in merchandising slots," he says. "When I took over the Mint in Las Vegas, I borrowed ideas from their slot operations. I've never worried about being original; I've been concerned with what works."

By 1970 he knew what everybody else in the Webb organization knew about gaming, but he also had a keen sense of business, something which, he believed, was lacking in that particular organization. In his mind he had formulated a dream: he would someday own a casino-hotel.

Mel Larsen, who worked with Bennett back then and became the head of marketing for CCE, says, "Before I met Bill Bennett I would never admit that I wasn't as smart as anybody else. But when I bumped up against him, I knew I had met the smartest man I ever knew. If Bennett asked me to run and jump off a roof, I'd just go and jump, because I'd figure he must be testing out a new kind of mattress or something. You have to realize, this is a guy who took the test to be a Navy pilot and scored one hundred percent. They told him nobody ever scored one hundred percent. That was on paper. Then he flew Navy bombers off of aircraft carriers, the real thing, and he still scored one hundred percent."

Though his success in running profitable hotels didn't earn him any greater salary than the guys who were running losing operations, Bennett had been able to acquire a good many stock options in the Webb company at two or three dollars. In 1970, knowing he was going to bail out of the Webb organization, Bennett borrowed money to exercise the options. The company asked him to stay longer, and by the time he left, the stock he had bought at two or three dollars was selling at seventeen. It was Bennett's first experience with gaming stocks.

A year or two earlier, Bennett had met a man by the name of William Pennington. Pennington owned Raven Electronics, a company that sold electronic keno machines and slot machines. One of his customers was Bennett, at the Mint in Las Vegas. Bennett and Pennington meshed perfectly. They were both sharp businessmen who could see that there was a lot more gold in the gaming mine. They knew from the beginning that they would be good in business together.

"At the time," Bennett remembers, "there was a company called Nevada Electronics, that had their license taken away from them twice. They had this electronic twenty-one game, with tables designed for two players. The company would place these games in bars and restaurants all over Nevada. The games were very popular but they just were not making enough money to justify the floor space they occupied. So the people who owned the company came up with a novel solution. They put in a cheating device, a gaff, so that when the dealer had a breaking hand he could not get a nine, ten, or picture card. The device just locked out those cards that would break the dealer. So of course the machine's win percentage went way up. Well, the state caught them, and yanked their gaming license for a year and a half. After they got caught doing this a second time, the company was finished.

"Anyhow, one day Pennington and I were talking about the company and the problem of this game not bringing in enough money. We were trying to figure out a way to make these machines make money without putting in the cheating device. Bill and I just came up with the idea jointly of the house winning pushes. [A "push" in blackjack is a hand in which the dealer and the player have the same card total.] Of course we mentioned this idea and almost everybody said the same thing, that folks just wouldn't play the machines."

But Bennett was convinced that he and Pennington had found a solution to the low-profit problem. They decided to test their theory. They got a bank loan for $100,000. With the money, they bought an option that reserved for them the right to purchase all the Nevada Electronics equipment for $750,000, which was about fifteen cents on the dollar. If it turned out that people would not play on a twenty-one machine that kept their money on a push, Bennett and Pennington would take a $100,000 bath. Plus interest.

"The state requires tests for new games and new game rules," Bennett says, "so I did the state-controlled test, at the Mint. Keeping the pushes didn't seem to make any difference. People played anyhow. The machines made a lot more money. They were a big success."

So Bennett and Pennington exercised their option and went into business together, forming a new company, Western Equities. But from the beginning they knew that the electronic games were only the means to an end. They wanted to raise money, and they wanted to use that money to buy their own casino.

"That was the whole idea, to build the company up so that we could buy a casino. But we found there were problems in buying hotels. Some people only wanted to give out drop numbers, saying that anybody who knew anything about the casino business could figure out the rest."

(The "drop" in a casino is the amount of money actually dropped into the cash boxes at each table. If you were to buy, say, $100 worth of chips at a blackjack table, that $100 would be dropped into a locked box, and it would increase the casino's drop for that day by $100, regardless of whether you won or lost with your chips. On average, and over time, a casino will win nearly 20 percent of its drop and you, the player, will cash in $80 worth of chips out of that $100 that you bought. Though Bennett doesn't say it, the implication of showing drop figures instead of profit is that some hotels were making more profit than they were reporting to the state and the IRS. Not exactly a shocker, since this was a time when casino skimming was still not uncommon.)

One of the first places Bennett looked at seriously was the Landmark, owned by Howard Hughes.

"I never actually met Hughes," Bennett says, "but then I guess nobody did during those years. We were very interested in the Landmark, but Hughes kept yanking us around. I had always been good at raising money and I had my investors lined up. I'd tell them, 'The Landmark is going to cost us so much.' They'd agree. Then Hughes's guy would come back to us and announce that the price was a million more than we'd already been told. So I'd have to go back to my investors and tell them, 'Hey, guys, it's going to cost us another million.' Well, you can do that just so many times. So we gave up on the Landmark."

There were a few more dry holes for Bennett and Pennington. Promises were broken. Deals fell through. This hotel was too small, that one too big. The men were getting frustrated and, in the process, lowering the standards of their dream casino. Then, in 1974, there came on the market a big, beautiful disaster of a casino hotel called Circus Circus. It was a nutty, schizophrenic big top, a poorly managed, wildly unfocused, mismarketed horror that had never had a profitable year in all its history. Everybody in town told Bennett and Pennington to stay away from it. It was, they said, the worst spot in town to try to make a dollar. The place was hemorrhaging money, and it would sorely test Bennett's belief that he could make money in the gaming business. But he and Bill Pennington decided to look into it.

And that moment, when William G. Bennett and William Pennington looked long and hard at this Las Vegas loser and concluded that they could make something of it, was the beginning of the new Las Vegas.

2

Days of Yore

Back in the twelfth century when John of Salisbury raised hell about "the damnable art of dice-playing," he was not onto something new. Gambling is as old as mud. Primitive people played games of chance by sunlight and firelight. Even more than contemporary man, they saw the world as a confusing place. It was a place where noises came from the sky, where fire spewed up from the ground; it was a place of mystery, and they no doubt found comfort in believing that the intentions of the gods could be discerned from the results of random events. The falling of a tree, the eclipse of the moon, the scudding of dark clouds across an afternoon sky all had meaning. No wonder, then, that they looked for the controlling hand of God in games of chance. "God likes me better than he likes you" is a belief that will inspire anybody to draw to an inside straight. It is not surprising that the instruments of divination have often been also the instruments of gambling: playing cards and tarot cards, runes and dice.

Of the thousands of forms that gambling has taken, many involve betting on animals. Cocks have fought, horses have raced, and frogs have jumped in Calaveras County, all so that gamblers would have something to bet on.

One of the less sensitive animal bets occurred in the 1940s when the Smith family, owners of Harold's Club in Reno, tried to secure a marketing edge on a product which was essentially the same as the competition's, by putting a mouse, instead of a silver ball, on the roulette wheel. The mouse's job was to run around the wheel until it dropped from exhaustion. Whatever number it dropped on was the winner. Business boomed. There were drawbacks, however, especially for the mouse. After the mouse collapsed, the roulette wheel would continue to spin, chopping off its tail in the process. This not only was disgusting to look at, it also gummed up the wheel, so it was stopped.

Almost as old as betting on animals is betting by lottery. Lotteries have been used throughout history to raise money for municipalities. Yale and Harvard universities both have had buildings erected with lottery proceeds. The Continental Congress used a lottery to raise funds for the Revolutionary Army. Even Moses, in the Old Testament, was inspired to divide up the Promised Land by lottery. Lotteries usually flourish in hard times and wilt when churches get on a morality kick about them, which is amusing, because over the ages a zillion churches have been built with lottery money. The churches, in fact, are probably the biggest operators of private lotteries, which they try to sanitize by calling them raffles.

In fact, for almost as long as there has been any kind of gambling there have been zealots condemning it. Over the centuries most of the condemnation has come, of course, from the churches, which have long feared that man would be brought down by this loathsome pastime, and might also gamble away the money he should be spending on lottery tickets to build the new rectory.

States have tried to regulate gambling in a number of ways. The state has made the beneficiaries pay taxes; the state has made gambling debts uncollectible; and sometimes, as in the present lotteries, the state has awarded itself a monopoly on this lucrative business, and kept for itself a percentage that La Cosa Nostra would have been embarrassed to ask for.

So there was gambling long before there was a Las Vegas, Nevada. But it was in Las Vegas that gambling was packaged, perfected, and made customer-friendly. Las Vegas did for gambling what Henry Ford did for the automobile: made it work efficiently, effectively, and at the lowest possible price. If you look at the gambling experience as a product to be purchased, then Las Vegas today produces the best and least expensive version of that product in the history of the world.

Las Vegas, which is Spanish for "the meadows," was once inhabited by Paiute Indians who, not having any televised baseball games, spent much of their time sitting outside their wickiups, rolling bones and colored sticks across the ground and making bets on the outcome.

In 1848 the area was ceded to the United States by Mexico in the Treaty of Guadalupe Hidalgo, a transfer which has been described by many as outright theft. From Utah, Mormon families headed for Nevada. But along with the Mormons came gold rushers, outlaws, prostitutes, and people who were mad as hell about something or other back home and weren't going to take it anymore. In other words, the type of people who might gamble, or at least not get too moral about other people doing it.

In 1859 gold was discovered not in Las Vegas, but around Virginia City, near Reno, a few hundred miles northwest of Las Vegas. When the gold miners found that the sludge they were mucking through was rich in silver, the California-bound wagon trains began detouring to Nevada. In time, Virginia City turned out $300 million in gold and silver. This helped to further define the type of people who would come to Nevada and eventually work their way down to Las Vegas. Jerome Skolnick, writing in *House of Cards* (Little, Brown, 1978), notes, "Gold prospecting did not draw men seeking stability and long-term work. The affinity between gambling and prospecting for gold is clear. Either way, one is seeking to strike it rich."

In May 1905 railroad officials, who for years had been selling worthless sagebrush to unsuspecting buyers, auctioned off townsites in Las Vegas, which, though it was characterized by one newcomer as "one of the dustiest places in all creation," did have a water supply and lay between Los Angeles and Salt Lake City.

Las Vegas was a town where prostitution and gambling were legal, so it naturally continued to draw characters who took pleasure in those particular recreations. Besides, it was out in the desert, so what else was there to do? (Though Las Vegans at the turn of the century had no television, they did, as a Cornell University report put it years later, "have their own CBS. Casinos, Bordellos, and Saloons.") Gambling in private homes had been legal in Las Vegas since 1879, but by 1910 morality took hold and gambling was made illegal. *The San Francisco Post* noted somewhat gleefully at the time, "With the close of the gambling houses in Nevada, one of the worst relics of the wild and woolly west has passed out." Probably during this time there was no less gambling than there had been, but more bribes had to be paid, and the games probably were more crooked.

The Las Vegas area grew in the 1930s when Hoover Dam was built, in the 1940s with the arrival of Nellis Air Force Base, and in the 1950s with the advent of atomic bomb testing. So maybe this city, which author Mario Puzo says "shouldn't even be there," would have existed anyhow. But Las Vegas has never been best known for the dam, the base, or the bomb. It has always been known for gambling, and over the years it has acquired a number of nicknames, all of them pejorative: Sin City, Electric Sodom, Modern Gomorrah.

In 1931, with a depression going on, the silver mines pretty much exhausted, and illegal gambling the only thing that seemed to make money, the Nevada state legislature once again saw the wisdom of legalizing gambling.

At first there was relatively little regulation. If you paid a tax to the local sheriff and the county commissioners, you could open a casino. For a small additional tax some officials could be persuaded to look the other way when a customer was being cheated. As time passed, however, the state began to see gaming less as a silver mine to be exhausted and more as a goose that would lay golden eggs forever if taken care of. So the state developed a sophisticated bureaucracy for ensuring that the games were honest, that the casino owners were respectable, and most important, that the state collected its full share.

Before the Second World War, the big gambling center was not Las Vegas but Reno, in northern Nevada, a town variously known as the City of Players, the Nation's Harlot, and the Biggest Little City in the World. But after the war Las Vegas came on strong. One reason was the rise of Southern California; Las Vegas was within driving distance of Los Angeles. Another was the invention of air-conditioning. The third, it turned out, was Bugsy Siegel.

If you saw the movie *Bugsy,* you get the gist of the story as it's been told over the years. Handsome gangster, who hates to be called Bugsy, drives through sleepy sagebrush town on his way to California, stops at a little nothing bar that has a low-rent casino, and has a vision that he can build a gambling palace in the desert.

Well, it wasn't exactly like that. Benjamin Siegel was good-looking and he did hate to be called Bugsy, but if he got out of his car in the middle of the desert it was probably to take a leak, not to have an epiphany on the road to Los Angeles. Bugsy was on his way to Hollywood to visit his boyhood friend, actor George Raft, and, he hoped, to become

34

a movie star. It happened that Bugsy had no acting talent, so he spent his time working with bookies. In that role he made trips to Las Vegas, checked it out pretty carefully, then announced his plan to build the Flamingo Hotel.

Bugsy not only didn't invent Las Vegas, he apparently didn't even invent the Flamingo. In 1991, after the movie *Bugsy* came out and was collecting Academy Award nominations, William R. Wilkerson, Jr., a Los Angeles writer and producer, wrote in *USA Today* about what he considered some of the myths of the movie. He said that Siegel was not the visionary behind the Flamingo.

"The vision of a grand hotel/casino in the middle of the Nevada desert belonged solely to William R. 'Billy' Wilkerson, my father," he wrote. "In 1945, he purchased the land, broke ground, and began construction. But in early 1946 he ran out of funds and, through a bizarre twist of fate, partnered with Siegel." Wilkerson Jr. also wrote that Wilkerson Sr. thought of the Flamingo idea in his Hollywood office, that after Siegel became majority stockholder Wilkerson was still the guy who made all the creative decisions, and that the name Flamingo had nothing to do with Bugsy's girlfriend Virginia Hill (Annette Bening in the movie) but came from Wilkerson's love of exotic birds.

In any case, investors were found, including gangsters like Morris Rosen, Louis Pokross, and Bugsy's boyhood friend Meyer Lansky. A builder was hired. He was Del Webb, the same man who would eventually hire William Bennett to work at the Mint. True to the legend, Bugsy did pull all kinds of strings concerning supplies and building materials, which during the postwar years were hard to come by through normal channels. In fact, many strings were also pulled by Wilkerson, according to author Dean Jennings in his 1967 Siegel biography, *We Only Kill Each Other* (Pocket Books). Jennings writes, "Through Wilkerson, who could and did apply strangleholds on movie executives, he got lumber, cement, piping and other material that came right off the studio lot." Siegel was manic throughout the building of the hotel, and Jennings writes, "In the history of building, the construction of the Flamingo probably is unique for the frenzy, the grand larceny and graft, and the accumulated errors that went into its construction."

Not only did the Flamingo run millions of dollars over budget, but when it opened it lost money, which is something that casinos are not supposed to do, especially when several of the owners are gangsters. This is almost certainly the reason why in 1947 a gunman blew Siegel's head off in Hollywood. After that the Flamingo made money, so one can speculate about the reasons it had been losing.

The shooting, however, stirred up the antigambling forces, and the gangsters quickly moved to seduce the churches with money, which partly explains why Las Vegas once had more churches per capita than any city in the country. The gangsters who had been in an illegal profession, gambling, were now in a legal profession, gambling, through the expedient of moving west. And they liked the respectability. They cleaned up the city, outlawed mob killings, and ran honest games. They did not, however, pay all of their taxes.

Ironically, the assassination of Bugsy Siegel, which helped create the popular image of Las Vegas as a haven for gangsters, is the singular event which would eventually lead to the extinction of gangsters in Las Vegas. The Nevada state legislature subsequently passed a law giving the state the right to approve or disapprove of any gambling license applicant. Though it would still be another three decades before the last gangster would pack his bags and head home to Chicago, the sides had been picked. It was the state against the mob, and the state would eventually win.

Bugsy Siegel was not the only colorful, and shady, character to get into the Las Vegas gambling business. There were dozens of them and they are typified, perhaps, not by Siegel, but by another Benny, Benny Binion.

Binion, who grew up on the streets of Dallas in the early 1900s, was running an illegal gaming operation before he was twenty. "Benny was a grown man since he was fourteen," says one of his longtime friends. "He had the whole town. He had all the games, craps, numbers, you name it."

Binion went to Las Vegas, where he developed a reputation as a man of honor who would walk through hell for his friends, but make life painful for his enemies. Now and then he shot someone or got into other trouble, which is why, when he built a casino, he was never the official licensee. His family-run casino became Binion's Horseshoe, a gaming joint that is steeped in legend and still survives in Glitter Gulch under the ownership of Binion's son Jack. Binion's was known for fast action and high stakes. In 1980 Binion let a bettor put $777,000 on the don't pass line at the crap table and the man won. Four years later the same bettor returned, dropped $1 million on the line, and lost. Binion was an innovator. It was he who established the practice of having waitresses give free cocktails to gambling customers. But he saw the formula for success simply. He once told a reporter, "I provide good food cheap, good whiskey cheap, and a good gamble. That's all there is to it, son."

Nonetheless, Binion was a promoter. After he saw people lined up to look at money at the U.S. Mint, he put $1 million in $10,000 bills on display in the lobby of the Horseshoe.

"Seemed to me," he once said, "that it would be a good investment to put a million dollars on display in our casino just for the heck of it. You'd be surprised how many people come by just to have their picture taken standing alongside all that money."

Binion also sent authentic stagecoaches to pick up tourists at the airport, and he gave fifteen-pound turkeys to all the cabdrivers in town every Thanksgiving. Not surprisingly, the cabbies tended to recommend the Horseshoe to first-time tourists. Binion, a longtime rodeo fan, also brought the National Rodeo Finals to Las Vegas.

Binion died in 1991 at the age of eighty-five, and with him died an era. There had been a lot of Benny Binions in Las Vegas history, but there probably will be no more.

While Siegel's Flamingo was the symbolic beginning of big-time Vegas, it was not, by a long shot, the first casino in Las Vegas, or even the first on what is today called the Las Vegas Strip. The Boulder Club had opened in 1929. El Rancho had opened in 1940. The Last Frontier opened on the Los Angeles highway in 1943. After that there were the Nevada Biltmore and the El Cortez. The Flamingo came in 1946.

And the Flamingo, which these days is the Hilton Flamingo, was certainly not the last. A year after the Flamingo, Clifford A. Jones founded the Thunderbird Hotel. In the fifties, the building of resort and hotel casinos continued. In 1950 Wilbur Clark opened the Desert Inn; Milton Prell followed two years later with the Sahara. The Sands was built in 1953. A year later came the Riviera, then the largest hotel in the country, a nine-story high-rise which broke the pattern of sprawling casinos in this desert where land was plentiful. In 1954 William Moore founded the Showboat on the Boulder Highway; in 1955 the Moulin Rouge was built in West Las Vegas. Downtown, the area known as Glitter Gulch, also grew. The Golden Nugget opened in 1946, and there were others like the Horseshoe Club, the Lucky Strike, the Bingo Club, the Pioneer, the Westerner, the California Club, the Monte Carlo, and the Las Vegas Club. The Fremont, the first high-rise downtown, arrived in 1956.

In the late 1950s Las Vegas saw another round of building. The Dunes, the Hacienda, the Tropicana, and the Stardust all opened between 1955 and 1959. By 1960 119,000 people were living in the Las Vegas area.

In the 1960s there was more building. The Mint opened downtown, and a year later the Four Queens. Later in the decade Las Vegas would see the Landmark and the Las Vegas Hilton open, marking the first time that "Strip" hotels were not actually on the Strip. But in 1961 something happened that would eventually lead to the new Las Vegas, the "Orlando of the West."

3

The Magician

One day in 1961, a gregarious bear of a man by the name of Jay Sarno flew from Texas to San Francisco via Las Vegas. Flying out of Las Vegas, Sarno noticed that not many people were on the airplane, and he wondered if maybe Las Vegas needed a few more hotel rooms.

Sarno, a designer and builder, was already a hotel man. His string of Cabana Motor Hotels was regarded as the best designed and among the best run in the country. In fact, his Palo Alto Cabana had been named the outstanding motel in the country by a leading travel magazine. Sarno had a fondness for plants and statuary, and plenty of both could be found at the Cabanas.

What Sarno had in mind for Las Vegas was something

far grander than a motor hotel. He was unimpressed by the Las Vegas hotels, which for the most part were mock Western in motif. "I felt it was time to do something more refined," he said. What he had in mind was a massive Greco-Roman shrine that would be called the Desert Palace.

Jay Sarno, who died in 1984, was a colorful figure in Las Vegas, a town that has seen more than its share of colorful figures. He was perhaps more in love with the image of being a big Las Vegas hotel operator than with the reality. He was a poor administrator, but he was also a man of great vision. Part hustler, part genius, he was a salesman without peer, and if he sometimes operated in shady areas, it seems now that he did so not because he was corrupt, but because he was naive and careless.

Victor Rogers, a friend and investor from the early days, says Sarno was "an Edison."

"Jay Sarno was a great man," Rogers says. "He was a great, competent man, an Edison who gave electricity to Las Vegas. He saw things that nobody else saw, he drew every section of the hotel in his mind before it was ever built. He was a magnificent presence, straight as an arrow. He was a kind, gentle person with a heart bigger than it should have been."

To this you can add: he was a gambler, a showman, storyteller, clever pitchman, resourceful money-raiser, visionary, and bon vivant. Current CCE employees Mike Hartzell and Joyce Gordon, who knew Sarno, describe him only in glowing terms.

It was Sarno's ability to sell an idea that made him a

Vegas legend. "When Jay Sarno pitched an idea, it was like a concert," Rogers says.

Sarno pitched his idea of a palace to people with money, notably the Teamsters' Union Pension Fund, and by 1965 building was under way on the first new Strip hotel in nine years, Las Vegas's most glittering jewel. What Sarno could envision he could create, and the hotel he created was every bit as garish, as overstated, and as successful as he had imagined it would be. Only the name was different. It was called Caesars Palace.

The complex was a reflection of its originator. The Sarno block, as the outer facade was called, was as innovative as he, with a latticework design that lowered the temperature inside the building. The casino inside also was a product of Sarno's architectural philosophy. Sarno thought about things like shapes and angles and the direction of light. Here, for example, is Sarno discussing ovals in a November 1979 interview with *Las Vegas Sun* reporter George Stamos:

Over the years that I have been creating hotels I've discovered that the oval is a magic shape. This is conducive to relaxation. If you examine Caesars' casino you will find that it is oval shaped. I even incorporated the oval design into the dice tables, which affects the dice angle geometry. Because the casino is shaped in an oval, people tend to relax and play longer. And the casino's intimate feeling is no accident, either; it is an optical illusion created by the twenty false columns encircling it.

In that same interview Sarno talked about the Caesars Palace statuary, "cut from the finest purest grade of Carrera from Florence." In fact, he filled Caesars with expensive art, and when his palace was complete he bragged to the world that he had spent $25 million, though in fact he had spent only $19 million. Unlike Circus Circus, which he would build next, Caesars Palace went directly to profit. In the words of former general manager Harry Wald, "We just opened the doors and never looked back."

Those doors led to a 34-acre complex with a 14-story tower featuring 680 rooms, 18 huge fountains along a 135-foot drive that was lined with imported Italian cypress trees, and an interior that featured an 800-seat theater called the Circus Maximus, statues from Italy, Brazilian rosewood, gold leafing throughout, white marble panels surrounded by black mosaics, and the world's largest crystal ceiling fixture, made from the finest German crystal. The era of the theme hotel in Las Vegas had begun.

Caesars, right across the street from the Flamingo, opened August 5, 1966, with a massive party. Celebrities and politicians gathered to gobble up two tons of filet mignon, 300 pounds of crabmeat, 30,000 fresh eggs, 50,000 glasses of champagne, and the largest single order of Alaskan King crab and Ukrainian caviar ever bought by a private organization. The party, with Andy Williams headlining, cost more than $1 million. But long before the champagne had run out Sarno was thinking of his next theme, his next hotel.

"At first he was planning an extension of the Circus idea at Caesars, but then he decided the idea was worth a place of its own," Victor Rogers recalls.

Nobody knows for sure how his place came to be named Circus Circus, but the apocryphal story is that Sarno was trying to explain to somebody what he had in mind.

"It will have a circus," he said.

"What do you mean, a circus?" his friend asked.

"A circus," he said in frustration, "a circus circus."

October 17, 1968, just two years and a pair of months after Caesars, Circus Circus opened on the Las Vegas Strip. The festivities featured clowns, confetti, VIPs, costumes, drum majorettes, arc lights, marching bands, and the highest fountain in the world.

The next day *The Las Vegas Sun* reported, "Jay Sarno, dressed elaborately as the ringmaster, led the invited mucky mucks down a slide from the first floor mezzanine to the main floor. High wire and aerial acts performed their feats of derring do directly above the gamblers and the high rollers hoped the somersaulters wouldn't crap out despite the safety net dangling below them."

This new casino hotel featured, along with those daring young men and ladies on flying trapezes, looping and diving barely above the heads of casino gamblers, an adorable baby elephant that had been trained to walk around the casino and yank slot machine handles with its trunk, and a very loud fourteen-piece orchestra that pleased the people who had come for the entertainment, but made it difficult for players to concentrate on their gambling.

Sarno was a good money-raiser and he had a strong imagination, but he owned about as much business sense as a Texas S&L manager. Naively, he believed that this new mix of circus acts and gambling would lure high rollers, so he geared his operation to accommodate them. Incredibly, to this wholesome circus theme he added nude dancers. If that wasn't loony enough, customers had to come in on the second floor and descend to the casino either by slide or by firepole. What's worse, they had to pay admission.

Mike Hartzell, who worked for Sarno and is today CCE's entertainment director, recalls, "One time when business was off, Sarno increased the admission price. I think it was three-fifty and he doubled it to seven dollars. And this was in the nineteen-sixties. At some point somebody counted eight hundred people who had walked away without coming in, so the admission charge was eventually done away with."

Hartzell also recalls one of the zanier entertainment acts of the early Circus Circus.

"We had a thing called the Sponge Plunge," he says. "A Hungarian guy by the name of Joe Gerloch would dive fifty or sixty feet from the top of the tent, into a giant sponge that was right in the middle of the casino. One time, in an effort to cut costs, Mr. Sarno hired a guy who said he could do the act cheaper. This guy was dressed up like an Indian and he called himself Chief Geronimo. Instead of a sponge, he had a giant airbag. Well, he had done this jump hundreds of times, so when he brought it to Circus Circus he didn't bother to test it. He made one jump. When he landed there was this tremendous whoosh of air that sent every card in the casino flying, and there was a huge uproar. After that, Sarno brought back the Hungarian."

Joyce Gordon, who also worked for Sarno and is now director of public relations for CC Las Vegas, recalls, "There was Tanya the elephant. Tanya would come around and pull

46

the handle on Big Bertha, the slot machine. Then Tanya would come to the crap table and throw the dice with her trunk. She was a wonderful, sweet little elephant, but sometimes she got bored and would wander off to the blackjack table. One time her trunk came across the table and sucked up chips like a vacuum cleaner. One player went running out. Poor Tanya was wondering, 'Why are they afraid of me?'

"And of course, there were the trapeze artists overhead. Imagine a dealer's eyes shifting back and forth to watch the trapeze flyers overhead, and you can imagine how much cheating was gotten away with."

Sarno had managed to put in at least one thing to offend everybody. His casino was an instant failure.

Certainly Dad wasn't likely to bring Mom and the kids down from Omaha to see bare-breasted women. Ladies in skirts and heels could find more convenient ways to enter a casino than slides and firepoles. And high rollers, while they might have enjoyed the bouncing breasts, probably shared the sentiments of Mario Puzo, who writes in his 1976 book *Inside Las Vegas,* "Personally I find it really unnerving to play a hand of blackjack as some guy in spangled tights goes flying over your head."

So the high rollers continued to take their fat bankrolls to other tables, other casinos.

"As anybody could have told Sarno," notes Daniel Seligman, writing in *Fortune* magazine in 1987, "those impassive Orientals at the baccarat table aren't looking for clowns and elephants."

Circus Circus was a textbook case of a mixed marketing message. It was neither a sophisticated den of sin nor a wholesome big top, and Sarno, like many before him and since, learned a hard lesson: you can't make money in the gaming industry simply by opening the doors. You've got to be a savvy businessman.

By 1974, not only was Circus Circus losing money, but Jay Sarno was wearing out his welcome with the Gaming Control Boards. Sarno wasn't doing anything felonious, but he had his own way of doing things and that was not always the Contol Board's way. "Sarno was not an out-and-out crook," says one of the men who knew him, now a casino executive, "but let's say he was not comfortable being confined to other people's rules."

In any case, Sarno's gambling license was in danger of being yanked. Clearly it was time to unload his latest debacle.

At first Bennett and Pennington, who were looking for a casino, did not appear to be the perfect buyers.

"I did not have the marketing idea for a family location like Circus Circus in my mind at the time," Bennett says. "I really wanted something along the lines of the Sahara, but there was not too much available. We had tried to buy the Landmark from Howard Hughes, but, of course, Hughes kept raising the price. Then Circus Circus popped up.

"I had met Jay Sarno but I didn't know him well. He was very close to bankruptcy. This was a place that had five and a half years of losing money, and had never had one single profitable year. All my friends said, 'Don't do it, that's the worst place in town.' But I felt that I had a knack for turning these places around. My first impression of Circus Circus was that Sarno had things all mixed up. The number one thing was that he had kids' games right next to slot machines. It seemed to me it would have been easy enough to divide the place up logically, put the adult entertainment on the first floor, put the arcade and midway on the second floor.

"Also, Sarno was trying to cater to high rollers. He didn't have high-roller players, but he had high minimums. He had a few high-minimum twenty-one tables and always one or two crap tables, some twenty-five-dollar minimums, some a hundred when it was crowded. In those days that was pretty high. He gave credit. He had baccarat. He was all over the lot. He didn't have any focus."

A number of complicated financing problems made it impossible for Sarno to simply sell the whole operation to Bennett and Pennington. So the two Bills bought the gaming equipment and leased the building and everything else, using their stock in Western Equities as collateral for bank loans.

(In 1977 Bennett and Pennington sold Western Equities to Si Redd, founder of IGT, the largest and most profitable maker of slot machines. In effect, Western Equities was a launchpad for IGT.)

Right up to the release of Circus Circus into Bennett and Pennington's control, Sarno remained flamboyant.

"Some way or other we had to decide who was going to pay the closing costs," Bennett recalls. "I don't know how the attorneys missed that. It wasn't a tremendous amount of money, about eleven thousand dollars. I just wanted us to split it or something. But Jay had another idea. Jay always had a deck of cards with him. He loved to play gin rummy. He said to me, 'Let's play one hand of gin rummy for the money.' I said, 'Jay, that's a lot of money for one game of cards,' but he persisted. He won, and we paid the closing costs.

"When I told Bill Pennington, he was not very happy. He said, 'Why did you do that?' I told him, 'Because Jay wasn't going to pay anyhow.' The only way he would pay would be if I beat him. He wouldn't pay a business debt, but he had gambler's honor, and he would pay a gambling debt."

Even though Jay Sarno no longer owned Circus Circus, Bennett had not seen the last of him.

"This place had no entrance right off the Strip when we took over," Bennett says. "Sarno didn't have the political clout to get a traffic light put in, so that people could turn left or right off the Strip and drive right into Circus Circus. After we took over, he came to me with a proposal. If we could get permission for an entrance, he would pay the cost of putting in a crosswalk and a light.

"In return he wanted to continue living in his suite here for two years. I wasn't real happy about that. He was a nice enough guy but I didn't like having him around. He said that he could not afford to live in a rented town house, and that he wasn't used to paying his own bills. Well, this crosswalk and light was going to cost about three hundred thousand dollars, which is a lot of rent to pay for two years, even with the fact that we would be supplying him with food. On the other hand, we had one suite in the hotel, and we were not catering to high rollers, so we weren't using the suite."

So Bennett made the deal and Jay Sarno lived at the Circus Circus hotel until 1977. He spent the rest of his life in Las Vegas. He was in and out of controversy for much of it. Not surprisingly, Sarno died with an unfulfilled dream. He spent most of his last years trying to get financing to create the largest resort ever, a fifteen-story, 6,000-room extravaganza called the Grandissimo. The theme: love.

(Actually, according to Mike Hartzell, Sarno had another dream, perhaps predating this one: he wanted to build another Circus Circus hotel, completely round, and prove that he could make the idea work.)

Once the deal was made for Circus Circus, Bennett and Pennington brought $2 million into the operation, a dangerously small stake for a business which had lost $400,000 in March 1974, the last statement that Bennett saw. "We could not afford to lose four hundred thousand dollars a month," Bennett says. And they could not afford to go long without profit. With Pennington concentrating on Western Equities, Bennett went to work straightening out the Circus Circus marketing message. The nude dancers were sent to the dressing room. The baby elephant was dispatched to a zoo. The trapeze artists stayed, and were joined by more clowns and jugglers, high-wire daredevils, stunt cyclists, and magicians. Bennett put a ceiling over the casino.

Though Bennett had little cash, he did have a vision of what would work. "Circus acts and kids and high rollers don't mix," he says. So he jettisoned the baccarat tables, abolished credit for players, and raised the circus acts to the second floor so that they were part of the ambiance, but not in the face of people who were trying to gamble. Bennett was doing something that ran directly counter to America's image of Las Vegas: he was building a family vacation spot for low-rolling, middle-class people who liked to include gambling in their itinerary. His guiding principle from the beginning was that the customer would get value for his or her money.

If Bennett was in conflict with Las Vegas's worldwide image, he was also in conflict with Circus Circus's own image, established during the Sarno years. The place had the smell of dishonesty about it.

"For example, there were jam auctions going on the mezzanine and one on the main floor," Bennett says. "The way it worked was a fellow would start out selling something cheap, two or three dollars. People would gather around, and he would say, 'Now how many of you would like one of these?' and he would hold up the item. People would raise their hands and he would go around and he would hand the item to people and say, 'Here, how about if we just give it to you.' He wouldn't charge them anything. Then he would come out with a sewing machine.

" 'How many of you people would like one of these?' he'd say. So, of course, people seeing what had just happened would raise their hands. Only this time the fellow would come around and he would take their money. People walked out of there shaking their heads, trying to figure out how they ended up buying a sewing machine."

While these auctions were private concessions, licensed by Circus Circus, that distinction was surely lost on the public, and it was not in keeping with the image that Bennett wanted to project. So the auctions were run out, too.

The first months were difficult, and Bennett's style from the beginning was definitely hands-on. "It was very iffy for a while there," says Glenn Schaeffer, who would join the company almost a decade later. "Bennett and Pennington went into Circus Circus with enough of a bank loan to survive for just a few months. If they could not turn a profit quickly, which looked to be impossible to outsiders, there would be no Circus Circus. Bennett is a man who makes big bets. The place had to make money in a matter of months or it was in big trouble. Bennett was there all the time. It was crisis management. He often didn't go home at night. He would be there twenty-four hours a day. He used to sleep in the cashier's cage."

Eliminating the auctions was not the only housecleaning that Bennett did. Sarno's management team was out, and in came the people who had impressed Bennett over the years.

"I cherry-picked Del Webb's organization," he says. "I picked the people I knew to be good: managers, shift bosses, department heads. I don't think Webb cared, because he never really believed in management. We covered every important area. We had a cage manager, but he couldn't be there twenty-four hours, so we also cherry-picked a shift manager who would be running the cage the rest of the time. Same thing with keno managers and slot managers and casino managers."

Drawing from his retailing experience, Bennett instituted daily income statements for every department, including the casino, the midway, and even the hotel's wedding chapel. (A few years later, when insurance rates went up, Bennett, ever cost-conscious, ordered executives to turn in their company cars.) Even his vocabulary suggested that something new was in the air. He referred to Circus Circus and the properties which would be acquired later as stores. He insisted that his company was selling a product, that the product was fun and excitement, and that management's job was to bring the customer into the high-margin section of the store.

Though many people in the business thought Bill Bennett had made a bet he couldn't win, he did win. The families came by the thousands. Bennett was practicing a hands-on, no-fat management style that would eventually turn Circus Circus into the most profitable and successful casino business on earth. What he did not only worked, it worked fast. Against all odds, Circus Circus went into black ink long before Bennett and Pennington's bankroll ran out.

"As it turned out, it was an easy turnaround," Bennett says. "We almost made money the first month. We bought it on May fourth, 1974, and we lost three hundred and something dollars the first month. The next month we made five hundred and sixty-five thousand dollars and change."

As a company, Circus Circus has made money ever since, tons of it, and over the years has grown at the rate of about one major addition or acquisition per year. And during that time there have been no mistakes, none of those multimillion-dollar miscalculations that sometimes come with speedy growth and can lead to early retirements and re-assignments. In fact, the company has rolled nothing but sevens, and almost all of the new properties turned a profit overnight. If nature abhors a vacuum, apparently so do CCE rooms. For twenty years customers have filled the new rooms and the old at an astonishing rate of 99 percent.

"We've always had an oversubscription rate," says Glenn Schaeffer, "so we were always confident that we could fill the rooms."

Mel Larsen, executive vice president, marketing, for

CCE, says, "When we build a new place the time is right, because we are filling up our other places. We never had big problems or worried about making money. Every place opened at one hundred percent occupancy."

Of course, the biggest Las Vegas acquisition of all was Circus Circus itself, which Bennett leased until 1983, when he bought it for $75 million. But the model for Circus Circus growth was there from the beginning. In 1972, under Sarno, Circus Circus had added a 400-room, fifteen-story tower. And by the time Bennett and company moved in, in 1974, the hole had already been dug for another fifteen-story tower, which would eventually contain 395 rooms and suites, bringing the Las Vegas property's total to 795.

In 1978 Bennett, who had long had his eye on the Reno market, saw his chance when an abandoned department store became available. It could be converted into a casino at an initial cost of approximately $30 million.

"I guess it was kind of Mickey Mouse moving into an old department store," Bennett says now, "but it was a chance to quickly get into the Reno market. We put in a hundred and three rooms. The law required at least a hundred. And we put up a huge circus tent in what had been the main body of the department store. That location was marginal for a few years, with just a hundred and three rooms, but in 1981 we added six hundred twenty-two rooms."

Half of the Reno purchase was financed with cash from Circus Circus Las Vegas, and half was mortgaged. Today Circus Circus Reno is a $125-million-a-year operation.

In 1979 Bennett was given the chance to buy fifty-one acres of land across the street from Circus Circus Las Vegas, and he grabbed it. For some time he had been fascinated by the idea of an RV park. Two hotels in town, the Stardust and the Hacienda, already had RV parks. Though Bennett did not think they were well run, he believed the parks had merit. Certainly they had done well for Disney. So the new property was turned into an RV park with 421 spaces, utility hookups, swimming pools, a Jacuzzi and saunas, a kids' playground, pet runs, a game arcade, a coin laundry, and a twenty-four-hour convenience store so that nobody who wanted to make a baloney sandwich would have to venture out into the streets, where other casinos would try to lure them in.

In that same year, 1979, Bennett made a deal which, while not his biggest, was arguably one of his best. Circus Circus's next-door neighbor, just to the south, was a small casino—a slot parlor, really—called Slots of Fun. "It was undermanaged," Bennett says. "And the people who were running it were not playing by the rules. They were playing 'one for me, one for the state.' They got caught and lost their license. So it was a fire sale."

We should all run into such a fire sale. Bennett bought Slots of Fun for $7.7 million, putting up only $700,000 in cash and letting the seller carry the rest. He enlarged the location, and almost every year since, the profit from Slots of Fun has been higher than the original purchase price. "We make about eight million a year profit out of that place," Bennett says. He thinks it over. "That," he says, "will keep you in wieners."

In 1980 CCE built again on the Las Vegas property, this time opening a self-contained little resort called Circus Manor, a complex of five three-story buildings containing

810 rooms with kitchenettes, a swimming pool, and its own mini-casino.

Of course, anytime you own two or more buildings on the same Las Vegas property, there is the terrible danger that a customer who is walking from one of your buildings to another will be enticed by a flashing billboard in the distance or seduced by the dinging of somebody else's slot machines. Particularly when he or she is losing, it is easy for a customer to believe that a pot of gold is waiting in some other casino. So in 1981, the same year that the Reno property was expanded, Circus Circus came up with a unique solution to the problem of customer leakage between the main casino and the Manor. The company built the Circus Sky Shuttle, which carries up to 1,200 customers per hour between the buildings in a Disney-like tram eighteen feet above the ground.

Also in 1981, CCE acquired and renovated Silver City about a quarter mile down the Strip, a small walk-in casino which has since become the first totally nonsmoking one in Las Vegas.

Through the 1980s there were frequent inquiries from Atlantic City. Would Circus Circus be interested in building on the Atlantic? A.C. could certainly gain some new players by adding the Disney of gaming to its mix. But the answer was always the same: "Not yet." For one thing, Bennett figured building a new operation in New Jersey would cost three times what it would cost in Vegas, so any move would have to be into an existing property. On top of that, New Jersey, like all of the emerging gambling jurisdictions, had higher gaming taxes than Nevada. And perhaps worse, there was the problem of too much regulation in Jersey.

"You've got to file papers just to move a slot machine in New Jersey," he says. "In our business there is constant change. But regulators restrict change. That's the nature of a bureaucracy."

By 1982 the original Circus Circus was ready for a face-lift and, as usual, the money was there to pay for it. A total of $7 million was put into expansion of the casino and dining areas, and a new front entrance marquee.

All of this building and expanding through 1982 was financed by cash and bank loans. There would be more building and expanding, lots more. In time Bennett would help to turn a town known as "Hell on the Colorado River" into a town known as "Boomtown USA." In time he would build the biggest entertainment building in the world. In time he would erect a high-tech pyramid in the desert. But all of this would come only after Circus Circus became a publicly owned company, an event which would be the last step in turning Jay Sarno's marketing disaster into the richest gaming company in the world.

4

The Kingdom

So what is this product that Bennett had to sell? It is, he will tell you, entertainment. And he's right. But it is entertainment that is different from a baseball game, a ballet, or a truck pull in ways that no prudent businessperson can ignore.

With this entertainment the customer sets the price. The customer decides when the show begins and how long it will last. And most depressing, if the customer is miffed for any reason, no matter how justified or unjustified, he or she can step outside and find a flock of competitors offering the same entertainment in an area the size of a neighborhood. Imagine ten movie theaters all in a row, showing the same film. How long would the theater with stale popcorn last? It's hard to imagine a customer for any product or service who could take his or her business elsewhere as quickly and effortlessly as the Las Vegas casino customer.

So this is not a business that forgives mistakes or poor management. One overcooked meal, one disgruntled dealer, one neglected telephone message, and the casino could say *adiós* to a customer who might have dropped 100,000 smackeroos on the tables over the next decade. The managers who didn't understand this are now running Taco Bells in Fresno.

And, as gambling spreads across the country at a frantic rate, gaming in Las Vegas is also not a business that forgives mediocrity, the way it once was. "Market position used to be no more than a Strip address," is the way Glenn Schaeffer puts it.

It is no longer enough simply to be "a casino in Las Vegas." You have to offer something that the customer can't find at the nearest riverboat or American Indian casino. The fact is that nobody has to go to Las Vegas anymore just to find a casino. That would be like going to Disney World just to ride Space Mountain.

There are new rules of business in Las Vegas, because there is a new Las Vegas. It began when Bill Bennett took the helm at Circus Circus. And if there is to be a single moment when a person can point to Las Vegas and say, "There, the new Las Vegas is fully realized," it will come during the fall and winter of 1993–94, with the completion of three major projects: Luxor (Circus Circus Enterprises), Treasure Island (Mirage Resorts), and the MGM Grand Hotel and Theme Park. The hallmark of the new Las Vegas is big themed hotels that offer entertainment, and damn near everything else, for the whole family.

Trip Gabriel, writing in *The New York Times Magazine* in December 1991, notes, "Las Vegas is drastically transforming its image. The city that was once perceived as the moral sinkhole of the country, home to the mob and every form of vice from gambling to prostitution, now feels, incredibly, like an acme of wholesomeness."

Gabriel also writes, "The new hotels, seeking the family crowd as much as the hard-core gambler, have borrowed a page from the Disney resorts. Every day Las Vegas looks more and more like a theme park."

And Steve Wynn, of Mirage fame, says, "I'm more of a Disney person than a casino guy."

These big new themed hotels are the places that are going to take the biggest slices of what should by then be a $4-billion-dollar-plus gaming revenue pie.

"By 1994," says Tom Hantges, a stock analyst who specializes in gaming stocks for USA Capital Management Group Inc., "fifty percent of all gaming revenues in Las Vegas will be generated by six properties, the three new themed hotels, along with the Mirage, Circus Circus, and the Excalibur."

It has always been true, but now more than ever, that the real product Bill Bennett and his colleagues have to sell is not just gambling, not just low-priced hotel rooms, not just dazzling revues. It is "the Las Vegas Experience," a treat for the body, mind, and spirit that tastes a little different to each person, but is always made from three necessary ingredients: the casino, the hotel, and the city.

At the time of the 1990 census, the city of Las Vegas was the fastest-growing city in America. The population of greater Las Vegas (Clark County) grew by 40 percent in the 1980s, to 700,000. Like most fast-growing cities, Vegas is being glutted by well-meaning people who want to escape from air pollution, traffic jams, overcrowding, and crime, zealous folks who have migrated in such grand numbers that they have created many of the same problems they hoped to leave behind. Yes, it's true that *INC.* magazine has rated Las Vegas the best entrepreneurial climate in America. It's true that Citibank, Lockheed, T. J. Maxx, and scores of other companies have all seen fit to set up shop in Vegas recently. But it's also true that Las Vegas has all the urban headaches. The water supply is dangerously low, the air pollution is bad, and there are even a few street gangs. Las Vegas isn't worse than the rest of America's tragic cities, but paradise it ain't.

Fortunately for the gaming industry, that is not the Las Vegas that people come to see. They come to see the "hallucination in the middle of the desert." They come to see the Las Vegas that has been called gaudy, cheap, brazen, glittering, sleazy, ostentatious, chintzy, flashy, garish, obscene, dazzling, tawdry, seedy, intoxicating, magnetic, and disgusting. Whether you look at those adjectives as reasons to come or reasons to stay away, it's clear that nobody means them to include the elementary schools, the churches, the drugstores, the small electronics firms, the shopping malls, the condominium developments, the candy shops, or the local charities.

Puzo writes, "Las Vegas is the big bet won, the miracle happening. An act of faith, possibly by the devil. There is no reason for Las Vegas to exist out there alone in the vast desert of Nevada. But its billions of watts of neon light are a Mecca for countless people from all corners of the globe."

Ninety-nine percent of the people who visit Las Vegas never see 99 percent of the city, except from a window seat in a 727 over McCarran Airport. Why on earth would they want to? What they come to see is a Las Vegas of the mind, an industry really, which directly or indirectly accounts for 55 percent of the city's jobs, but occupies just a few square miles of the land. The Las Vegas that drew 21 million people in 1991 is comprised of Glitter Gulch (downtown), the Strip (Las Vegas Boulevard), and a dozen or so casinos that would be just a chip shot from the Strip if there were any grass in this desert community. (In fact, the Strip isn't even in Las Vegas. It is part of an unincorporated area of Clark County.)

Furthermore, the Las Vegas that's been called gaudy, etc., is the old Las Vegas, and if it is not dying, it is at least sucking some serious wind. There's a new Las Vegas blooming out there in the desert, and it's rising from a seed that William Bennett planted twenty years ago. It is called "Disneyland with gambling" more often than "tawdry," and "the Orlando of the West" more often than "glitzy."

Las Vegas is a city that in 1990 drew 20.3 million visitors. According to polls conducted by the Las Vegas Convention and Visitors Authority, 75 percent of them were repeat visitors, and 35 percent were Californians. Forty-two percent flew into McCarran International Airport, eighteenth-busiest in the nation, on one of the 575 daily flights, where they were immediately greeted by slot machines rumored to be the stingiest in town. McCarran is uncommonly close to the action, so these visitors were at their hotels fifteen minutes after yanking their luggage off the carousel. They stayed, for the most part, in the city's 63 major hotels and 214 motels. They spent about $13 billion on hotels, meals, transportation, and entertainment, and left behind almost $4 billion in gaming losses, more than half of it in the city's 85,000 slot machines. A hundred and fifty thousand of them got married in the city's thirty wedding chapels, which gave them something in common with Bruce Willis, Elizabeth Taylor, Frank Sinatra, Joan Collins, and Jon Bon Jovi.

The average visitor to the city was a forty-seven-year-old married man who had gone to college and earned between $20,000 and $40,000 a year. He stayed for two or three nights, lost $533, and played for five to six hours a day. His loss was offset somewhat by the fact that his room cost about half what it would cost in another major city, and his meals probably less than a quarter of what he would pay elsewhere.

If Mr. Average Visitor got tired of eating at casino restaurants, he might have gone off to some of Las Vegas's better nonhotel restaurants, like Manfredi's, Kiefer's, or Pamplemousse. If he got to town in time he might have seen the Lido de Paris show at the Stardust, before it closed after running for thirty-two years through 2,200 performances, for more than 19 million people. Lido de Paris was the first show to feature what was called "female upper-body nudity." In any case, Mr. Average Visitor could catch any of maybe five dozen live shows. And if he didn't care for live performers, he could see a number of dead ones, including Elvis Presley, Judy Garland, Marilyn Monroe, Bobby Darin, and Buddy Holly, all of whom live on in Vegas in the form of impersonators. If there was not yet a Mrs. Average Visitor, and he wanted to get married, he could do so in one of the many churches or chapels, or for that special wedding he could tie the knot in a motor home cruising down Las Vegas Boulevard, in a thirty-five-foot limo equipped with a Jacuzzi, or at a drive-up window wedding chapel.

If Mr. Average Visitor brings the wife and kids he may have to put in a few hours away from the tables. He has choices. He can drive out to Lake Mead, thirty miles from Las Vegas, where he will find the largest man-made reservoir in the western hemisphere, more than 100 miles long, with 550 miles of shoreline. There the kids and the wife can go swimming, water-skiing, and boating while he works on his new crap system.

Or, also thirty miles from town, he can take the family to the spectacular Hoover Dam. While he is memorizing his souvenir "basic strategy at blackjack" card the wife and kids can take the tour, on which they will learn that the dam, which was built in the 1930s, is the equivalent in height of a sixty-five-story building. It supplies juice to Arizona, Southern California, and of course Nevada, where about 10 percent of its generated electricity is poured into the Las Vegas hotels, mostly for air-conditioning, and about one percent of the juice goes to light up the town.

There's more, if he cares. There's Red Rock Canyon, with its impressive geological formations, the Valley of Fire, and old mining towns. He can take the family to the Liberace Museum, to the chocolate factory, or even on a tour of the marshmallow factory outside of town.

If Mr. Average Visitor is a sports fan he's in luck. Along with the sporting events that are telecast at sports books all over town, and of course the occasional live boxing match at hotels like the Mirage and the Hilton, a number of live events are held in Vegas. Vegas is the host city for the National Rodeo Finals, which has the richest purse in rodeo and brings in 150,000 spectators for the nine-day event every December. In the summer the AAA Las Vegas All Stars, the farm team for the San Diego Padres, play baseball at Cashman Field Center. The PGA comes in for the Las Vegas Invitational in October. In the spring the Seniors Tour and the LPGA also hold tournaments in Las Vegas, one of the few cities to get all three professional golf tours. And, of course, Las Vegas is host to events that are more in line with what Mr. Average Visitor came for in the first place: the World Series of Poker and the World Blackjack Championship.

But let's face it, the main thing for this guy is to find time to gamble, and he will, even if he has to pass up a trip to the chocolate factory to do it. Though he might choose to play roulette at a casino where there are no costumed characters roaming around, and where gambling still feels a little bit sinful, this forty-seven-year-old fellow will still come to the new Las Vegas because he likes to gamble, and because gamblers like to be where the action is. In fact, he might come more often because instead of having a wife who says, "You're going to Las Vegas again, sweetheart?" he'll have a wife who says, "Las Vegas! Yes! I've always wanted to see that Luxor pyramid, and the kids would love Treasure Island." If he's not in Las Vegas for a convention, chances are that the city itself, not the particular hotel or casino, will be the main attraction for Mr. Average Visitor and his family. In 1991 Las Vegas had four "must see" attractions: Circus Circus, Excalibur, the Mirage, and Caesars Palace. In 1993, with the addition of Luxor and Treasure Island, there will be six, and when the MGM is completed in early 1994 there will be seven. This is a city that already has eight of the nine largest hotels in the world (the Excalibur, the Flamingo Hilton, the Las Vegas Hilton, the Mirage, Bally's, Circus Circus, the Imperial Palace, and the Stardust). The new MGM, with an Emerald City and movie theme and more than 5,000 rooms, will be bigger than all of them. So maybe in the future this forty-seven-year-old guy will see more of the marshmallow factory and the Liberace Museum than he cares to, but overall his experience won't change much. If he wants to sit at a blackjack table and gamble for five and a half hours, there will be plenty of tables to accommodate him. The new Las Vegas is definitely not going to muck around with the games that are played in the casinos. As they say in the World Series, you go with the guys that got you there.

5

The Castle

Two old friends ran into each other in Las Vegas. One guy said to the other, "Where you staying?" "No place," the other replied, "I'm only here for three days."

It's an old joke that says a lot about the relative importance a hotel room used to have in the old Las Vegas. A room was a place to sleep, if you slept. It was not designed to make you want to spend time in it. In fact, not until the 1960's did most Las Vegas hotels put TVs in the rooms, and some today don't even have cable. That's changing. The room, and particularly the hotel itself, are becoming a more important part of the package.

The most successful Las Vegas hotel of today, and possibly the only successful hotel of the future, is a full-service resort without golf. (There is golf in Las Vegas, and major tournaments are played there, but let's face it, golf is not as important in Las Vegas as it is in, say, Hilton Head.) This Las Vegas hotel is a place where you can sleep in comfort, eat cherry pie at six different restaurants, take in a show, shop for gifts, order flowers, make airline reservations, get married, swim ten laps, get your hair styled, buy a loaf of bread, leave your kids in a safe and entertaining place, and, of course, bet $100 on the Boston Celtics to win the NBA championship the following June.

It is simply no longer enough to offer a bedroom that is indistinguishable from all the other bedrooms in town. You've got to create a place that will draw people to it like ants to a picnic, and then pamper them so thoroughly and so cheaply that they will think it pointless ever to leave your building while they are in town.

"You must have a signature building," Glenn Schaeffer says, "something that says, 'Come into the place because this is really something special, and we won't let you down when you come inside.' Our company, we believe, is the most outlandish in terms of signature buildings and theme architecture. That is a big part of our success."

Long before the end of the 1980s, Jay Sarno's fifteen-story, 400-room circus dream on the Strip had been shaped into just such a hotel by William G. Bennett. Circus Circus, situated on sixty-six acres, had grown to 2,793 rooms in four buildings, two casinos, eight restaurants, a sky shuttle, the largest array of carnival games ever assembled under one roof, thirteen hours a day of free circus acts, the wedding chapel, the convenience store, the swimming pool, even an

RV park. It had become a full-service gambling resort for the whole family, with room left for more construction. Indeed, in late 1992 the company embarked on another dramatic addition to Circus Circus Las Vegas. This was to be called Grand Slam Canyon, a five-acre water-theme park under a huge dome.

Though the company had bought or built new properties in Reno and Laughlin, and even within Las Vegas, the Circus Circus Las Vegas hotel was still the big jewel in the CCE crown. But this was a growth company with buckets of cash and a chairman who yearned to outdo himself at least a time or two before he packed it in. It was time for CCE to build a signature building that would top all signature buildings.

"Of course, we didn't know right away what we would build," Bennett says. "We knew it had to be something with an enduring theme. You couldn't, for example, build a three-hundred-million-dollar hotel with a disco theme. The theme must be timeless. Like a circus. Everybody went to Barnum and Bailey as a kid. And we knew that we wanted to expand in Nevada, not Atlantic City. So we talked it over. These things are never one person's idea. I listen to a lot of intelligent people. I don't like yes-men and I don't think I have any. Usually when we end up deciding to do something, we can't go back and figure out whose idea it was. There's lots of ideas that get discussed; it's a very complicated process. You just bounce ideas around in a group and it all sort of comes together."

Bill Paulos, general manager of Circus Circus Las Vegas, who will be the first GM of Luxor, puts it this way:

"Ideas get thrown out. Let's build a big boat, let's make

the Colorado Belle in Laughlin three times as big as it already is, this time on the Las Vegas Strip. Okay, that's good. Or that stinks, let's leave that one on the wall. Let's build a Wild West place, no, that doesn't work, okay, how about a castle, yeah, how about a real castle."

Glenn Schaeffer recalls, "Initially, we wanted to do a first-rate Western-themed hotel, and we pursued the idea for a while. But an Old West hotel was difficult to pull off, particularly if you build high. A Western theme, particularly, should be spread out. Land on the Strip is too expensive these days to build something low and spread out. Big hotels in Las Vegas used to be eight hundred or a thousand rooms, but you're not in the ball game these days if you don't have a couple of thousand rooms. So how do you build a high-rise Old West hotel? What do you do, put a big cowboy on top, like the Dolphin or the Swan at Disney's Orlando park?"

So the Western theme was jettisoned, along with several others. But Bill Bennett recalls, "I had been wanting to build a castle-themed hotel for years. In fact, I'd had renderings done of different castles."

Bennett and his troops kept coming back to this castle idea. What started out as a rendering soon became a corporate vision. Yes, a castle would be just the thing. A castle that would enchant people from all over America, bring them back to the age of chivalry and romance. It would have towers and turrets and a medieval fantasy fountain that was three stories high. It would be like something out of, well, Disney.

It was decided. CCE would build the Excalibur, a massive hotel resort with a Camelot theme. Like Circus Circus, it would have free entertainment all day long, costumed characters, places to eat and shop and play nongambling games. Like Circus Circus, it would be a full-service operation with emphasis on the most important word in the corporate vocabulary: value. And furthermore, it would be the biggest hotel in the world.

To design the Excalibur Bennett turned to Veldon Simpson, the architect who had designed the Colorado Belle and the Edgewater in Laughlin and had supervised the expansion at CC Las Vegas.

"Mr. Bennett came to me and he said he wanted a castle," Simpson recalls. "So he sent me and Mel Larsen, who was then the director of marketing, off to Europe to look at castles. We went everywhere, England, Germany, Ireland, Scotland, Austria. All we did was look at castles. We saw over three hundred castles in ten days.

"Bennett wanted to do something that would have its own character, and he wanted to try very hard not to do anything that would resemble Disney World. The King Arthur idea had already been decided upon. He wanted a romantic castle, a fantasy, and he wanted it big. The unique thing about Las Vegas is that you can put up such huge buildings that you have to visualize what you are building from quite a distance. We knew that with four thousand rooms, we had to build the castle on such a large scale that it didn't get lost in the sheer size of the building."

Typical of CCE, the corporation used as much cash as possible. Of the $290 million needed to build the Excalibur, CCE borrowed $100 million and paid the other $190 million in cash from its wallet. By keeping a lid on debt, the Excalibur could survive the bread-and-water days if they ever came, and could get by on a daily nut that was about one-fourth of that needed by the Mirage.

But the bread-and-water days never came. The rendering of a castle evolved into the most stunning debut in Las Vegas history, and in hotel history. In June 1990, the Excalibur, the largest retail establishment in the country, opened for business, and 70,000 customers walked through the door on the first day. The hotel had four twenty-eight-story towers containing 4,032 rooms, most of them under forty-five dollars, and all of them were filled every night in the first year of operation. In fact, for a while the hotel was getting 4,000 calls a day from people who wanted room reservations.

"In our first year we drew just about as well as Disney World in its first year," Schaeffer says. "In 1972 Disney drew about ten point eight million. Excalibur attracted somewhere between ten and eleven million."

(Incredibly, CCE was getting all this business without much help from the popular press. While the daily newspapers and *USA Today* ran stories, *Time* and *Newsweek* have pretty much ignored the biggest hotel in the world. There is, says Glenn Schaeffer, a strong anti–Las Vegas bias among the top news magazines.)

The Excalibur, with its theme of Camelot, King Arthur, and all things medieval, has everything that a hotel of the new Las Vegas should have, including a 7,000-car parking lot. It has seven restaurants with names like Sir Lanca-Lotta-Pasta (dubbed by Mrs. Bennett), Sir Galahad's, and the Sherwood Forest Cafe. It has shopping at the Fantasy Faire, where you can buy glass wizards and pewter dragons. It has a theme atmosphere, with costumed jugglers and damsels and fools roaming about the building all day long; it has the Canterbury Wedding Chapel, even convenience stores so customers don't have to run out to buy milk and cookies for the kids.

And, of course, it has a casino, 100,000 square feet of it, with 2,800 slot machines and 100 table games under high ceilings and gold heraldic banners, where dealers and cocktail waitresses wear the costumes of the realm and the chairs at the slot machines are upholstered in royal purple.

The other major ingredient in the Las Vegas hotel experience is food. If Las Vegas is famous for anything besides gambling and entertainment, it's food, and lots of it.

In 1990, for example, the Excalibur served the juice of 6 million oranges, more than 50,000 gallons of coffee, almost 7 million extra-large grade-A eggs, more than a million pancakes, more than 5 million pounds of roast beef, 600,000 pounds of ham, 800,000 pounds of chicken, and about 1.5 million bagels.

The longest lines in Vegas are for the legendary buffets. (The second-longest lines are for the ATM machines.) Every hotel has one, and the competition to be the best is hot. (The word around town from buffet aficionados, as of fall 1992, was that the Golden Nugget had the best.)

There are two widely held, and indisputable, beliefs about the quality of food in Las Vegas. One is "The food is awful." The other is "The food is great."

However, there is no disagreement about the price of a restaurant meal in Las Vegas casino-hotels. It's low.

Even in 1993 it was quite easy in Las Vegas to find a complete breakfast for less than three dollars, and dinner, with everything from salad to strawberry shortcake, for less than five dollars. Given the fact that you can get a room at a number of casino-hotels for less than forty dollars, you could probably live in a Las Vegas hotel for less than it costs you to live at home, if you didn't gamble. In fact, there are buffet-hoppers, people who don't gamble but just go to Las Vegas for two- and three-day eating orgies.

Las Vegas hotel restaurants are different from restaurants everywhere else in one significant way. They are not there to make a profit. Circus Circus, for example, loses about seventy cents every time it serves a meal. Las Vegas hotels are in the gaming business, not the hotel business, and certainly not the restaurant business. The restaurants were put there originally to keep hungry gamblers from walking out the door. But in time the hotels discovered that restaurants could do more than that. They could be used as loss leaders to draw people into the casino, and if the question is "Excuse me, could you tell me where the coffee shop is?" the answer is usually "Just walk through the casino." Almost any frequent Las Vegas visitor can tell you about the four-dollar dinner he had that cost him fifty-four dollars because he dropped fifty dollars at the roulette table on his way back through the casino.

One way that Las Vegas restaurants are used to increase casino business is through differential pricing, reducing the already low price even further at certain hours. The *Las Vegas Advisor (LVA),* a newsletter that is devoted to helping people get the most for their money in Las Vegas, publishes its top ten values every month. In June 1992, for example, two of the bargains were at the Horseshoe, downtown: a complete New York steak dinner for $2 from 10 P.M. to 5:45 A.M., and an enormous ham-and-egg breakfast for $2.50 from 4 A.M. to 2 P.M.

Bill Friedman gives an example of this differential pricing in his 1982 book *Casino Management* (Lyle Stuart), which is the bible of the industry, read by anyone who wants to get ahead in the gaming business. Friedman writes about the Showboat Hotel, which is three miles from downtown and the Strip, and caters mostly to locals:

> *In 1956 it inaugurated a premium quality $.49 breakfast from 12:00 P.M. to 6:00 A.M. During the following fifteen years, The Showboat served almost three million of these breakfasts, almost five hundred a night. These meals, a bingo game, and a bowling alley, created a profitable late-night business for the casino.*

Bill Bennett says, "We make money on hotel rooms, but not enough to be proud of. We lose money on food and beverage. The profit center is the casino. A lot of Las Vegas operations got in trouble because they forgot what business they are in. We try to keep the place full, low-priced buffet, low-priced rooms, and so forth. Some people in this business try to make money on everything they do. It's that corporate mentality that every department must show a profit. You can't run a place like this from a corporate boardroom in New York or Los Angeles."

6

The Court Jesters

The father of Nevada casino entertainment was a man named Newton, but it wasn't Wayne. And he wasn't from Las Vegas or Reno. He was Newton Crumley, Jr., of Elko, Nevada.

When Crumley's father bought the Commercial Hotel in Elko in the early 1940s, young Newton decided to make his mark in the business by booking an act touted simply as "a female dancer" into the Commercial lounge. Crumley's dancer packed the place. So Crumley went looking for even bigger talent. He signed big-band leader Ted Lewis.

Nancy J. Jackson, in a 1976 book written for Nevada's celebration of the U.S. bicentennial, writes, "When this startling announcement hit the local papers it shocked the residents of Elko and Elko County. It was the general feeling that the brash young man would send the Commercial Hotel into bankruptcy."

The opposite occurred. Not only did Lewis draw people to the casino, but it was rumored that he and his band members gambled away more than $12,000. So Crumley went on to book Paul Whiteman, Sophie Tucker, Jimmy Dorsey, Chico Marx, the Ritz Brothers, Phil Harris, and Lawrence Welk.

Crumley was just a step ahead of William Harrah, the innovative gaming pioneer of Reno and Lake Tahoe. By the 1950s Harrah was hiring entertainers like Sammy Davis, Jr., and Frank Sinatra, who would forever be linked in the public mind with Las Vegas.

"The important thing," Harrah said, "is to hire stars that bring in the customers and to keep those stars happy so they come back."

Having said that, Harrah began a tradition of pampering casino headliners with private jets, limousines, carefully researched gifts, and we can only fantasize about what else.

(Bill Cosby once turned the tables at Christmastime and bought a Mercedes for Harrah, who had amassed the most famous collection of antique cars in the world.)

From the beginning, entertainment in Las Vegas, like food, has been seen as a loss leader. You don't hire Frank Sinatra so you can make a few bucks selling tickets to his show. You hire him because more people will come to Las Vegas if big-name entertainers are playing in town, and they will especially come to those casino-hotels that have the big names flashing on huge neon signs out front, and while they are there they will gamble. This explains why a Las Vegas headliner can make a hell of a lot more money singing for 900 people in Las Vegas than he or she can singing for 15,000 in Hammond, Indiana.

Over the years the choice of hotel entertainers has been regarded almost as a science. The question was never simply "Who will attract a lot of people?" but also "What kind of people?" It has long been accepted as holy writ that two stars of equal magnitude could attract the same number of fans, but that you could pay the mortgage off of one star and file for bankruptcy thanks to the other. In other words, some idols bring in crowds that gamble, and some bring in crowds that don't.

Conventional wisdom in the gaming industry has it that Frank Sinatra is the all-time king at bringing in high rollers, that Elvis Presley drew huge crowds that didn't gamble much, and that Barbra Streisand is a great singer whose fans didn't leave ten cents on the tables. Implicit in this belief is the further belief that an entertainer can create for a hotel a market that is not already there. It is a belief which is given great credibility in Las Vegas, and one that John Giovenco says is "horseshit."

Giovenco was the president of Hilton's gaming division, one of the most important players in the Las Vegas entertainment game. Hilton, which pays about $250,000 a week to Wayne Newton and $500,000 weekly to Bill Cosby, has four Nevada locations. Incredibly, the two Vegas operations, the Las Vegas Hilton and the Flamingo, account for 70 percent of the profits of the entire Hilton corporation.

"They used to say that Elvis didn't draw a gaming crowd," Giovenco says, "but we made more money when he played than with anybody else, because he drew tremendous crowds. He was always our top superstar. We used to keep charts on how various entertainers did and with him I understood what they meant by 'off the charts.' It is a myth that there is a direct correlation between the entertainer you have and the level of casino gambling. The idea that Sinatra draws a better gambling crowd I think is mostly bullshit. What you need is a large number of people."

Giovenco says the market dictates the entertainer, not the other way around.

"Entertainment is a marketing decision made by a property, to provide an enjoyable experience for the guests that fit the market niche of that property. In Las Vegas hotels, entertainment is tailored to fit the various market segments. At the Hilton Las Vegas, we cater to conventioneers and premium players. Therefore, we have a star policy, Wayne Newton, Bill Cosby, and so forth. At the Reno Hilton we combine the production shows and contemporary concert acts because of the market segment there. At the Las Vegas Flamingo, we have 'City Lites,' the big revue. It's been running for eleven years and it sells out every night. The Las Vegas Flamingo customer is a tour-and-travel customer, and that show is sold in conjunction with the room, as part of a package. But at the Flamingo in Laughlin we have a customer who wants to see Gladys Knight, Frankie Valli, the Four Tops, and the Temptations, so that's what we book. The point is you hire entertainment that will appeal to your particular segment of the market."

Though entertainment is still a major ingredient in the Las Vegas mix, most old hands will tell you that it is not what it used to be. Vegas has always been famous for big, glitzy shows with lots of tall, bare-breasted females. You can still find them, certainly, and "City Lites" is an example. But those shows are getting expensive, even by Las Vegas standards, and even when they are produced, these days they are often scaled down. The fact is that nightclub entertainment has been declining everywhere and Las Vegas is reflecting that.

"One of the problems," says Giovenco, "is that the big stars of the fifties, sixties, and seventies are not being replaced. You don't have the Frank Sinatras, the Andy Williamses, Dean Martins, or Liberaces that you used to. And the contemporary acts, like Paula Abdul and Billy Joel, play in arenas and stadiums. Most Las Vegas showrooms are in the six hundred to a thousand capacity range. We seat fifteen hundred and we're the biggest in town. By today's standards that is much too small. Of course, you're not trying to make money with entertainment, but you're trying to lose just a little."

Giovenco says another reason for the change is that the casino itself is becoming more entertaining.

"Now you've got all these interesting new slot machines and slot tournaments and so forth. So guests don't need that entertainer as much; it's not as much of a 'must do' on a trip as it used to be."

There is one form of entertainment that Giovenco is bullish on: boxing. The Las Vegas Hilton, like Caesars Palace and the Mirage, pays big bucks to land major boxing matches.

"Boxing also qualifies as entertainment," he says. "If

you get a good crowd for boxing you are going to make a lot of money. Boxing brings in a special crowd, the crowd you specifically invite. If you have a big star playing you don't go out and invite all your high rollers to come and see him, but in boxing you do invite them for a big match. You invite a large number of people and it is more profitable than other forms of entertainment."

Las Vegas may not be creating new stars, but you could cast a year of *Murder, She Wrote* episodes with the old ones who are still playing at the hotels. In fact, if the question is "What ever happened to?" the answer can often be found on a drive along Las Vegas Boulevard. Among the veterans strutting their stuff in the fall of 1992 were Donald O'Connor and June Allyson at the Dunes; Jerry Lewis, Debbie Reynolds, and Dean Martin at the Desert Inn; the Four Lads and the Four Aces at the Four Queens; and Don Rickles at the Golden Nugget. From a slightly newer generation you could find George Carlin at Bally's, Kenny Rogers at the Mirage, and Diana Ross at the Las Vegas Hilton. And still more up-to-date, Louie Anderson and Rita Rudner at Bally's, David Copperfield and Jay Leno at Caesars, and Kenny G. at the Las Vegas Hilton.

But you won't find big-name stars or sexy revues in any of the CCE hotels. In the matter of entertainment, Circus Circus has marched to the beat of a different drummer since the beginning, and the history of that company's entertainment tells us a lot about the new Las Vegas.

The director of entertainment for the Las Vegas Circus Circus and the Excalibur, Mike Hartzell, is a former acrobat. In his forties, Hartzell is a youthful, athletic-looking guy who still works out on the trapeze in his garage, but in point of service he may be the senior Circus Circus employee, having arrived two weeks before the hotel even opened. He came for a three-month stint and became a ringmaster under Sarno, then a production manager under Bennett, before taking charge of the entertainment. He is now into his third decade with CCE. Hartzell has seen the evolution of entertainment at Circus Circus, and what he has seen is a reflection of both the overall marketing of CCE and the evolution of the new Las Vegas.

"When I first came to town before Circus Circus even opened, I saw a big billboard for the hotel, which I assumed was a family-oriented operation," he says. "But this billboard had a picture of a beautiful red-headed girl climbing over the top of it, and it said 'Circus Circus opening in October,' and 'Circus Circus ain't kid stuff.' I don't think Sarno quite understood what he had. He was trying to mix this Circus theme with the sophisticated Las Vegas nightlife."

Hartzell's assumption that a circus theme would produce wholesome family entertainment seems as obvious as sand in the desert, but Sarno apparently missed it. Certainly the circus theme did dominate the entertainment under Sarno. In fact, Sarno had an image of himself wearing a ringmaster's uniform printed on all the casino souvenirs, and he did provide his customers with aerialists, jugglers, and clowns.

"But," Hartzell recalls, "Sarno also had a peep show where you put in a quarter and you would see a seminude girl dancing. And he had something called 'The Bed Toss,' where you had a lady lying on a large sofa. You'd throw a ball at a target and if you hit it, the lady would get up and dance for you, nude. And he had the 'Ooh La La Theatre,' where there was a nude girl supposedly frozen in a block of ice. Not only that, but he had all these adult elements mixed in with the family elements."

Bennett and Pennington, of course, took the family route and gave the nude ladies their pink slips. Since that time entertainment at Circus Circus has been primarily provided by an array of jugglers, contortionists, clowns, slack-wire stars, and other circus acts that Hartzell brings in from all over the world.

However, the most striking difference between Circus Circus's approach to entertainment and that of the rest of Las Vegas is not that the entertainment is wholesome. It is the fact that the entertainment is free, and that it goes on all day long, not in an isolated theater (which traditionally is situated so as to release its audience right into the casino) but throughout the hotel. Entertainment at Circus Circus is not a low-priced loss leader; it is part of the package.

When CCE and Hartzell began to consider the entertainment package for the Excalibur, they faced a problem, and made a decision, which might be unique in the history of Las Vegas.

"We looked at renaissance fairs across the country," Hartzell says, "and they seemed too adult, too bawdy. The customers who come into our place can be sensitive to what they perceive as less than family entertainment, the off-color remark, and so forth. So we had to come up with something that was a compromise between the real thing and what was presentable at a Las Vegas hotel."

Too adult? Presentable at a Las Vegas hotel? Las Vegas,

it seems, had come full circle. Here was a major casino-hotel actually *toning down* the sexual content of an entertainment to make it appropriate for its Las Vegas audience.

With construction of the Excalibur, CCE continued the tradition of free entertainment, in the form of strolling minstrels, jugglers, madrigal singers, and a mezzanine theater that runs all day long, but the company added to the mix a couple of paid shows. At King Arthur's Tournament, guests cheer for their favorite knight, dine without silverware, and witness a medieval wedding ceremony every night. It is an audience-participation show which has, says Hartzell, "a story line instead of a chorus line." There is also an afternoon show featuring the Lipizzaner Stallions.

"Everybody said forget afternoon entertainment in Las Vegas, it's dead," says Hartzell. "But I went to see the Lipizzaner Stallions when they came to town, and they had eight thousand people for an afternoon performance. So I signed them up."

So it is true that nightclub entertainment in Las Vegas is fading, and casinos are, as Giovenco says, getting more entertaining. But entertainment is not losing its importance as a major element in the Las Vegas experience. Entertainment has become not less important to Las Vegas, but more important. With each new Las Vegas project that comes off the drafting table, more emphasis is put on entertainment and less on pure gambling.

Bennett says, "As gaming continues to proliferate nationally, our edge lies in the entertainment side. We will compete most effectively by raising the total entertainment factor;

using more attractions for the enjoyment of the widest possible audience."

The MGM Grand will have a theme park and twelve rides. The Mirage's new project, Treasure Island, will have a pirate extravaganza on Las Vegas Boulevard every day featuring live actors. And CCE's new Luxor will present what Glenn Schaeffer believes is the future of Las Vegas entertainment.

The Luxor will be a pyramid-shaped casino-hotel with Egyptian architecture, and hieroglyphics, and a "mysteries of ancient Egypt" theme. But much of the entertainment will be as new as the theme is old.

"Market futurists, like Faith Popcorn, predict that trips with high tech will be a rising element of the tourism business," Schaeffer says. "Our high-tech adventures at Luxor will be the most advanced of their kind. But we have to keep in mind that technology by itself is not family entertainment. Along with the technology we need creativity, story, and a sense of adventure."

"In a way," says Bennett, "we are in the excursion business. The pyramid, for example, will take customers on memorable trips once they're inside. More and more, people want the sense of having traveled to someplace special, but they don't like the trouble or risk or cost of going terribly far. This is the idea of cruise ship vacationing. For example, our total entertainment environments work the same way. And we use exotic or historic themes to help carry off this illusion. But this isn't just something for kids to do while the parents use the gaming facilities. Good entertainment is a matter of aiming for the child in all of us."

7

The Arena

Author and self-help coach Anthony Robbins says that when you boil it all down, everything we do in life, we do to acquire a state change. He says we don't really want money, or a new bicycle, or a girlfriend or boyfriend. What we want is a feeling, or state, which we believe those things will give us.

The experience that Las Vegas offers is the feeling of being a king or a queen. The deal is simple: I will gamble at your tables. In return you must pamper me, make me feel special. You must send attractive cocktail waitresses to the gaming table with free drinks for me, you must give me meals at such low cost that they seem to be free, you must park my car for me when I arrive and fetch it for me when I leave. You must make my bed; sing, dance, and juggle for me; and now and then, when I am playing the games, you must drop stacks of colorful and valuable chips in front of me.

This is the deal and this is why 93 percent of the people who leave Las Vegas, almost all of them with less cash than they brought, report that they had a good time. The money they lost paid for the excitement of gambling, and everything else was damn near free.

"The customer understands this," Glenn Schaeffer says. "Sure, sometimes they will tell you about how much money they won, but mostly they will tell you, 'Look, I lost a little money, I had a good time, and it was worth it.' "

A casino is a place cut loose from time. It is a place not touched by apprehensions about matters beyond the casino doors, a place where you don't have to hear about famine in Ethiopia, or who's divorcing whom in the royal family. It is a place of music, of color, of emotions just barely under control, a place of hope and superstition. It is also a place in which it is easy to get disoriented. North, east, south, and west are as hard to figure out as the time of day. There are no clocks.

Within this arena, and within the Las Vegas experience, there is a singularly intense experience that comes with gambling. It is not as good as sex, but for many people it is better than going to a movie, eating peanut butter pie, or riding a bicycle. It is often called juice. That juice, as much as anything, is the product that Bennett and his colleagues have to sell. Like any product, it can be sold profitably or at a loss, depending on how savvy management is about packaging, pricing, and marketing.

But a business can't measure the degree of restlessness in a customer's soul, the voltage running through his or her veins. It can only bring its skills to bear on the observable product. In the casino business the most observable product is the games, and that's why it is called the gaming industry.

The principle behind all of the games, except poker, is the same: We, the casino, will give you, the customer, a fair chance to win money, and we will play any game with you at any time, twenty-four hours a day, seven days a week. But because we have to pay for the lights and the music and the dealers and still make a profit, we will set the games up so that we have a slightly higher probability of winning than you do.

That higher probability is called the house advantage, and it really is slight when you compare it to a state lottery, which often keeps 50 percent, or even a horse track, which drags 15 to 20 percent right off the top. This house advantage can be seen as the price of gambling. And the fierce competition of more than sixty casinos from the interstate to Glitter Gulch has done to the price of gambling what competition does to the price of anything: kept it down, and made casino gambling in Las Vegas the best gambling bargain in history.

A higher house advantage, by the way, does not necessarily correlate to a higher house profit. Twenty-one, for example, has a very low house advantage, but it is the most profitable table game in the casino. A slot machine that returns only 75 percent of the money dropped into it will be less profitable than a slot machine that returns 96 percent, because the one that returns 96 percent has provided more gamblers with more positive gambling experiences and it's going to get used, while the one that returns only seventy-five cents on the dollar is going to get ignored.

The effect of the house advantage on any given day is measured by three numbers: the drop, the win, and the hold.

The drop is the total amount of money spent on chips or lost in cash. (Cash bets don't occur much at the tables, only when some eager hunch player is trying to get a bet down before the dice are thrown or is making a single bet on his way to the men's room. Quarter, nickel, and penny—yes, penny—slot machines are also cash bets, but tokens are used for the $1, $5, $100, and $500 slot machines.) The drop figure, naturally, is nowhere near the amount of money gambled in a day, because a man or woman with $100 could bet thousands of dollars by winning and losing all day long. The total amount of money gambled is called the handle, but you'd have to post two full-time mathematicians at each table just to keep track of it, and even then it would have no particular value.

The win is the amount of money the casino has when the amount of chips cashed in is subtracted from the drop.

The hold is the same as the win, but it is expressed as a percentage of the drop.

So if you went to the Circus Circus hotel in Las Vegas and brought $100 worth of chips at a twenty-one table, the dealer would drop that $100 into a locked box under his or her table, and $100 would be added to the day's drop, no matter how your luck ran at that table. If you played for ten minutes or ten hours, then left the table with eighty dollars in chips, which you then cashed in at the cashier's window, the casino would have a win of twenty dollars from you and a hold of 20 percent.

The win, of course, is not profit. From that win the casino has to pay the dealers, the floormen, who watch the tables, the boxmen, who watch the craps action, the security guards, the company that sells the cards and dice, the people who vacuum the carpet, the electric company, the people who fix the slot machines, the company that makes the slot machines, the bankers who lent the money, the executives who manage the casino, the state that taxes it, the commission that licenses it . . . and so forth. And let's not forget, there is the cost of all those free cocktails you sucked up while you were playing twenty-one. A casino could have a win in the millions and still not make a profit. In fact, many casinos in Las Vegas and Atlantic City are doing exactly that.

The house advantage is sacred in the industry. But the reality is that if a casino set itself up to make money on its rooms, restaurants, and shows, it could conceivably make a casino profit without any edge at all. Consider this: the house advantage at a Las Vegas casino runs from a high of 25 percent in keno to a low of 6.7 percent with certain craps bets, and the advantage on most table bets is less than 4 percent. And yet casinos generally keep around 17 percent of the money that is bet at tables. (The average slot hold on the Strip is 6 to 9 percent.) What this suggests is that the greatest generator of money for the casino is not its mathematical edge in the games, but rather the habits of people who gamble. The casinos would go down in flames tomorrow if gamblers obeyed one simple rule: quit when you're ahead. (And the chances of being ahead at some point in a session are excellent.) But gamblers, for the most part, are not people who come to win. They are people who come to play.

And so they recycle money. The result is that people who lose their bankroll have no money left with which to win, and people who win now have bigger bankrolls to lose.

While Las Vegas casinos vary greatly in size, there are certain principles about the arrangement of furniture that a casino violates at its own peril. Tables games, slot machines, rest rooms, restaurants, etc., are all positioned for maximum casino profit.

Here is Gary O'Keefe, who runs the casino at CC in Las Vegas, explaining: "The rule of thumb is you try to put your table games in a high traffic flow area, toward the center, around the cashiers' cage. You've got a bar close by. In fact, if you stand in a pit where there are craps and twenty-one tables, you can probably see a bar and a cashier's cage close by.

"Slots are all over the place. If you come out of a restaurant you will see slot machines. If you leave a bar you will see slot machines. If you park your car in the lot and come in a side door, you will see slot machines. You wouldn't put a pit in some side area where it can get lost, but you put slot machines everywhere."

In *Casino Management,* Bill Friedman elaborates:

The highly profitable $1 slot carousels are often placed near casino entrances. Since crap tables have the highest per-unit revenue, they are usually situated near the showroom exit and cashier's cage on the Strip; in downtown Las Vegas, they are typically placed near the cage and the casino bar. The *cage should be placed as far as possible from the casino exits, to force winners to walk through the entire casino after they cash out. This is also a security feature—a robber would have to run through the entire casino to make an escape.*

Restrooms are a necessity. They should also be far from the exits, in the lowest and least marketed traffic area, to require customers to walk back through the entire casino operation after using them. Entertainment and dining facilities and elevators from the rooms should be at the opposite end of the casino from the exits, to draw patrons through the whole operation. This layout design affords the greatest game marketability, induces the greatest impulse play, and maximizes revenues and thus profits.

8

The Games

On Monday, March 9, 1992, Glenn Schaeffer arrived in his office early, as usual. He found on his desk what he and all the CCE top executives find on their desks every morning: the reports on the previous day's operation at all seven CCE locations. These collections of numbers are the corporation's medical chart. How fast is the heart beating, what's the blood pressure? How does the patient feel right now, this moment? If there have been any significant security problems over the weekend, there will be a report to tell Schaeffer about it. If there have been any significant maintenance problems, there will be another report to tell him about that. If anybody has won a huge keno or slot jackpot, there will be a report about that, too.

But foremost among the reports are the Daily Managerial Reports.

"The Daily Managerial Report," Schaeffer says, "is the heart of CCE management. Bennett is a quick-response kind of guy, and this is him at his best. The daily reports tell us exactly what is happening in the properties, almost on a real-time basis."

March 9 was a Monday, so on that day Schaeffer had in front of him the reports for Saturday and Sunday. He picked up the Excalibur Daily Managerial Report for Saturday, March 7. This particular report was seven legal-sized pages filled with numbers. By glancing at those numbers Schaeffer could see how much money the Excalibur made on Saturday, how much it had expected to make, how much it spent to make that money, where the money came from, how many employees worked that day, and how the totals for the month compared to the same date a month ago and the same date a year ago.

By reading the Saturday report Schaeffer learned that the weather had been rainy and cool, that 1,945 employees had worked in the hotel that day, and that 928 had worked in the casino.

Because the Excalibur is a major tourist attraction, it draws an enormous amount of walk-in business that is the envy of every hotel in town (with the possible exception of the Mirage, which is also a top attraction, and CC Las Vegas). Because the Excalibur lures in so many thousands of people who are not staying at the hotel, there was no way for Schaeffer to compute how many people actually gambled in the casino that day. But he knew that those who did gamble played seven major games: twenty-one, craps, keno, poker, roulette, sports betting, and slot machines, which includes the highly successful video poker machines. That's where 99 percent of the casino money came from. In fact, about 90 percent of it came from twenty-one and slots.

The most popular casino game in the mining camps and cattle towns of the nineteenth century was faro, a good percentage card game that was played on a layout called a faro bank. Faro is a bit slow and complicated by today's standards, and it would be easier to find a snow bank than a faro bank in Las Vegas today. But for the most part, casino games do not go out of style. Folks come to Las Vegas to play the familiar blackjack, craps, roulette, etc., and generally they cast a cynical eye at any table that promises a new gaming experience.

Nonetheless, there are legions of game salespeople out there trying to get their wares into casinos.

"I get dozens of people in here every month, trying to sell us on new games," says Gary O'Keefe, who runs the casino at Circus Circus Las Vegas. "They come in with ideas for games that are so confusing that nobody would play them. A game has to be simple. People don't want to spend a lot of time learning how to play a game, especially when mistakes are costing them money. Or others will come in here with a game that is such an elementary variation on an existing game that it doesn't really offer anything new.

"Had one guy come in here with an idea for a game called Nevada Mines. He had a layout for roulette with the names of a bunch of gold mines here in Nevada on it, and various payoffs for each mine. He thought this would really push up the drop on roulette. People will come in with even simpler ideas, like, 'Let's put colored boxes on the crap table,' or 'Let's make the roulette numbers pink and green instead of black and red.' These are ideas that don't really change anything."

If an entrepreneur wants to sell a new game, he or she must first go to the gaming commission for approval. The game won't be approved if it has too high a hold percentage, or if it is deceptive to the point of looking crooked. If the game is approved, its owner then has to convince a casino to put it in for a 90-day trial. After that the game's creator can make the rounds up and down the Strip and try to sell the game to casinos. If a casino takes the game, the owner will get a percentage of the drop on the game or, more likely, a monthly fee for every layout of the game in the casino.

One game making some headway in Las Vegas is Caribbean Stud. "People will play it because it is a variation on poker, which they already know," O'Keefe says. "The owner of the game has rights to the layout and provides all the gadgetry that goes with it. It's very popular at some casinos. We don't go in much for new games here, though. Why pay for games when nobody owns blackjack, or craps or roulette?"

In recent years many casinos, including the Excalibur, have made space for Asian games like pai gow poker and sic bo, to please huge numbers of Asian gamblers who have been rushing to Las Vegas to help reduce the trade deficit. But those seven major games are still to CCE what Chevrolet, Buick, Cadillac, Oldsmobile, and Pontiac are to General Motors.

And just as cars come in a variety of colors, models, and

100

options, but ultimately are the same thing, casino games come in a variety of shapes, rules, and paces, but offer the same thing: juice.

TWENTY-ONE

The game of twenty-one, played in casinos, is usually called blackjack. But that is incorrect. In blackjack the deal rotates from player to player; in twenty-one it does not. The essence of the game is this: you accept or reject cards offered to you by the dealer, with the goal of having a higher point total than the dealer without going over twenty-one. This is simple but not always easy, and the "basic strategy" of the game is to know the likelihood of your going over twenty-one (busting) on the next card, compared to the probability of the dealer's busting or getting a higher point total than you. The only other thing you need to know is that the player makes all the decisions and the dealer makes none. The dealer, representing the house, must take a card if she has a total of sixteen or less, and she cannot take a card if she has a total of seventeen or more. She could just as well be a robot, and perhaps someday she will be.

Casino twenty-one is unique in two ways. It is the only casino game in which the player can make decisions that affect the outcome of the game. (Of course, the player can do that in poker, too, but the casino has no stake in the outcome of the poker game.) In other games the player can make decisions about how much money to bet and what kind of bet to make, but cannot change the destination of a roulette ball or dictate the roll of the dice.

Twenty-one is the most lucrative table game for the casino. It is played legally for money in Nevada, New Jersey, and at least a dozen other states, as well as Puerto Rico, parts of Canada, much of the Caribbean and South America, many European countries, the Middle East, Macao, Sri Lanka, Botswana, and many countries that nobody has ever heard of and which cannot be easily pronounced.

Twenty-one has also been one of the most popular illegal games for years because the only equipment required is a deck of cards, which can be easily hidden, and it offers the player a decent chance of winning if the game is not rigged.

The game in some form goes back at least to the 1500s, but it started showing up in U.S. casinos in Indiana in the early 1900s.

Like all gambling games, twenty-one inspires irrational beliefs. Many players, for example, believe that a poor player at the table hurts their chances of winning. The fact is that an unwise decision by another player has as much chance of helping your hand as it does of hurting it. This ignorance would be harmless enough except that it sometimes brings out the obnoxiousness in players, and it's not unusual to hear some loser grumbling that he would have won if the other guy had known how to play the game.

(And while we're on the subject of obnoxious people, it is worth noting that Las Vegas has a far lower obnoxious index than Atlantic City, and Atlantic City has a far lower obnoxious factor than, for example, the Foxwood Casino in Connecticut. There are many ways to interpret this, but one that comes to mind is that the shorter the average visit to a casino, the higher the obnoxious level. People in Las Vegas are staying for three days; in Atlantic City, for one whole day; in Foxwood, for perhaps a few hours. They become less patient with a slow game, more anxious for success as the clock ticks. A major study will have to be done on this phenomenon someday. In the meantime, the more fascinating observation is not that people are sometimes rude, crude, and stupid, but that almost everybody in Las Vegas is pleasant and polite almost all of the time, even though at any given moment most of them are losing money.)

Twenty-one also has the distinction of being the only game in which the player, in theory, can get an edge on the casino. The edge comes from card counting. Card counting can be done by the carpenter from Des Moines who keeps track of how many tens have been dealt, or by the astronomer from Boston who tracks tens, aces, fives, and categories of cards to which he has assigned values such as "high," "medium," and "low." The controlling idea in either case is that if you know what's been dealt from a deck or a shoe containing four decks you can generalize about what is left in it and from that you can extrapolate your chances of getting winning cards, and bet accordingly.

If you'd like to know more about this, there are about 9 million books on the subject, and you can get a list of them from the Gambler's Book Club in Las Vegas. The books will tell you that an expert card counter can get a 1 percent edge on the casino. This does not seem to worry the casinos. One reason is that for every player who plays basic strategy and counts cards, there are fifty who play basic strategy and don't count cards, and another fifty who don't play basic strategy, and another fifty who never even heard of basic strategy, and another fifty who can't even count their fingers.

"As a pit boss, I see amazing things," writes professional gambler Mike Goodman in his book *How To Win* (Holloway House, 1989). "One gentleman sat down at a table, ordered a drink, opened his tie, and bet $100 on his cards. He did this about half a dozen times and lost each time. Then he turned to me and said, 'Say, how do you play this game?'"

ROULETTE

Though roulette is the most popular casino game in the world, Las Vegas loves it less than slots, twenty-one, and craps. Roulette is a game in which a silver ball is rolled one way, a wheel of numbers is spun the other way, and the ball eventually tumbles into one of thirty-eight numbered resting places. Bettors place chips on various combinations of numbers, then pray that their combination includes the winning number. The payoff odds vary, but the overall house advantage is just under 5.25 percent. The casinos estimate that one player out of five leaves the roulette table with a profit. Albert Einstein said that you cannot beat the roulette wheel unless you steal chips off the table.

Roulette, as near as anyone can figure, is the oldest of the games being played in the casinos. Credit for inventing the game has gone to the usual suspects: the Chinese, the Italians, and the Egyptians, along with a score of mathematicians and snake-oil salesmen. The word "roulette" comes from the French word for wheel, and it seems that gamblers have been playing some form of the game as long as there has been something to spin. The Romans, for example, used to turn their chariots on their sides so they could spin the wheels and make bets.

The game as we now know it first lured bettors in Paris in the mid-eighteenth century. To this day it remains far more popular in Europe than in the United States. Certainly one reason for that is that in Europe the wheels have no double zero slot, which shaves the house edge down to 2.7 percent.

(Which, as in the case of the 75 percent slot machine versus the 97 percent slot machine, doesn't necessarily mean that European casinos make less money at the game. In 1842 François and Louis Blanc hightailed it out of France when gambling was outlawed and went to Bavaria, where they opened a casino and reduced the house advantage on the roulette wheel from 5.26 percent to 2.70 percent. They beat hell out of the competition and made big bucks. François eventually opened a casino in Monte Carlo, and ever since that time European casinos have practiced the "less is more" philosophy, which Las Vegas, for the most part, has ignored at the roulette table.)

Roulette came to the United States in the 1800s through New Orleans, where the first entrepreneurs unwisely raised the house advantage by adding a third zero slot, thus setting the standard for roulette greed in America.

Roulette in Europe has always been a fairly elegant game, played by gentlemen in tuxedos and ladies in gowns. And in its early days in America it was largely a game of the elite, wealthy patrons of posh spas, people with clean finger-

105

nails who looked down on blackjack and craps. That distinction, of roulette as a game for the upper class, has pretty much gone the way of dress codes and carriage houses. In fact, roulette itself might be bound for oblivion if U.S. casinos don't do something to reduce the house edge. Some casinos have already added features that slightly reduce the house roulette advantage.

Jerry Patterson, one of the country's top gaming instructors, says in his book *Casino Gambling* (co-authored with Walter Jaye, Perigee Books, 1982) that roulette will never be as popular in the United States as it is in Europe:

> *Although casino gambling is expanding, roulette's share of the action continues to decline each year as consistently losing players become disillusioned with the game when they come to realize the inordinately high percentage they must face. Compare this to Europe, where roulette has been offered successfully for nearly 150 years. If roulette is ever to compete again with blackjack or craps, or even baccarat, the single-zero wheel with the European option of prison or surrender must be adopted.*

In the July 1991 issue of *Casino Journal,* Laurance Scott offers his plan for resurrecting roulette in Las Vegas. He suggests that the house edge be reduced. This, he says, will give the players a more favorable impression of the casino and will attract more players.

Scott also says the game should be speeded up. At the average roulette table there are only thirty-five spins an hour.

Scott says the problem is that roulette dealers are spending too much of their time mucking, that is, stacking the losing chips. He suggests that there be a mucker at every table, and points out that mucking is a job that could be done by handicapped and otherwise unemployable people, which would create much goodwill.

And finally, Scott says casinos should encourage system play. Many players like to place their bets after the wheel has been spun, because they believe that at that point they can calculate where the ball will end up. Some casinos don't allow bets to be placed after the wheel has been spun. Scott says they should.

CRAPS

It is said that today's game of craps is descended from a long line of games that stretches all the way back to the days when idle caveman tossed six-sided bones around in some form of gambling. It is difficult to imagine how anthropologists figure these things out, but for sure craps is a lot older than most games. Dice have been found in pyramids and other ancient graves, and while Jesus Christ was throwing the money changers out of the temple, Mark Antony's grandson Claudius was writing a book called *How to Win At Dice*. And, of course, it was Mark's pal Julius Caesar who gave us the immortal phrase, "The die is cast." The name craps apparently comes from the word "crabs," which was the appellation given to the two, three, and twelve when the game was played in twelfth-century England.

In America the game of craps entered through New Orleans, came north on Mississippi riverboats, and spread east and west on many boring train rides, where it was introduced to newcomers by various traveling reptilian gentlemen whose dice were less than perfect.

Craps, an almost exclusively male game, looks complicated to the novice, but is not. Dozens of possible bets can be made on the roll of the dice, and almost all of them have colorful nicknames. Eleven is "Yo," four is "Little Joe," ten is "Big Dick," twelve is "Box Cars," and two, as almost everybody knows, is "Snake Eyes."

The simplest craps bet, a line bet with double odds, carries a house advantage of 0.6 percent. The house advantages on the other bets vary all the way up to 16.67 percent, bets commonly referred to as sucker bets.

(This business of sucker bets deserves a little scrutiny. The premise behind the phrase "sucker bet" seems to be "You're stupid because you're going to lose 16 percent of your bankroll during a day and I'm smart because I'm going to lose only 4 or 5 percent of my bankroll." Hmmn. In fact, if a sucker bet means a bet you cannot win in the long run, then all casino bets are sucker bets. On the other hand, if we look at the casino customer as a person who is buying an entertainment experience, then the term becomes irrelevant. Who's to say that the bettor who plays a long shot and gets a big payoff now and then is not being entertained as thoroughly as the one who plays a conservative bet and gets small payoffs more frequently?)

Craps is the fastest-moving game in the casino, draws a lot of premium players, and offers some of the best betting bargains. Nonetheless, it is waning in popularity, and many people in the gaming industry think the game is dying. Inasmuch as it is an enjoyable game with a small house advantage, it seems that the only logical explanation for its demise is the same one that explains why publishing has come upon hard times and why the Navy has to print instructional manuals in the form of comic books. Americans more and more have a terrible fear of actually using their brains. Whereas a person with only three brain cells could play a slot machine, craps to the novice looks as if it requires excessive thinking. It doesn't. It has, after all, been played on the streets for years by high school dropouts.

Sometimes even the people who play the game think there is more to it than there is. They convince themselves that they are good shooters or bad shooters. In fact, the only skill required in tossing dice is the physical strength to throw them hard enough so that they will hit the back wall of the table and bounce off it. Though it is comforting for the shooter to believe he is controlling his own fate, the fact is the chances of a given number coming out are exactly the same whether the shooter is Carl Sagan or a trained squirrel.

The casino's edge in craps is determined by the pyramid of crap numbers. There are thirty-six possible combinations with two dice. Six of them total seven, five of them total six or eight, four of them total five or nine, three of them total four or ten, etc. The payoff on a number that is bet is always slightly less than the probability of that number's winning.

Playing craps, or "rolling the bones," is also the closest you can come in a casino to being on a team with a bunch of rowdy, drunken friends. Though each gambler is playing against the house, almost everybody plays the "pass line," which is kind of the basic craps bet, and that puts all the people around the table in direct competition with the casino. Interestingly, the "don't pass" bet is, mathematically, a slightly better bet, but few people play it because it is psychologically unsatisfying. If you bet the "don't pass," your interests run parallel to the casino's and against most of the players, which is kind of like rooting for the Yankees in Fenway Park.

Twenty-one, roulette, and craps are bunched together in CCE daily reports under "Games," a category which also includes some of the less popular games, like Red Dog, but does not include poker, slots, the sports book, or keno. On March 7, the Daily Managerial Report for the Excalibur showed Glenn Schaeffer that these games had a drop of $684,981. The daily report does not use the term "win." Instead it uses "hold" both for the win and the win percentage. The hold for "Games" was $126,181, which was 18.45 percent of the drop. This would amount to the revenue generated on the "Games" before any expenses.

POKER

When you play poker in Las Vegas, you are not playing against the house. You are playing against the other players. The house just deals the cards and takes a small percentage of each pot. Poker rooms in Las Vegas are not big moneymakers. They are put there more or less as a courtesy to players, who, the casino hopes, will play a few other games while they are in town.

On our typical day, March 7, the Excalibur had poker revenues of $10,709.

SPORTS BETTING

In America $37 billion a year is bet illegally on sports. Or maybe it's $197 billion. These are two of the figures you hear, but who the hell really knows? One thing is certain, it's a lot, and whatever the figure, it makes Las Vegas's almost $4-billion win look like chickenfeed. Illegal sports betting is by far the biggest gambling operation in America, and according to some of the people who figure out these things, it has greater total revenues than the seventy-five largest industrial organizations in the United States.

One inevitable result of all this sports betting money changing hands has been that by the beginning of the 1990s state legislators were falling all over themselves trying to legalize sports betting. In California, for example, state assemblyman Dick Floyd collected signatures to get a sports gambling initiative on the ballot. "It's time we woke up to what's happening all around us," Floyd told *USA Today* in June 1991. "Legalized sports gambling is on the way nationwide in one form or another, and I'd just as soon it gets here first."

And, of course, there were legions of people who thought that the legalization of sports gambling was a bad idea. Among the reasons listed in *USA Today*'s editorial the next day: it encourages gambling among kids, it can lead to crime, the odds are lousy, it preys upon the poor, it could lead to fixed games, and when states run any kind of gambling the money often doesn't go where it is supposed to go. All of which is true.

Sports betting in Las Vegas is done in sports and racing books, large sections of the casino which are populated by mostly male bettors, some of whom actually pay the mortgage by picking winners. There a gambler can sit in a comfortable chair, order a free drink, make his bets, then relax and look up at a wall of television screens. Without leaving his seat he can watch a dog race from Flagler in Miami, a baseball game from Three Rivers Stadium in Pittsburgh, a horse race from Santa Anita in California, and a boxing match from some unpronounceable city halfway around the world. If there is a heaven for sports fans it looks like a Las Vegas sports book. In fact, the sports book at the Las Vegas Hilton is, arguably, the best place on earth.

Las Vegas race and sports books, which have been allowed in casinos since 1975, keep 4.55 percent of the handle. Writer Bill Friedman explains it this way: "If two customers each wager eleven units on opposite teams in a contest, the sports book will win one of their twenty-two units, as it pays out twenty-one of the twenty-two units to the winning customer—eleven units wagered plus ten units won."

However, the nature of the animal is such that the house advantage does not manifest itself in a nice, even flow. It is more like rain, consistent in the long run, but with a lot of droughts and torrents in the meantime.

The head of the race and sports book at the Excalibur is Sid Diamond. Diamond has been with the Excalibur since it opened in 1990, and before that he worked the sports book at

CCE's Edgewater Hotel in Laughlin, Nevada. It is Diamond's job, along with his assistant, Vince Dimari, to set the odds or establish point spreads on sporting events. Racing odds, of course, are set by the bettors.

"What we are trying to do," Diamond explains, "is create a balance. Ideally, we would like to have an equal amount bet on either side in a game. The idea behind giving one team points, or paying better odds for one team, is to divide the public into two even camps, those who bet on one team and those who bet on the other."

The person who sets the odds at a Vegas hotel has to consider a lot of information. Who's pitching? Are there any injuries on the team? Who's got the home court advantage? Does this guy choke in the big games? Is the goalie involved in a paternity suit that could distract him from his game? But the book manager is not reviewing this information so he can figure out who is going to win. He's reviewing the information so he can try to figure out who the public will expect to win. The book manager's concern is not with the thrill of victory or the agony of defeat. His concern is, What does the public think and how will they bet? In a perfect world half the money in a football game would be bet on the Giants and the other half on the Redskins.

"But that doesn't happen," Diamond says. "In football, if I can get sixty percent betting one way and forty percent the other, I'd call it a success. In basketball, it's common to have seventy percent betting one way and thirty the other. My goal is to try not to gamble. But, of course, we have losing days."

March 7 was a losing day for the Excalibur race and sports book. In March the football season is over but the baseball season has not yet begun. For that day the Excalibur lost $4,782 in its race and sports book before departmental expenses.

SLOTS

How would you like to run a business where you had thousands of tireless employees who were willing to work three shifts a day, 365 days a year, without pay? And what if these employees never took maternity leave, asked for no benefits, stole nothing, and only rarely got sick? And what if their only job was to make change all day long, and for every dollar they changed they gave back only ninety cents?

There are such employees. They are known as slot machines.

A Las Vegas casino can buy a slot machine for less than $6,000, and if the casino markets its business correctly, that slot machine will turn over to it $50,000 a year without a peep or a whine.

Slots are by far the most productive money-makers in a casino. The industry overall derives about 60 percent of its casino revenues from slots, and at CCE the figure is closer to 70 percent. At the Excalibur slots take in more money than all other games combined, and have the smallest labor cost. Plus, they don't require health insurance, won't go on strike, and don't drive cars that take up valuable spots in the parking lot. There is no license to steal in Las Vegas, but slots come closest.

Gary O'Keefe, CC Las Vegas's casino manager, says,

"About ten years ago table games were still tops in the industry, and slots were not. Since then slots have become the
prime money-maker of casinos. Craps has dropped because it
is a tough game to learn and new generations don't want to
take the time to learn it. So the craps players are dying off.
With slots it is easy to sit at the machine and put in a quarter
or a dollar. You're not intimidated, you're not inhibited. That's
why video poker machines have taken off so well. Also you
can make a bigger score on the slot machine with your coin
than with twenty-one. With twenty-one you get a dollar for a
dollar. With slots you could get three hundred dollars for a
dollar."

Actually, for shoving a dollar into a slot machine you
could be rewarded with a lot more than $300. One thing that
the casino business has learned from the lottery business is
that people like the idea of huge payoffs, even when the odds
of winning are a zillion to one. You didn't have to be a business whiz to see that ten lottery winners of $100,000 never
got the folks lined up at the 7-Eleven the way a single
million-dollar winner did. So Las Vegas has installed the extremely popular progressive slots, computer-linked networks
of slot machines, in which a percentage of each deposit goes
into a long-shot pool and the payoff can run into hundreds of
thousands, or even millions, of dollars.

(And while we're on the subject, keep in mind that the
idea that only certain games, such as slots and keno, offer
huge payoff possibilities is an illusion. Any casino game will
give you a huge payoff if you defy the probabilities to the
same extent required for a major slot payoff. David Louis, in
2201 Fascinating Facts (1988, Outlet Book Co.), says that in

1950 at the Desert Inn in Las Vegas, a craps player made twenty-seven straight passes, that is, wins, with the dice. The odds against his doing that were 12,467,890, but he did it anyhow. If he had bet the house limit on each roll he would have earned $268 million. As it happened, this poor gob left the table with $750 and the satisfaction of knowing that his dice would be enshrined on a velvet pillow under glass.)

While craps and table games are played primarily by men, the slot players far and away are women. There are a number of theories about this, probably all of them true. One is that women like to bet smaller amounts and the slot machines allow that. CCE casinos still have nickel slot machines right alongside the quarter and dollar machines. There are still casinos downtown where you can find penny slot machines. (A cynical person might conclude that a casino cannot make money on penny machines, and is only using them to train people into the slot-playing habit.)

And there is the theory that women are intuitive, and less inclined toward percentages, overlays, hedge bets, and the like, so that while men are agonizing over their betting strategies, the women are simply dropping coins and hoping for the best.

The payouts on Las Vegas slot machines average in the 90 to 98 percent range. If a machine is paying back 96 percent, for example, that means that, on average, for every 100 silver dollars that is poured into it, $96 will come tumbling down into the payoff return tray. These are long-term probabilities, based on the setting of reels inside the machine. The excitement, of course, comes from the short-term possibilities, the fact that you could put in a $1 and get $300 back while the pathetic schmuck next to you puts in $300 and gets $27 back. You might lose $100 on one machine and win $1,000 on the next.

Slots are computerized these days, and the combinations of reels that come out are the result of a random number generator. The machine has no sense of fair play. It doesn't know when it last paid out and it doesn't care. The result is that if a female plumber from Sarasota and a professional wrestler from Kyoto stand side by side at identical machines, and one of them has pulled the handle a hundred straight times without a win, and the other has just scored nine wins in a row, they both have exactly the same probability of winning on the next pull.

(Though, if you want to be technical, they will probably be pushing, not pulling. Slot machines still have handles, but they also have buttons, and most people push the buttons because you can get more shots of juice per hour and less chance of developing bursitis in the right shoulder.)

Here's a math quiz. If a man with $100 walks up to a slot machine that has a 95 percent payoff return, how much money will he have when he walks away from that machine? If you said $95, you are wrong. The answer is: probably nothing. Slot players also come to play, not to win, and they will recycle that money until the 5 percent each time has eaten it all up. There is a very fast way to learn why slot machines make so much money in casinos. Walk through a casino at four o'clock in the morning. Look at the slot machines. How many of them are showing winning combinations? In other words, at how many machines did the player leave on a win? The answer: damn few.

For this, Glenn Schaeffer was thankful when he looked at his daily managerial slot sheet. He saw that on March 7, 1992, the Excalibur had a win of $335,306.

KENO

Keno, with a house advantage of 25 percent, is the worst bet you can make in a casino, except, of course, for a wager on the Red Sox or Cubs to win the World Series. But thousands of people still play Keno. They like the keno parlor atmosphere: comfy chairs, free drinks, and, as with slots, the possibility of a humongous payoff. (And besides, if nobody played it, then something else would be the worst bet you could make in a casino.) And because keno tickets are sold by keno runners, keno also has the distinction of being the only casino game that you can play while you're eating pancakes in a hotel restaurant.

The game was brought into the country by Chinese laborers who worked the railroad in the last century. It was known then as the Chinese lottery, but it hasn't changed a whole lot, except that there is now electronic equipment, to help casinos get through more games per hour and generate income faster.

In keno, a player picks anywhere from one to fifteen numbers from a ticket that contains eighty numbers. The selection of winning numbers is similar to the selection process you see on televised state lottery programs. The numbers are printed on plastic balls. The balls are in a transparent cage known as a goose, where they are kept in constant circulation by a current of air. Twenty balls are selected, one at a time, and as each number arrives it is called out and flashed on electronic screens in the keno parlor, the restaurants, and perhaps a few other locations in the hotel and casino. (In *Casino Management* Bill Friedman says there are 3,535,316,142,212,174,320 different combinations to be made from those twenty numbers, which gives you a pretty good idea of your chances of winning the state lottery.)

The total number of winning numbers or "catches" you have will determine your payoff. Your chance of getting all fifteen numbers is 1 in 428,010,179,098.

On March 7, the Excalibur had a keno drop of $34,040 and a win of $14,429.

BACCARAT

The other major game played in Las Vegas casinos is baccarat. (It's pronounced "ba ka *ra,*" by the way.) Baccarat is a simple enough game in which two hands are dealt. One is called banker, the other player. You bet on one of them, and whichever comes closest to nine is the winner. It is believed that baccarat is based on the Roman legend of nine gods. However, the number nine has had mystical significance in many times and places—nine Muses, nine rivers of hell, nine earths—so perhaps it was inevitable that some game based on the number nine, besides baseball, would emerge.

There are a number of baccarat rules concerning whether or not additional cards will be dealt, but your knowledge of these rules will have no more effect on the game than daylight saving time. One beauty of baccarat is that it can be played by people who just fell off the turnip truck. It is a game in which your only decision is which hand to bet on. After that, no options are presented, no decisions are made. Though the game lacks the rowdiness of craps and the decision-making of blackjack, it does have odds that make professional gamblers salivate. The banker hand is the better bet, with a house advantage of only 1.06 percent, but even the player hand, with a house advantage of 1.23 percent, is one of the best gambling buys in town.

Baccarat is usually played in plush parlors for high stakes by people who are well dressed. But many casinos also offer mini-baccarat, a low-stakes version for the great un-washed. Circus Circus hotels offer no baccarat. For one thing, it does not appeal to their middle-market customer. For an-other, baccarat has that exceedingly low house advantage, and being the game of choice for high-rolling, credit-using play-ers, tends to have wild variations in its hold percentage. In-deed, it is a game at which many casinos get laundered from time to time.

"Bill Bennett put the ax to the last baccarat table years ago," Schaeffer says. "It was too much like gambling."

9

Lords and Ladies

The gaming customer comes in all shapes and sizes. There is, for example, the customer who doesn't have a clue.

Mark Leffert, a craps dealer at the Rio, tells this typical story: "This Indian guy walks up to the table and he puts ten one-hundred-dollar bills on the pass line, doesn't even ask for chips. He's all agitated and everything, like he just lost some money at another table. As it happened this guy was the next shooter. So the stickman passes the dice to him. The guy picks them up and looks at them as if they're objects from another planet. It was clear that this guy didn't have the vaguest idea of what to do with the dice, or what game he had just bet a thousand dollars on. I figure maybe he didn't even know how much he was betting. Maybe he thought each of those hundred-dollar bills was rupees or something."

Then there are the customers, surprisingly rare, who get peeved to the point of violence when they lose. Dave Hardy, director of slots at Circus Circus, says, "People sometimes act out; they get frustrated and hit the slot machines. We have one machine called Smash Hit and there have been a few times when a player got frustrated, maybe had a few drinks, and punched the glass out of it."

But most Las Vegas customers are people who put some thought into their gambling. Everybody's got a system. In fact, the dedication of many gamblers to the games has nurtured an entire sub-industry of information and advice. There are books, magazines, newsletters, audiotapes, videotapes, and computer software on how to play the casino games and, most important, how to win. This sub-industry has its own gurus of inveterate gamblers, mathematical geniuses, and computer whizzes. Many of its leaders come from business, law enforcement, and universities. Some are well known in other industries, like publisher Lyle Stuart, who is also the author of books on gambling.

Some studies have shown that gamblers are more likely than nongamblers to be book readers, and a trip to 630 South 11th Street in Las Vegas would strongly suggest that's the case. There you will find the Gambler's Book Club, a Las Vegas landmark, a hangout for casino habitués, and a place which is often crowded with colorful characters yapping about point spreads, overlays, clutch players, and dice that were as cold as a witch's tit. There you can buy old copies of *Gambling Times* magazine, which now is *WIN* magazine, new copies of *Casino Player* and *Casino Journal,* and books on every aspect of gambling.

In the GBC catalog, which is mailed monthly to thousands of gamblers all over the world, you will find more than 1,000 books on twenty-one, craps, baccarat, slots, poker, and the racing of thoroughbreds, quarter horses, and greyhounds. Many of the titles begin with the word "beat" (as in *Beat the Odds, Beat the Wheel, Beat the Four-Deck Game, Beat the Casino,* and possibly the most famous gambling book, mathematician Edward O. Thorp's *Beat the Dealer*) or "winning" (as in *Winning Systems, Winning Without Counting,* and *Winning By Computer*). Most of the books present systems for winning at specific games, and many are about how systems don't work. Most will tell you how to win more, and a few promise only that you will lose less.

Though many of the titles sound as if they were composed by televangelists, the books, for the most part, are rational and not ruined by hyperbole. While a few are fallacious and dishonest, most are simply optimistic. Though none can guarantee a consistent winner, it's reasonable to assume that the population of gamblers who read these books cashes in more chips than the people who don't read them, if for no other reason than that the books teach you how to play the game and present you with the odds on each bet.

There is one other type of customer, one that Las Vegas would rather not talk about. That is the compulsive gambler. Though some sociologists insist that compulsive gambling will be the addiction of the 1990s, compulsive gambling is not a subject that comes up much in discussions with gaming executives. Now and then in a casino you'll see a slogan like

"Bet with Your Head, Not Over It," or perhaps a sticker with the phone number for Gamblers Anonymous, but by and large compulsive gambling seems to be an issue of more concern to people outside gaming circles than inside.

There are addictive or compulsive personalities, of course, and some of them binge out on credit cards and some on gambling. But there is nothing intrinisic to gambling itself that causes addiction, so far as clinical studies have shown.

Gambling is not like alcohol and it's not like tobacco. It's not even like coffee. All of those are inherently addictive. Compulsive personalities are a small number—studies show they make up maybe two percent of the population—and those people clearly don't belong in a casino. But for the rest, gambling is basically a lifestyle decision which can be made without the help of moral police.

One Las Vegas executive recalls:

"I was speaking to a group of politicians in a southern state that's been debating casino gambling, and I was asked, 'What sort of program does your company have for problem gamblers?' I said, 'We don't have one.' This city counselor said, 'Well, don't you think you should have one?' I said, 'Hard to know. For one thing, these people don't identify themselves, they don't come up and say, "Hey, I've got a gambling problem." ' 'Okay,' he says, 'don't you think you should make an effort to identify them?' I said to him, 'How so? Why don't you call the manager at your local department store, and have him identify, before he sells the next bottle of perfume, which customers are almost maxed out on their credit cards. Have him quiz his customers. "Do you really need perfume, don't you smell good enough already, what's

124

the credit limit on your card, I don't think you should spend your money, what are you up to, do you really think today is the best time for you to buy another piece of clothing, why don't you go home and cool off?" ' The fact is that most people conduct themselves very well and wisely. We are a society where the consumer makes his own choices."

Most nongamblers seem to have an exaggerated idea of just how much compulsive gambling there is in Las Vegas. Simply being a gambler doesn't make you a compulsive gambler, any more than being a drinker makes you an alcoholic. Nonetheless, compulsive gambling is a problem to be reckoned with, particularly with all the new gambling venues around the country.

It is a problem that can reach bizarre proportions, as it did in the case of Brian Moloney, a Canadian bank manager who in one four-month period won $450 million and lost $457 million, mostly playing baccarat at Caesars in Atlantic City, which he financed with a complicated scheme of dummy loans from his bank. His exploits are recounted, and the subject of compulsive gambling is well articulated, in a fascinating book, *No Limit* by Gary Ross (Ballantine, 1990).

But the vast majority of casino gamblers are not compulsive gamblers. Many only gamble once a year, or even once in a lifetime. If they are seeking a state change, it seems that they are seeking the state change that comes with winning. Winning does feel good, no question about it. But that doesn't explain why all those losers say they had a good time in Vegas.

If a generalization can be made about casino gamblers, it is perhaps that they are as superstitious as cave dwellers.

There is something about letting chance baby-sit your money that brings out the superstition in almost everybody. No matter how rational a woman is, it is difficult for her to walk along a line of slot machines without finding one that "calls out" to her and others that are "putting out bad vibes." In fact, you could argue that making any bet in which the odds are against you is an act of superstition; you are behaving as if something in the universe favors you more than it favors its own laws of probability.

Superstitious behavior among gamblers, which is almost universal, assumes that the something which favors the gambler will withhold approval in certain circumstances; if a player loses a baccarat hand three times in a row when a waitress comes by to take drink orders, he will pull his money back the next time he hears her voice. If a dealer gets blackjack right after a new player joins the game, half the players at the table will blame the new player. If a craps player accidentally hits the dice and they come up losers, everybody blames him even though his klutziness could just as easily have knocked the dice into a winning combination. And if the dice fly off the table, many players will call off their bets on the next roll; if you ask them why, they will tell you that a losing seven always comes up after the dice fall from the table. (Interestingly, though they act as if this is true, they apparently don't really believe it. If they did, they would call off their bets and also make a huge bet on seven, and they never do.) Some men won't shoot craps if there is a woman at the table; others increase their bets when a woman is the shooter. There are blackjack players who won't play when it is raining, roulette players who won't play number thirteen and won't bet on any red numbers, and many slot players have a favorite machine and get edgy as hell when they find someone else playing it.

Maybe the man who said, "The next best thing to playing and winning is playing" was right. Maybe the state that we are really seeking when we gamble in a casino is neither winning nor losing. It is that little jolt we get at the moment of uncertainty, that adrenaline rush that shoots through us during the split second when the dice are in the air, when the twenty-one dealer is about to flip over the hole card, when. the metal ball is about to drop onto a number on the roulette wheel, when the reels are still spinning on the slot machine.

Much of life has become as predictable as the sunrise, so we crave the dramatic experience, and gambling is a way to get it. Like the plot of a good novel, the gambling experience must have stakes that are significant enough for the outcome to matter, which explains why a short-order cook can play the $1 tables at Circus Circus and get the same thrill that a tax attorney gets from laying $2,000 on the pass line at the Mirage. Gambling is a safe way to go into the woods and see if you come out alive, jump out of a plane and see if your chute opens, put the pistol to your head and see if it's loaded. It is a make-believe life-and-death experience. But when it's all over you're still alive and you're as healthy as when you walked in the door. If you've lost, and you probably have, all you've really lost is money.

10

The Bazaar

A guy by the name of Homer Taylor, from Albuquerque, New Mexico, says, "One day, couple of years ago, my wife and I were at Circus Circus for a few days. We like to come up and gamble two, three times a year. We're not big gamblers, we just come for the fun. So we get on the tram to come over from the Manor to the main casino, and when we're getting on, my wife bangs her head somehow. So we're sitting there on the tram and my wife's head is hurting and we're rubbing it, and this fellow comes over to us, well-dressed guy, I didn't know who he was. He asks what happened. My wife banged her head, I tell him. Oh, he says, and then he starts asking us are we having a good time at Circus Circus and is everything okay with our room and all. And we told him, sure everything is great. Then he asks me what do I do for a living and where do I live. So we're going along like that, and when we get to the other side, the guy reaches in and hands me a hundred-dollar bill. Here, he says, take your wife to dinner. He didn't say his name or anything, but I asked someone who he was, and they said, oh, that's William Bennett, he owns this place."

Bennett doesn't remember the incident. He smiles and shakes his head. "That fellow must be dreaming," he says.

Maybe. But it's a story that is consistent with the Bennett gospel of marketing: know your customer and never let him or her go away unhappy.

KNOWING THE CUSTOMER

If the Las Vegas product were simply gambling, then one casino's customers would be interchangeable with another's. After all, a jackpot is a jackpot whether it falls into a slot tray at the Tropicana on the Strip or one at the Horseshoe downtown. But because the product is a total entertainment experience, it divides its market into different customers, looking for different experiences, who require different kinds of casinos.

In a March 1987 *Fortune* magazine article about Las Vegas, Daniel Seligman writes, "It is plainly important to have a coherent marketing strategy, but impossible to state crisply which strategies work best. Arresting detail: Two casino companies with polar opposite strategies are, arguably, the two most profitable in the industry."

Seligman is talking about Circus Circus Enterprises, Inc., which remains the most successful, and Caesars World, Inc., which has since been rivaled by the Mirage.

So you make money in Las Vegas gaming not by identifying and targeting the "one true market." You make it by understanding the market that you aim for, and providing the experience that your customer wants.

"That," says Tom Tomlinson, who heads up marketing for Circus Circus Las Vegas, "has always been the genius of Bill Bennett. He has an incredible sense of just what people want from the experience."

A tour of Las Vegas casinos can be as full of contrasts as a tour of Europe. The differences in the Las Vegas market are not all subtle; many are obvious to the casual observer. When you walk into a new casino you are immediately struck by the different demographics. There are differences in dress, vocabulary, age range, manner of speech, amount of cigarette smoke in the air, kind of music being played. At the Mirage, for example, you can almost smell the wealth. You see gorgeous blonds of both sexes, many of them dripping with jewelry, some of them movie stars. At the Gold Coast, just on the other side of the interstate, the ambiance is more reminiscent of a bowling alley in Tallahassee. Lots of dungarees, cigarette smoke, and country music. Go to one of the small casinos downtown and you'll see the old-timers, many of them seeking out their favorite slot machine and swapping tales about big bets won and streaks as cold as an arctic winter.

"You have to know your market," says general manager Bill Paulos. "And you must have a definable difference."

131

PREMIUM AND GRIND CUSTOMERS

There are many ways of dividing up the Las Vegas market in order to discuss it.

One is by betting level. In this division, the market is divided into premium players and grind players.

Premium players are the people who make higher than average bets, and this group includes, of course, the high rollers, some of whom are "whales," people who literally bet millions on a gambling trip.

A premium player is probably playing $25 or $100 chips, or higher. It is not unusual to see a player at the Mirage, for example, bet a stack of black $100 chips on one roll of the dice or one hand of blackjack. At the Mirage, the Las Vegas Hilton, and Caesars Palace you can even find $100 slot machines. At Circus Circus, where $500 could be a player's entire trip bankroll, such machines would just take up space.

The premium players, of course, are courted zealously by the hotels that cater to them. In a March 1987 interview in *Fortune,* the Mirage's Steve Wynn provides a little insight into the kind of money these people bet, by describing two groups as he sees them.

One was "the Texans":

They come up to Las Vegas in their DC-9's. They come with their wives or girlfriends, sometimes both. And they want to raise hell. I'm thinking of guys with a quarter of a million dollars worth of credit, but an acceptable amount of money to lose, in their minds, is maybe 100 G's.

132

The other group is "the foreigners":

The stories you hear about people losing $20 million, or $4 million, in a weekend, are mostly about Chinese, sometimes Arabs. . . . and probably several hundred Mexicans and South Americans. That whole family of foreign players amounts to maybe 1,000. That's 1,000 people known by first and second name at a few high-end casinos. Last week one of them won a million and a half at the Golden Nugget in Las Vegas. He could come back and lose $2 million in a week.

Wynn is a man who ought to know about high rollers. His success, according to Jack Binion, owner of the Horseshoe Casino, "lies in having created a hotel within a hotel for the super players from Asia."

The New York Times adds:

Accommodated in special suites that have their own gardens, statuary, swimming pools and putting greens, these gamblers—mainly from Japan but also from Taiwan, Hong Kong, and Thailand—are capable of gambling as much as $12 million an hour on baccarat, according to several casino executives.

The casinos that cater to these high rollers like to know as much as possible about them. Their taste in drinks, their favorite games, their idiosyncrasies, and so forth, are all tracked by computer. Is this one a football fan? Let's invite him when we have an NFL coach giving a talk before the Super Bowl. Another is a Jay Leno fan? Let's make sure he's invited when Leno plays Caesars.

More and more these days, "high roller" is synonymous with "international player." While it was American high rollers who created much of the Las Vegas mythology, the number of American big spenders is dwindling. One reason is the economic condition of the country. The other is the IRS, whose regulation 6A requires casinos to reveal the name of any player with a credit line of $10,000 or more. Gamblers in general, and high rollers in particular, like to minimize the amount of information they share with the Internal Revenue Service.

Today one key to getting high rollers into your hotel is knowing which ethnic group to go after. There was a time when Mexicans and South Americans were bringing the loot to the party in Vegas, but when oil prices went south, a lot of players from the south could no longer afford to come north. The South American and Mexican players' bankrolls dropped, as did the bankrolls of Texans and Louisianans. Then the Mexican peso took a pounding, and after that the Mexican equivalent of the IRS started looking too closely at the habits of gamblers who came north. So the Japanese became the foreigners of choice in Las Vegas's international marketing departments. Not as many yen are being left in the counting rooms as a few years ago, but the Japanese still account for the majority of the high rollers at some hotels, such as the Mirage.

But by 1993 Las Vegas was looking more and more toward China to help it replace the American high rollers—and toward countries with large Chinese populations, such as Malaysia, Singapore, and Thailand.

Hilton, for example, has had great success by pursuing the Chinese players aggressively with customized individual packages, Chinese hosts, and an emphasis on wish fulfillment. If there are no premium junkets for these players it is because today's high roller is a busy man with many commitments who can't always meet a carefully planned travel schedule. Most likely, he is also private and would like to keep his gambling habits to himself.

The reason Las Vegas is salivating for the Chinese player is simply that the Chinese seem to gamble more than anybody.

Michael Stirling, vice president of international marketing at the Las Vegas Hilton, says, "The Chinese people like to gamble, and they make no apology for it. The casinos in Macao are unbelievable. The Lisboa Hotel may have a hundred rooms, and we have three thousand—but they do far, far more in table game business than we do in this place. The racetrack in Hong Kong will do in one day what many racetracks in the United States do in a year. It's incredible."

The players who bet small amounts are known as grind players, and the hotels that cater to them, such as all the CCE properties, are called grind houses. Though "grind" sounds pejorative, it shouldn't. A grind house, by reason of the smaller bets it accepts, gives the customer a lot more product for the money. Unless the customer's luck is unusually bad, or someone has placed a curse on him or her, the grind player is going to take a long time to lose the money. And that's how CCE wants it.

"Our philosophy," says general manager Bill Paulos, "is that the customer came for entertainment. He has a certain budget for it. He expects to lose money. People will tell you, 'I can lose fifty dollars a day,' or 'I can lose a hundred dollars a day,' whatever.

"We want his money, but we want to give him his entertainment. That is why the rooms are so inexpensive. That is why food is so cheap that we lose money on it; it's part of the entertainment that we are selling. If a guy has a hundred dollars to lose, I don't want it when he's only been here for ten minutes, because if I have it that soon, he's an unhappy customer. If he's got a hundred dollars to lose that day, I don't want the hundredth dollar until just before he goes to bed, because that means for his hundred he had a good time."

Glenn Schaeffer also sees the customer as someone who sticks around for a while. Schaeffer, a former college boxer who is drawn to the sports metaphor, puts it this way: "In a mall you have a customer who has an intention to shop. The customer walks in the store and he announces, 'I am bringing money, now you have to figure out how to entice it from me.' We have to say to our team, 'Okay, team, how do we do it?' The longer we have the customer in the store, the more likely we are to win."

Casinos can, of course, subtly shift their marketing strategy from the high end toward the low end, but losing one market doesn't guarantee that a casino will attract another. Las Vegas is full of nearly empty casinos that were once the cat's meow. Caesars Palace, however, is a good example of a premium house that has successfully gone hunting for smaller game. For years Caesars was known as a high-end casino, but with the opening of the Mirage next door and the drop in the economy, Caesars has seen fewer sheikhs and oil barons. So the company has reached out more for the middle-market customer. It has done this by expanding its casino, boosting its tourism value with a glitzy new mall and specialty stores and an animatronics attraction, installing a people mover that draws walk-in traffic from the Strip and the Mirage, and putting in more five-dollar tables. The result is a lot more people playing for smaller stakes. According to one Caesars exec, the hardest part of the transition has been getting the staff to appreciate the grind customer, whom they used to look down on.

CONVENTIONEERS, LOCALS, AND VACATIONERS

Another way to divide the market is to ask yourself why the customer is in Las Vegas. Three answers cover almost everybody: the customer is on business, the customer lives here, or the customer is on vacation.

The person who is on business in Las Vegas is probably attending a convention, or is in town for one of the big trade shows. The Las Vegas Convention and Visitors Authority (LVCVA) operates one of the largest convention centers in the world, and also operates Cashman Field Center, which has a stadium for 10,000, a theater for 2,000 and 100,000 feet of exhibition space. Vegas is a leading convention town, and there are hotels, notably the Las Vegas Hilton and the Sands, that survive on that market. Las Vegas welcomes more than 1,000 conventions a year, the LVCVA estimates that those conventioneers spend $800 to $1,000 each, not including their gaming losses.

Circus Circus does almost no convention business. "We don't even have meeting rooms," William Bennett says. Bennett has sometimes been accused of being anticonvention. But that, he says, is a misstatement of the facts.

"There's a lot of confusion about what I am and am not against. I'm not against conventions. We don't happen to be in the convention business. We don't have convention rooms. But a lot of conventions are designed for work and fun, and they're good. Conventions usually don't hurt us until they occupy at least twenty-five-thousand rooms in the city. What I'm against is huge trade shows like the Consumer Electronics Show, that come in and take every room in town and put pressure on the casinos. These are people who displace tourists. They spend the whole day working and the casinos are empty."

Though Bennett has been speaking out about the scheduling of the huge trade shows for years while others have only extolled their virtues, in recent times other Las Vegas hotels have echoed his concerns.

"The shows used to come in December and January," Bennett says. "Which wasn't bad, because those are the low tourism months of the year. Then they moved it up to October, which is often the best month of the year for tourism business. The town is finally waking up to the fact that these big trade shows can squeeze out the best customers. After one big show came in October, I think every major spot on the Strip signed a petition to have it moved back to December or January. Many of these shows are big computer shows where they introduce the new computers and so forth. These people *have* to come to this, and they would probably come even if it was held the day before Christmas."

Another reason that a customer could be in Las Vegas is simply that he or she lives there.

Jay Sevigny, general manager of the Rio, says, "With the growth of the city of Las Vegas, the local business has become an increasingly important part of the market. All the hotels get some share of the local market, but some really go after it, like Arizona Charlie's, Palace Station, and the Rio."

Sevigny is the guy you see on those Player's Club commercials with Telly Savalas. The all-suites Rio opened in 1990 with 424 suites, quite small by today's Las Vegas standards, but has seen both its revenue and its stock climb steadily, largely due to the local market. One way to spot a hotel that does a lot of local business is by its check-cashing promotions.

"People get paid on Thursday or Friday night," Sevigny says. "They want to go out and have a good time; they need a place to cash their check. We provide that service and give them a chance to win a big prize by cashing their check with us. It's a way of getting the local business into our casino."

The tour-and-travel customer is of course the person who is traveling for pleasure. If this customer is just in for the weekend, he or she is probably from California. If coming from overseas, as is often the case these days, he or she has an excellent chance of being a Flamingo Hilton customer, because of Hilton's worldwide reservations system.

While CCE aims for the leisure time or vacation time customer, he or she is less likely to have flown any great distance to get to the big top or the castle.

"The majority of our customers live within a radius of three hundred miles," says Tomlinson. "We find that the customer who comes from anywhere further than the Midwest is likely to travel with children. He spends more on a hotel and about the same amount on gaming as our customer. Most of our customers drive to get here, and that tells me to concentrate my advertising efforts on reaching that customer. We advertise mostly in newspapers, and mostly in California and the Southwest. We don't do much electronic advertising, except when there is a special need for it."

What's true for Circus Circus Las Vegas is true for the other CCE hotels. Mel Larsen says, "We concentrate on a radius of five hundred miles because if I spend a dollar to reach a guy in Phoenix or Albuquerque, he has the ability to come three or four times a year. If I spend that same dollar to reach a customer in London, we might see him once a year or once in three years. The same goes for New York or Miami."

As CCE's reputation for colorful signature buildings grows, the circle of customers seems to be widening. Larsen says, "We've got to broaden that base because every day we are trying to fill eleven thousand, two hundred rooms." Tom Tomlinson, head of marketing for Circus Circus Las Vegas, notes, in the summer of 1992, that advertising in Chicago, Houston, Dallas, and San Antonio is lately proving very profitable for the company. However, so far CCE has not gotten a big piece of the foreign market.

"Our business is mostly the American traveler and not from far away," Schaeffer says. "The foreign market is not a huge part of the Las Vegas business right now, but it does bring a lot of premium players. Generally, the farther someone travels to get here, the bigger the budget he brings to town."

THE MIDDLE MARKET

The most inclusive term for the CCE customer is "middle-market." It denotes a person, says Tomlinson, who is middle-class, not a high roller, and not a local. This person comes to Circus Circus about three times a year, and six times out of ten he or she is not staying at the hotel.

But "middle-market" is a fairly imprecise term which takes in almost everybody whom you see walking along Las Vegas Boulevard. In fact, the middle market is so large that it is broken down into three segments: the low end, the middle, and the high end. With the completion of the Luxor in 1993, CCE intends to have three Las Vegas hotels that span this diversity within the middle market.

Bill Paulos says, "Circus Circus Las Vegas caters to the lower half of the middle market. You can get breakfast for a dollar ninety-nine or dinner for three ninety-nine. The Excalibur caters to the middle of the middle market. There you can get a buffet that's at a slightly higher level for a slightly higher price. And at Luxor you'll pay a little more and there will be a high-end buffet, a Golden Nugget kind of buffet. Or take room service as another example. At Circus Circus Las

Vegas we do almost no room service business at all. At the Excalibur there is limited room service. At Luxor we will have a full room service menu."

Other differences reveal themselves even to the casual observer. At Circus Circus, except for the Steakhouse, the restaurants are of the coffee shop variety. At the Excalibur there is more in the way of fine dining. At Circus Circus there is no paid entertainment; at the Excalibur there are two paid shows.

"But it's all still middle market," Paulos says. "It's not high rollers, and it's always the best possible value. Among the properties there are subtle differences, because those differences exist in the market."

One reason we probably won't see Circus Circus building any high-roller operations, according to Glenn Schaeffer, is that there is still plenty of middle market to be tapped.

"One of the big lessons of the past year, with the Excalibur," he says, "is that this market will grow when you expand the category and show the customer something he hasn't seen before. Right now fewer than fifteen percent of Americans have been to Las Vegas on vacation. Disney World is still the obligatory vacation trip. We think in the next decade Las Vegas will be on the 'A' list for American vacationers."

While any discussion of the middle market in Las Vegas inevitably includes words like "wholesome," "family," and "children," it would be a mistake to think that the CCE marketing strategy is aimed at kids in the way that, say, a Mc-Donald's strategy is. The fact is that kids can't gamble, and kids are in school eight months out of the year, while Circus

Circus is fully occupied all year long. The LVCVA says that only five percent of the city's visitors are less than twenty-one years of age.

"The kids are here during school vacations and during the summer," Paulos says, "but the rest of the time, eighty percent of our rooms are occupied by people who don't have children with them."

While Las Vegas is more than happy to think of itself as the Orlando of the West or Disneyland with Gambling, those appellations are somewhat misleading about the role children take in the new Las Vegas. Las Vegas is never going to be a children's playground that comes with something to amuse the adults. Orlando, for the most part, is like McDonald's, marketed to the kids, who will bring their parents. Las Vegas is more like Wendy's, marketed to adults who will bring their kids.

The importance of building themed hotels that appeal to kids as well as adults is not to attract a lot of children. It is to make it possible for parents who want to vacation where there's gambling to do it in an environment where they can bring their kids. It is unlikely that there are many people saying, "Gee, Marian, let's take up gambling now that there are places for the kids."

However, there may be a far more important point to all these kid-appealing theme hotels, and it is something that Glenn Schaeffer discussed in a paper titled "How Does Nevada Compete?" presented to the Nevada state legislature in 1992. Schaeffer, discussing trends in the industry, wrote:

One trend will reflect a desire of these consumers— many of whom will be traveling with children (and grandchildren)—to act more like kids themselves: thriving on spontaneity, on impulse activities that make them feel less grown-up. Circus already knows that many adults like to behave as children: over the course of a full year, fewer than 25% of the customers on Circus Circus' midway are actually children. The market futurist Faith Popcorn calls this trend "down-aging"—a return to innocence, free play, escape from complication and duty. Come to the fantasy environment.

Schaeffer's point is important. After all, what could be more liberating or childlike than putting five bucks on number twenty-two and crossing your fingers? While it is obvious that Circus Circus would lose a lot of customers if no children were allowed, Schaeffer seems to be saying that Las Vegas might lose customers if no "acting like children" were allowed. In other words, a big part of the market might be people who would not otherwise be in Las Vegas. Just as there are people who want their gaming sophisticated and are repulsed by the idea of clowns and jugglers in a casino, there are also people who insist on being surrounded by magic and story, and would be bored at the Hilton. For them "juice" occupies less space in the total equation.

So Las Vegas knows a lot about who the customer is. Marketing, however, does not mean knowing who your customer is. Marketing can more fairly be described as all the things you do to make your product desirable.

The Las Vegas Club in downtown Vegas is a small,

funky old casino, seedy in an appealing sort of way. When you walk into it, you feel as if you have walked into the Las Vegas of the forties. But the experience of going to the Las Vegas Club cannot, by any stretch, compete with the experience of going to the Excalibur, the Mirage, or the Golden Nugget. So the Las Vegas Club advertises "the most liberal blackjack rules in Vegas." The casino allows players to double down on any number of cards, pays double for blackjack, etc.

That is an example of a casino trying to compete on the price of gambling. There are other examples around town, bonuses for three sevens at blackjack, 97 percent return on slots, and the like. But overall, because the house advantage is often thin to begin with, and because gaming regulations are strict, there isn't much a casino can do to compete on the price of gambling. It must compete on the price and quality of the total experience.

PROMOTIONS

Promotions are a significant marketing tool for most Las Vegas casinos. The simplest form of promotion is a coupon that entitles you to a free drink or a free bet. This costs the casino little and it gets the customer into the store. But promotions come in all shapes and sizes.

In the summer of 1992, for example, you could get a Caesars MasterCard, win a Mercedes by playing the five-dollar slots at Harrah's, win his/hers Chrysler convertibles at Bally's, get free meals by entering the $200,000 slot tournament at the Stardust, play multiple-action blackjack at the Four Queens, and stay at any number of casino hotels for practically nothing, including air fare. And from the irrepressible Bob Stupak, one of Vegas's more flamboyant casino owners, you could get a "virtually free" vacation package to his Vegas World hotel and casino which, he said, was worth $1,200 in cash and action.

The string that is attached to all of these promotions is, of course, playing time. The overall philosophy is: get the customer to the tables, and the law of averages will do the rest.

At CCE, Bennett has made more money than everybody else by going against the grain on many issues, and promotions is one of them.

"Mr. Bennett is not big on promotions," says Tomlinson. "I do some mailing to travel agents and distributors throughout Southern California, and we have our own in-house coupon book which we distribute at various locations on the properties, but overall we don't do much. There's really not much point when you're running at ninety-nine or one hundred percent occupancy. Word of mouth happens to be CCE's strongest form of advertising."

COMPS

Comps are those little freebies you get for playing at a particular hotel. Everybody, of course, gets free drinks while playing. But depending on the size of your bets, you can get a free room, free meals, free shows, and at the high end, a free jet to pick you up in Hilton Head and fly you to town.

To comp or not to comp? That is often the question. And if so, how much? The decision is made through a process called rating. Rating is not a highly significant activity at CCE hotels, with their bargain-seeking, low-end players, but even CCE will rate players who buy in for more than $1,000, and reward them with dinners and shows. Rating can be crucial at stores like the Mirage, the Golden Nugget, and the Hilton, which are trying to attract premium players, or hang on to the ones they have. When a Casino is rating a player it means that casino personnel are keeping track of how much the player bets, what kind of bets he or she makes, how long he or she plays, and whether he or she plays with cash or credit. All of this information is noted by pit supervisors, and much of it is stored in casino computers. This of course will also put the player on the appropriate mailing lists for upcoming promotions, such as slot or blackjack tournaments.

In order to rate a player, the casino has to know who he is. The casino gets Gary Gambler's name by issuing little plastic comp cards that identify him as a regular customer. Gary hands over his comp card when he begins to play, and the pit supervisor makes a note of the time, or runs the card through a computer scanner. Even the one-armed bandits these days are wired to keep track of how long a player has been yanking the handle, if the player lets the computer know he or she is there by sliding the comp card into a little slot on the machine.

If the casino sees a player it wishes to rate it will ask for the card. If the player doesn't have one the casino will offer an application for one as a way to get his or her name, often with an accompanying bribe such as a ten-dollar coupon or a free meal.

Of course, the duration of a player's gambling is only part of the rating. More important than how long is how much. Does this gambler play "nickels," "quarters," or even "black" ($100 chips)? And how does he or she play? A player who splits tens and doubles down on twelve at blackjack is going to add a lot more to the casino's bottom line than a basic strategy player. So the pit supervisor will keep an eye on the player. All of this is a way of rating how valuable the player is as a customer, which in turn tells the casino how far it should go to keep him or her happy. If the player leaves the pit, the casino supervisor will call other pits and tell them what this guy or woman looks like, how much he or she is carrying in chips, and whether or not he or she has any markers. All of this, of course, must be done discreetly. The last thing you want is a premium player storming out of the casino because an overzealous pit supervisor hovered over him or her like a hawk circling a chicken.

Not all players have to be rated, but any player can be rated. The casino will rate any player who is using credit, a player who buys in for $200 or more, anyone who asks for a comp or asks to be rated, or anyone making an average bet of more than $50.

Most casinos have a formula that ties the amount of comps to the amount of playing time and the level of betting. One hour of $100 bets might be worth dinner; two hours at $1,000 and you might find yourself in a suite. Robert

Renneisen, president of the Claridge in Atlantic City, in his book *How to Be Treated Like a High Roller . . . Even Though You're Not One* (Carol, 1992), writes, "There's a misconception that comps don't cost the casino anything. That is simply not true. A $100 dinner really does cost the casino $100. And if the comped diner is taking up a table that could be used by a paying customer, the cost could be even higher."

Managing comps in the casino business is an art. If you're too soft, you'll lose money. If you're too hard, you might alienate good customers. But if you do it right, you can make it pay. In 1983, for example, the Golden Nugget, then with two locations, increased its comps by $12.8 million, and increased income by $31.1 million, a 40 percent jump over the previous year.

Clyde Turner, CFO, told *Business Week* at the time, "When comps go up, it's not all bad. But if you don't understand which of your customers are your best, you're misallocating your resources."

Bill Bennett apparently agrees.

"Where you go crazy with comps is with the high rollers, putting them up in elaborate suites, flying them in corporate jets, and so forth. It really can get very expensive when you get into that. We don't cater to high rollers. We are very liberal with comp drinks for people who are playing at the tables and slots. We are fairly liberal with food, but our comps are a tiny percentage of our revenue. Three or four percent of our total casino revenue is comped, a small percentage compared with the rest of the industry. It is twice that, or more, in other places."

CREDIT

Bennett also parts company with his competitors on the matter of credit. At premium houses like Caesars, the Las Vegas Hilton, and the Mirage, credit is an essential marketing tool. Players are evaluated, credit lines are established, and cash is put in the hands of players who otherwise could not play. In some casinos 40 to 50 percent of the business is credit, and they could no more live without credit than Sears could.

CCE, however, is not Sears. More than one business magazine has called it "the K mart of the gaming industry." So credit is not important. Good thing, too, because Bennett is not crazy about it.

"We don't believe in credit," he says. "In my opinion most casinos get hurt more than helped by credit. There is something that I think most casinos don't seem to understand. If a bank loans you fifty thousand dollars, the most they can lose is fifty thousand dollars and some attorneys' fees for trying to collect it. If I give you fifty thousand dollars in credit and you have no intention of paying it back if you lose it, you might go right down to the casino and play like a wild man, and you might win two hundred thousand dollars or a million dollars, and walk out the door with it. It's like giving a man a gun so that he can shoot you. And if we beat you for the fifty thousand, we have to beat you twice. First at the tables, and then we have to collect it. So, rather than credit, we cash a lot of checks.

"If I were running a different establishment, like the Mirage, I would give credit but I would control it better than they do. It has changed considerably in the last ten or twelve years. It used to be that a million-dollar line of credit was a big line of credit, a jumbo. Now there are ten-million-dollar lines of credit. I think it can be controlled better. One of the problems with credit is that the hotels don't seem to be working well together. It used to be that if a guy came in and wanted a fifty-thousand-dollar line of credit, you'd put in a call to Central Credit and you could find out his credit history. Maybe a guy is good for fifty thousand dollars, but if he's got that much credit at four hotels, now that's two hundred thousand dollars. The problem is a lot of hotels don't check because they don't want anybody to know they've got this high-rolling customer. Or maybe the host who brought him in is sure that, well, yes, I know this guy has some problems at another hotel, but he really likes us and he'll pay us first, and so forth.

"It used to be that gambling debts were not legally collectible in Nevada. And then Atlantic City came along and they made them legally collectible, and Nevada finally did the same thing. Some of the high-rolling places wanted that. But it's a terrible idea and we were against it for years. We don't want gambling debts to be legally collectible. Is this what we need, some casino taking a guy's business away? Wouldn't that be great for our image.

"If the debts are not legally collectible then the casinos will be a little more careful about how they issue credit. If you're doing your job right from a marketing standpoint, you won't get into a position where you have to be chasing people for debts. One of my primary rules is 'Never hurt your customer.' "

"Credit," says Glenn Schaeffer, "is a marketing tool that,

given the type of customer we attract, is not very useful to us. There are other hotels that feel the same way, but we think we are the stingiest in the business. Now, at another type of casino you might have a different philosophy. A Cliff Perlman, for example, the former head of Caesars, might say, 'Hey, if a guy comes in here and loses fifty thousand dollars at craps and I lend him fifty thousand more, I've just turned a fifty-thousand-dollar customer into a hundred-thousand-dollar customer. And usually, he'll pay the money back.' Credit can be a very profitable tool if used wisely, but it's not the route for us. And refusing credit has helped CCE keep our operating expenses down, which the organization is famous for. When you're not in the credit business, you cut down enormously on the number of decision-makers around the casino. You don't need all those hosts and supervisors on the floor judging some player's credit quality."

VALUE

"I learned a few lessons from the furniture business," Bennett says. "The company that really taught me something was Levitz. They were just a little smarter than me and they came in and killed my business in certain areas. They had moved into Phoenix and Tucson, and they had a pricing policy that was unusual. They would sell for twenty-five or thirty percent less than my stores would, and make a profit. Half their store was showroom and half was warehouse, so they had lower operating costs than we did. You'd come in, pick out what you want, and throw it into a pickup truck and drive it home. Levitz would mark up something less, and sell it for less. People would get more value for their money and come back. We had a higher operating cost, and we had to spend more money on advertising than they did, because they had a very loyal following. Everything in the store was a value, so they had a lot of repeat customers, instead of living from sale to sale. Meanwhile, I had to 'buy' my customer for every visit, and that's very costly in retailing. The lesson is that it is better to make ten dollars off a customer who keeps coming back than to make twenty dollars off a customer that you never see again. That's why at Circus we compete on everyday value, not periodic 'sales.' Word of mouth is our most productive form of advertising."

Bennett's formula for getting repeat customers has always been contained in one word: value. In fact, "value" is the mantra of Circus Circus Enterprises, and it is a word rarely omitted from a Bennett discussion of business, or from an interview with the people who work for him.

In the gaming industry you cannot add value to a central product which is a prisoner to the rules of mathematics. You can't, for example, start a campaign that says, "At Circus Circus we will pay double for red roulette numbers," or you would be out of business in six hours. So the value has to be delivered everyplace else.

It comes in room prices, food prices, and entertainment prices. It comes at the games in the form of minimum bets. At Circus Circus and the Excalibur it is still possible to play blackjack or craps for a buck, and you can even buy fifty-cent chips at the roulette table. These stakes can be found in some of the older and seedier downtown spots, but they are virtually unheard of elsewhere on the Strip.

Although there are noticeable differences of style between Bennett and his heir apparent, Schaeffer, the emphasis on value is not one of them.

While Bennett walks through the casino to learn about his customers, Schaeffer tends to view things in larger contexts. "People are demanding more value for their dollar," he says. "If you look at the decade of the eighties, despite all the talk of consumer materialism, the fact is that the companies that grew fastest were the discount or off-price companies. The winners were names like Wal-Mart, Costco, Food Lion, Home Depot, and Circus Circus."

So if there is a simple Circus Circus marketing formula, it is: Entertainment Plus Value Equals Profit. Or, as Richard Stevenson put it in *The New York Times,* "The company's goal is not to make money on rooms or meals—and it does not. It simply wants to attract mobs of people on the theory that almost all of them will ultimately gamble."

11

The Midas Touch

William G. Bennett has put behind him more than a quarter of a century in the gaming industry. Like Midas, he has turned all that he has touched to gold, using not a wand but a set of principles. Long before American business knew about one-minute managers and the seven habits of highly effective people, Bennett had his own ideas. And though he has never codified his rules of management, it is possible by looking at his handiwork and listening to his subordinates to come up with what might be called Bennett's five rules of success in the gaming industry, or in any retail industry. If such a list existed, it might look like this:

1. Know the difference between spending and investing.

Though Bennett has spent some of his personal fortune on a few extravagances like speedboats, expensive cars, and model airplanes, complete with a model-plane airport on his Nevada ranch, he does not part easily with company money.

"We run lean and mean," says marketing head Mel Larsen. Larsen, who worked with Bennett at the Mint, has been with Circus Circus from the beginning. In fact, he was technically on the payroll a few days before Bennett himself. "I came down a few days before we took over to see just what we were getting into," he says. Larsen says that over the decades Bennett's style has always been to get the most for CCE's payroll.

"We don't have excessive management," he says. "Each person covers a lot of bases."

Bennett himself is fond of saying, "You can't pay too much for a good manager, but you can pay too many managers."

Down in the casino at Circus Circus Las Vegas, Gary O'Keefe sees the same philosophy at work.

"A lot of our cost control is in how we staff employees," O'Keefe says. "I went down to Main Street Station shortly before they went into bankruptcy. It was a great-looking hotel, but I felt that they were overstaffed. In just one bar there were three bartenders and there weren't three customers in the whole bar. There's a fine line between customer service and being overstaffed.

"Here in the casino we don't have five or six guys running around watching tables. We don't have a host running around. We don't have credit people, because we don't give much credit. When we do give it, the shift manager can okay it, or I can okay it. So we've eliminated some top-paying positions. Most hotels have two boxmen at a crap table. We only have one. Most hotels have one floorman for every table; we have one floorman for two tables."

The dice from those tables, by the way, are another example of Bennett economics at work. The dice are retired at the end of the day and sold in the gift shop, after holes are drilled in them, so that they can't be rigged and slipped into another game. The same with playing cards. O'Keefe's casino uses about 500,000 decks of playing cards a year, none of them for more than one day. While many of the decks are donated to charities, the rest are resold in the gift shop. CCE pays about sixty-two cents for a deck of cards and resells them for fifty cents. This is a practice of virtually all Las Vegas casinos.

Bennett in many ways is like the customers he caters to. Though he is richer than they are by some hundreds of millions of dollars, he likes a lot of the same things. At home he watches television. At work he eats his lunch every day at the Pink Pony coffee shop at Circus Circus Las Vegas. Away from the office, one of his favorite treats is a bag of Church's fried chicken. Bennett is also a man who demands his money's worth. He studies the prices of the things he buys, and often he will keep a new camera or some other small product on his desk so that he can quiz his executives about the price. "Bill Bennett," says Glenn Schaeffer, "could probably be the all-time champ on *The Price Is Right.*"

One of CCE's competitors has said that Bennett's genius is in spending exactly what is needed, but not more, to make his product highly profitable.

Perhaps nowhere is Bennett's demand for value so obvious, and so important, as in the building of new hotels. Long before the first shovel of dirt had been lifted to build the Excalibur, for example, Bennett had decreed that if CCE, Inc., was going to make money from the Excalibur by selling product, the company was also going to make money by not spending it frivolously, a charge that has been fired at Donald Trump and Steve Wynn, two casino titans who are less successful, but better known, than William Bennett. As Bennett sees it, a major distinction between himself and the two more public figures is that he doesn't simply "spend," he "invests." Investing, he says, means putting money into things that the customer sees and pays for.

By the time the Excalibur was conceived, CCE had gone public, and Bennett spent stockholders' money the same way he had always spent his own: carefully, efficiently, and with a pretty good idea of where every nickel went. As a result, the Excalibur was alive and breathing on schedule, with a price tag of only $290 million, compared to $730 million for the Mirage and more than $1 billion for Trump's Taj Mahal in Atlantic City.

Buildings are a reflection of the people building them. Ego becomes a problem for some people. For whatever reason, when people come into money they either want a restaurant or hotel. There's something about having a public building that's important to them. A lot of ego hotels were built in the 1980s.

"We are pretty tight," Glenn Shaeffer says. "We know how to build properties, because we've done more of it in less time than anybody in the history of the gaming industry.

158

We don't stick in a lot of marble and brass and other high-cost elements. Steve Wynn is, in part, an interior designer and vivid creator, but he does it by putting money in places where we don't. We build for a look and a feel, an atmosphere, but we do it on a budget. We also avoid change orders. If you get going one way and then you say, 'Hey, let's do it a different way,' that's very expensive. To make changes in the middle of the process runs the meter up unmercifully."

Though Bennett has generally spent money wisely, he is quick to acknowledge that he has made mistakes. "Not every idea is a good idea," he says. For years Bennett tried to put Circus Circus into the hobby plane business, for example, but this pet project never made money. In February 1989 Bennett decided that enough was enough, so the hobby business was converted to Bennett's personal ownership, with no loss to CCE.

2. Feed the troops.

"Feeding the troops" is Bennett's phrase for treating employees as well as he wants them to treat customers.

No gaming company in Las Vegas, including CCE, can be overly proud of the wages it pays to low-level employees. The hotels that are awash in profits, as well as the ones that are losing money, pay dealers minimum wage, or close to it. It is not enough that casino customers lose their money, they are also expected to subsidize the casino's payroll cost with tips. In fact, most of a dealer's salary is tip money, which, thanks to the IRS, must be pooled and declared. According to one Las Vegas casino manager, dealers at a busy casino make about $60 to $100 a day in tips.

"Being a dealer is a tough job," Schaeffer says. "We don't have a quota, exactly, but we know when a dealer is not putting down enough hands. So here's this dealer, on the one hand he is like a factory worker, but he is also dealing with the ultimate consumer. The customer wants the game to go at his pace, not our pace, and the dealer needs to keep the customer happy, while at the same time trying to get out so many hands per hour, and we're telling him, 'Here's how you deal,' and 'Put a hand down this way,' and so forth."

Dealers in Las Vegas have no union, which is understandable. A union might wreak havoc with the casino's security procedures. Every time a dealer got caught palming a chip, the union could howl. However, one might argue that the barring of a union is a reason that dealers should be given better wages. Bennett could argue, of course, that dealer wages are a function of the free marketplace; nobody has to work if he or she doesn't want to, and Bennett has an obligation to the stockholders to keep all costs down.

In any case, after the wages and tips are counted, the average dealer makes about $30,000 a year. The additional benefits, at least at CCE, bring it up to $40,000, which puts dealers well ahead of workers in other service industries.

But the fact is that historically the gaming industry does not have the greatest record in the world with labor.

"We try to put a lot of emphasis on employee relationships. We have great benefits," Gary O'Keefe says. "We try to treat people fairly, which the industry has not always done. When I was coming up, if you were an unlucky dealer and your table lost money for a couple of days, you would be fired. If the dice on a crap table lost money consistently, they would fire the whole crew. A lot of people in this business are superstitious. But the superstition only goes one way. If a table makes a lot of money, they don't give the crew a bonus."

Barney Vinson, writing in the March 1993 issue of *Casino Player*, recalls some of the superstitious behavior of oilman Major Riddle, who took over the Dunes in 1957:

Not only was Riddle losing at the poker tables, but the win percentage in the casino was starting to drop. Riddle retaliated in some rather bizarre and unorthodox ways. If a slot machine paid a jackpot, he disconnected it. If the stickman on a dice game called too many winners, he replaced him with a dealer from another game. A dealer in paint-spattered overalls once happened to be in the casino on his day off. Riddle walked up to him and told him to take out the stickman at a nearby craps table.

"Like this," the dealer asked, gesturing at his overalls.

"I don't care what you look like," Riddle barked, "just get in there."

The dealer took the stick and immediately called a winner, six, much to the delight of every player at the table. Suddenly, he felt another dealer tapping him on the shoulder.

"Mr. Riddle said you could go home now."

On another occasion, Riddle was alleged to

*have chopped a dice table to pieces with a fire ax
after a losing day.*

Gary O'Keefe says there is little superstition among casino executives these days, and in any case it is not indulged to the detriment of employees. "But when I was a dealer there was a lot of superstition," he says. "I remember one pit supervisor who used to walk around with a salt shaker and he would sprinkle salt around certain blackjack tables to make sure they were lucky for the house. And lots of times if a crap table was making money, they would make the stickman stay in place instead of rotating, because they thought if he changed positions the table might go cold."

Not surprisingly, all of the executives at CCE say that CCE takes particularly good care of its employees. They can hardly be viewed as reliable witnesses. But there also seems to be a good deal of outside evidence that Bennett and his company are more enlightened than many of their competitors. The people on the front lines of Las Vegas, the dealers and the cocktail waitresses, speak with great admiration for Circus Circus. Almost without exception, they will tell you that it is the best company, or one of the best, to work for in Las Vegas. It's not that they make any more money under the big top, but they seem to have a feeling that they are listened to, respected, and given a fair shot at promotions. Bennett is not a man to coddle his help, but he has apparently earned their respect.

Bennett recognizes the fact that because of the proximity of competition, a happy work force is of paramount importance in a Las Vegas hotel and casino. A snooty desk

162

clerk or foul-mouthed roulette dealer can pour cold water on any entertainment experience and send the customer looking elsewhere for a good time.

"When you walk into McDonald's you have maybe a four-minute experience," he says. "You walk up, you get your order, you pay, you get your food, you leave. There is not a lot that can go wrong. But here, people come for three and four days. We have a point of sale at the front desk, we have a point of sale at the slot machine, at the restaurant, we have a maid changing the beds. We have a lot of interaction with the consumer and a lot of ways to disappoint, but also a lot of ways to triumph. This is day-to-day merchandising. We have motivated people in this company. The question is how do you get people to do more, how do you make them want to?"

Bennett's supporters might argue that one way he motivates them is to stand up for them. In 1983, for example, when the unionized Las Vegas hotel workers were on strike, William Bennett broke ranks with other hotel operators and gave his people the raises they wanted. He had agonized long and hard about the issue, he says, but in the end decided that his loyalty to his employees was more important than his loyalty to other hotel operators. At the time he told a reporter, "How could a man like myself, with my employees who know how well the property is doing, largely because of them, how can I go to them and not give them a raise?"

He says now, "We have excellent employees who keep our customers coming back. We invest in people in this company just as we invest in bricks and mortar. We try to treat our people as a kind of customer, too. How people treat each other within a company will usually influence how the outside customer gets treated."

In 1992 Bennett supported striking Culinary, Bartenders, Teamsters, and Operating Engineers unions at the Frontier. When his own workers mentioned the tough conditions of friends at the Frontier, Bennett sent a Circus Circus lunch truck down to feed the strikers.

He told a reporter for *The Las Vegas Sun,* "If I had the time, I'd get a stick and sign and go out there and picket with them." Bennett said he had studied the Frontier contract, and that the hotel was trying to "take things away" from its employees. "We have been paying wages higher than the Culinary scale for a number of years," he said. "This irritates the hell out of me. They say they can't make money, and they are paying a damn sight less than we do, and our earnings aren't too bad."

Bennett has also parted company with many of his competitors by coming out against Nevada's "employment at will" doctrine, which says that an employee can quit at any time, without reason, by saying, "I quit," and an employer can fire him or her at any time, without reason, by saying, "You're fired."

"I have a different view," Bennett says. "Employees should know that their jobs are secure, unless there is a valid reason for layoffs, such as bad economic conditions. Other than that, an employee should be terminated only when there is just cause, and he should be told exactly what that cause is."

At CCE there is a policy that any terminated employee

has a right to a hearing by a council of peers, and the right of appeal to Bennett, or to Glenn Schaeffer.

None of which should be construed as saying that Bennett is a pussycat. Pussycats don't get to be billionaires. Circus Circus seems to be a hard-driving company. There's not a lot of politics, but it's not a chummy atmosphere, either. There is an edge to it. CCE only has a use for producers. They staff very lean and each manager must cover a lot of ground. If you lose a step, or the desire to go full-bore all the time, you'll be on your way out.

"For managers Circus Circus Enterprises is a tougher place to work than many companies," Glenn Schaeffer says. "When you draw a big check from this company, your first duty is to this company. You put in the time. In this company a top executive can easily go a couple of years without any real time off. Bennett is like a head coach who's relentless in extracting performance from his players. He's not a nag, but he'll call you at home if there's a problem. Bennett pushes people. He wants to see how much he can get out of them. Bennett's formative experience, in my judgment, was his stint as a combat pilot when he was still in late adolescence. When you fly missions, he's told me, every day has meaning.

"Every day here has meaning. We see management as a perpetual skirmish line. And we push people to the front. We want people to reach their potential. Bennett wants to see who'll duck, or who'll run, or who'll dig in, or who'll charge. Adrenaline is one of our management tools. We don't push too hard, but we push enough. Our managers love it, but I'm sure there are days when they hate it. A consultant who's worked with us on supervisor training once asked Bennett if he 'set the bar high.' Bennett just looked at him and said, 'Yes.'

Many CCE executives say that Bill Bennett is highly critical by nature, and that is part of the CCE culture.

Schaeffer says, "He once told me that the CEO must be the 'pickiest devil alive,' because if he isn't, no one else is going to be, and it will eventually turn up as a weakness in the company. Bennett never raises his voice, which, maybe, makes him all the tougher. He is a kind of logician. If something hasn't worked out, he takes a manager through it by the numbers, and he doesn't care about hurt feelings. Okay, explain this to me, he will say. He wants to examine the train of thought that brought you to this result. He's very good at spotting the fallacious turn in your thinking. And he is an expert listener, that is one of his strengths. He won't interrupt you, he won't argue. When you are done, he will respond.

"Sometimes you'll explain to him what you want to do, in your department, or with a contract or policy. Then he'll lean back and think it over, and he'll say, 'Well, that's not the way I would do it. But we're going to do it your way.' This means that you now own it, you've just acquired equity in this thing, and you'd better see that it turns out well. 'And,' he will remind you, 'I reserve bitching rights.' "

Bennett's style with managers is well suited to a bias of his, and that is toward youth. He prefers to grow his own team, not buy players on the market. "I think the likelihood of getting new ideas, high energy, and personal sacrifice is higher from hungry young people on their way up," he says. "Our executive corps is pretty young by industry standards, though pretty well experienced by now. I like to get that surprise performance, more than I counted on, from the younger person. I promote them fast and give them plenty of responsibility."

3. Keep your hands on the wheel.

"Mr. Bennett walks through the building all the time, always looking around," Gary O'Keefe says. "If he sees something that's not right, he will say so. I remember one Sunday he came in, and the porters had really let down on the job. I guess they figured, it's Sunday, there's no boss around. Well, Bennett found the place a little bit messy. He was not happy. Now Bennett never yells, and he never really fires anyone. But when he's unhappy, you know about it. So he got a couple of porters together and he put in a call to the department head, and made sure it all got taken care of right away."

Tom Tomlinson tells this story: "Mr. Bennett went into the breakfast buffet the other day, and he felt that the food was a little cold. So he walks into the kitchen and grabs a thermometer and tests the temperature of the food. He was right. It wasn't as warm as it was supposed to be. Now maybe this was just a fluke thing, where his food happened to be a little cold, or whatever, but the point is he had the food and beverage executive there all weekend, testing the equipment to make sure everything was working properly to keep the food hot. One of Mr. Bennett's maxims is 'Do it now. Fix it today.' "

Everybody has his favorite Bennett story, but they all seem to be about the same thing: Bennett roaming the building, testing the product, talking to the customers. Dan Lee, who used to be a stock analyst with Drexel Burnham and is now a Mirage executive, has said, "When Bill Bennett eats from the buffet, and if the fried chicken doesn't taste right, he raises hell. It's little details like that which make his company so successful. He has impeccable personal tastes and he knows what his customers want."

Bennett is big on getting out of the office and into the store, so it's not surprising that he would hire people who do the same thing, or perhaps encourage them to do it if they are not so inclined.

Tomlinson says, "I like to go down and watch the customers, see who they are, find out where they come from."

Paulos says, "I spend as little time as necessary in the office. The rest of the time I'm out there, on the floor."

And Glenn Schaeffer says, "I stand by the entrance sometimes and watch people put quarters into the slot machines. They win. They lose. But they're having a good time, which is the real product we provide. This environment is for fun.

"We have a Ringmaster's Club. This is a group of regular slot players who come for slot tournaments, and I often have breakfast with them. There's a lot of kibitzing that goes on. I'll say to them, 'Now make sure you lose some money today. We can't build Luxor without it.' And they'll tell me I'd better load up the machines because they're going to get my money. We have a lot of fun. And, just as important, they will tell me how we can make the whole experience better for them."

Customers are not the only ones who tell Bennett and his executives how to improve the product. Bennett is a greater believer in "benchmarking," and his employees are expected to observe the competitors' stores and practices, to pick up fresh ideas. Is somebody doing something better than CCE does it? Does somebody have an idea that CCE can use, or even improve on? If so, Bennett wants to know about it.

4. Get employees into the game.

Bennett, recalling the Del Webb system, whereby a successful casino manager would get the same salary as an unsuccessful one, put his incentive theories into play as soon as he took over Circus Circus. From the beginning Circus Circus has tied a big slice of employee compensation to the profitability of the company.

"Because the Webb company did not treat employees very well, I was able to cherry-pick my people from there," Bennett says. "All I could offer them was the same salary they were getting with Webb, which was pretty low, but I instituted a bonus program. I never imagined the bonus program would take off the way it did, and those people who were with me at the beginning are doing very, very well."

In 1992 the average wage and benefit at CCE, below the executive level, was about $25,000 a year, compared to say, $27,000 at Caesars. CCE was pretty tightly bunched with the majority of Vegas operations. From the supervisory level up CCE's pay improves relative to the rest of the industry. But in keeping with Bennett's strong beliefs about incentives, most of the pay is in the form of bonuses and stock options.

"For people at senior levels we pay relatively low salaries," Glenn Schaeffer says, "but they are in a bonus program which is based on profits at their store. The bonus

169

program across the company reaches pretty deep, including hundreds of people. Most of them will make the majority of their compensation from bonuses, which are paid quarterly.

"We think that the company should make a certain amount of money based on its shareholders' investment. The stockholder is first in line; then a percentage of profit also goes into the employee bonus program. People coming up see it as something to shoot for. Our stock options are strong by the standards of the industry, but they are tied to merit. Mr. Bennett, by the way, has never taken a single option on a single share of stock. His rewards have all come from his original ownership stakes in the company. This is an unusual practice in corporate America, but he just feels that he is making enough money."

One result of these practices, according to Mel Larsen, is that the executive team stays in place. "We are well compensated," he says. "So nobody hires us away. We don't have the massive changes you see in some other organizations."

One of the reasons that people like Mel Larsen are well compensated is not that they are drawing big salaries, but that the stock on which they've profited through options has performed so well, a performance for which Glenn Schaeffer is given his share of the credit. "Glenn has helped to make us all millionaires," Larsen says.

In fact, one difference between Bennett's discourse and Schaeffer's is that when Bennett talks about CCE, the listener hears reasons that a customer should sleep and gamble at a Circus Circus property, and when Schaeffer discusses the same subject, the listener also hears reasons that an investor should own CCE stock.

Here, for example, is Schaeffer on the subject of executive compensation:

"T. Boone Pickens founded a group called Shareholders United. One of the things they measure is corporate performance relative to executive compensation. In 1991 Circus rated twenty-third out of one thousand public corporations. We are in the top two percent of American companies in growth in shareholder value relative to executive compensation, and we are number one in this industry. Despite that, the company has made a lot of people, including me, rather wealthy, because it has performed so well."

While CCE is well-regarded on Wall Street for its executive compensation package, the gaming industry is certainly not immune to some of the questionable executive compensation packages which have offended stockholders in recent years. While still in bankruptcy, Bally's gaming division, for example, paid their company president 2.9 million dollars. Many gaming executives were amazed that a company strapped for cash would give almost three million dollars to its president.

5. Stay on your toes.

Napoleon Hill, in his famous study of successful men, learned that one quality of almost all multimillionaires was the ability to make decisions quickly. Bennett, though he has to spend much of his day dealing with legal issues and being politically sensitive in this highly regulated and privileged industry, seems to have that ability. He has a reputation for being able to respond quickly, whether it is to a problem with the toilets or to the sudden availability of land where a hotel could be built.

"The key to fertility of ideas," Bennett has written, "comes from continually pushing ourselves to the next level. That's a bias in this company, the next level. We don't operate by a comprehensive strategic plan, laden with schedules, a sort of self-restricting view of the future. Instead, we try to meet the future by relying on both a restless and responsive spirit that says, let's find something new."

Schaeffer says, "Bennett's philosophy is that managers are basically problem-solvers. The way he sees it, is that most people don't become good managers because they just are not willing to confront problems. In life, he says, people don't like to confront problems. They hope a problem will go away or heal itself but it won't. If you want to get crosswise with Bill Bennett, I can tell you that one proven track is to be a shirker or an excuse-maker. He'll explain to you that early on, the problem used to be this big, but now, due to in-action, it's gotten this big. He will tell you that small things that are not taken care of right away have a way of bringing large, ugly consequences down the line.

"Bennett does not blame you for finding problems. He blames you for not attacking them. And you're going to live a lot better around here if you walk up to him and say, 'We've got a problem,' or 'We've made a mistake.' He will usually say to you, 'What are you going to do about it, and when will it be done?' "

Perhaps the most influential instrument of this "quick response" mentality is the Daily Managerial Reports. These financial statements, with their figures on yesterday's profits by property in each operating department, compared with the monthly projections as well as last year's performance, are a kind of early-warning system.

Bill Paulos says, "We have tremendous accountability, in that I get a complete profit and loss statement right down to the dollar in every single department and every revenue generator in the house. I know where everything is, right down to all the money spent. I don't think anyone in the business is as detailed as we are. And that's been the case since day one."

"That daily report is the bible we go by," says director of entertainment Mike Hartzell. "Everything we do is a response to how well we are doing. If we're not making money at something, we have to decide, should we spend more money to attract customers, should we advertise more, change what we're doing, or just quit spending money on something that isn't worth it?"

The daily report in the casino industry, by the way, is not a Bennett invention. In *William Fiske Harrah* (Doubleday, 1982), Leon Mandel gives credit for daily casino reports to Maurice Sheppard, who in 1946 went to work as a bookkeeper for Bill Harrah, whom Bennett would later describe as the only man he admired in northern Nevada gaming. Sheppard, Mandel writes,

> *was developing something that would come to be known as the Daily Report. It listed department grosses, interest accrued daily, and pretax operating profit. It revealed immediately whether or not the company was within budget. It compared cost*

year to date to the same period of the year previous.

Mandel later writes:

The Daily Report did, in time, turn into an immensely sophisticated tool; enough so that The Wall Street Journal *would remark on it in a major piece done on Bill Harrah in the last year of his life. Even in 1946, though, Harrah thought it was a wonderful device. In the months and years to come he would encourage Shep to work out supplemental reports on each slot machine, and then each table.*

Bennett is also big on responding to customer feedback.

"We are always taking the pulse of the place," Tom Tomlinson says. "For example, we have guest comment cards in the rooms, but we also have them in the lobbies, near elevators, in the casino, and near entrances. The response percentage is amazing. With a mailing piece, if you get a ten percent response it is stupendous, but we get a much higher percent of response from guests. I'd say about fifteen percent of the respondents have some sort of complaint. If it's an in-room card it is usually the drapes, or the carpet or whatever. First those cards would go to housekeeping, then to us. Our publicist looks them over, then gives them to me. She pulls out certain key ones, and I'll pull out what I think needs to be immediately tended to. I'll send them to the general manager. If a card says, 'Well, I played twenty-one and the dealer,

Harry Jones, was surly,' then Harry Jones will probably get a call and it will go on his record.

"We analyze these cards overall, every quarter or every six months, and we look for patterns. For example, you'll find that certain equipment only lasts five years, and some ten years, and all of a sudden you're getting comments about a certain piece of equipment. It is attention to details; we are always comparing ourselves to last year."

"Mr. Bennett reads many of these cards and so do I," Glenn Schaeffer says. "If there's a complaint concerning your department, you'll get a call from on high; it's as simple as that."

For Bill Bennett, staying on your toes also means knowing why you are successful. "The worst curse in business is to fail and not know why," he says. "The second-worst curse is to be successful and not know why. Business success comes from doing a few things extraordinarily well and spending your time and resources just on those things. Customers expect a handful of things from Circus Circus: low prices, good value, enthusiastic people, consistency of product, and creative themes. If customers want, on the other hand, doting room service or large lines of credit, they should pick a competitor."

12

Protecting the Goose

The most enduring myth about Las Vegas is that it is a mob town, and that gaming is a mob-controlled industry. In this, the age of information, it is shocking to see how slowly the information that Vegas is clean has traveled to the hinter lands.

"Going to write a book about Las Vegas? Watch yourself," said people who never issued a warning when the author was off to interview psychotic killers. "You won't get anywhere without the mob's permission," others said knowingly, without the benefit of having actually been to Las Vegas.

The cigar-chomping Las Vegas mob boss, running a casino hotel and dealing harshly with anybody who gets in his way, is a bit of mythology on a level with channeling, palm reading, and surefire stock tips.

In his *New York Times Magazine* piece, Trip Gabriel writes:

> *Though in the popular imagination Las Vegas is still associated with the Mafia, it's been years since an organized crime figure was hauled into court on casino-related charges. Today many of the hotels are owned by squeaky clean image–obsessed companies like Hilton and Holiday Inn. They are staffed by bean counters and micro managers who live in the suburbs.*

Unfortunately not all newspapermen are as well informed, and many, out of ignorance or a desire to appear clever, perpetuate the myths. Here, for example, is columnist Dan Bernstein writing in the Riverside, California *Press-Enterprise* in 1992:

> *Type one Americans not only love Vegas, but routinely come up with amazing packages that include roundtrip air fare, four nights in a tall hotel, meals, drinks, gambling money, and tickets to Nudes on Ice. All for $24.95. Anywhere else, this would be exposed as a con-artist scam. In Vegas, it's viewed as the best good-faith offer the mob can make in tough economic times.*

To understand why the use of the word "mob" is an anachronism here, you must first see Las Vegas gaming for what it is: an enormous magic goose that lays golden eggs. When you are as powerful as, say, an entire state, and you have such a goose, you don't let anybody, including the mob, screw around with it.

The mythology about Las Vegas mobsters is not, of course, without basis. The town has been home to many gangsters over the years—most notably Bugsy Siegel.

As noted in Chapter Two, the assassination of poor Bugsy helped to create the popular image of Las Vegas as a haven for gangsters, while it was also the first domino in a series that would lead to the exodus of gangsters from Las Vegas gaming.

Dean Jennings, in *We Only Kill Each Other,* writes:

In Nevada the political leaders suddenly saw the Siegel murder as a threat to their growing gold mine—the gambling business that supplied the cash they couldn't get in taxes or any other way from the state's meager population, then about 140,000.

It was not just the killing that made them uneasy. It was the sudden realization that the big money was coming from the underworld, that they knew very little about the hoodlums in their midst, and that any homicidal thug like Siegel could get a gambling license merely by applying to city authorities.

So Nevada passed a law giving the state approval over

all gambling licenses. "Thus," writes Jennings, "the state got complete control of gambling and gambling taxes."

The protection of the magic goose had begun. But with all those golden eggs being laid, the crooks would not be routed easily. Las Vegas was probably never as tainted as middle America thinks, but neither was it as clean as the state would have liked. If a gangster couldn't get a license or own a hotel, he could often slip in the back door by lending large amounts of cash to an honest casino operator. Cash in large quantities is always a corrupting influence, and it worked its way through the system. Bribes were paid to politicians, questionable alliances were made between license holders and guys named Lefty, cash was skimmed, suitcases full of bills were delivered, and now and then bullet-riddled bodies were found rotting in the sagebrush.

Sanitization came only gradually. By the late 1940s and early 1950s, Las Vegas had lived through more scandal than Warren G. Harding. In 1951 Tennessee senator Estes Kefauver, who was investigating organized crime, linked Bugsy Siegel with Eastern mob figures who, unlike Siegel, were still breathing, and when Kefauver's focus turned to Las Vegas it revealed, among other things, that a member of the Nevada Tax Commission, which was supposed to be policing the gaming industry, was a part owner of the Last Frontier Hotel, so at least one fox was guarding the goose house. In that same year, murder attempts were made on Benny Binion and Lincoln Fitzgerald, casino men whose names still sit atop Glitter Gulch casinos.

In 1954 *The Las Vegas Sun* ran gaming industry exposés that shocked the state legislature into creating the Gaming

Control Board, which would serve as the investigative arm of the Tax Commission. Even this was not enough, and the legislature later created the Gaming Commission, with the Gaming Control Board under it. This is the bureaucracy that today polices the Nevada gaming industry, and though many in the industry bristled at the additional controls, few gaming executives today don't give both the Commission and the Board high marks.

While there are millions of people today who think gangsters run Las Vegas, there are also millions who understand that Las Vegas flushed the wiseguys out of its system long ago. For many, the message was delivered through two highly publicized events. The first involved Frank Sinatra.

"In 1960," writes Jerome Skolnick in *House of Cards,* "a loose-leaf binder was compiled by the Gaming Control Board with the names and pictures of eleven men the board thought to be of 'notorious or unsavory reputation.' "

The list became known as the Black Book, and the Gaming Board told casino operators that guys in the Black Book were to be banned from all casino properties. Knowingly let one in the door, and you would lose your license; it was that simple.

Around this time Frank Sinatra had bought a piece of the Sands Hotel in Las Vegas and the Cal Neva Lodge at Tahoe. One Cal Neva guest was mobster Sam Giancana, whose name was in the infamous Black Book. When the Gaming Board brought this detail to Sinatra's attention, the singer swore up and down that he didn't know Giancana had stayed at the hotel. The Gaming Board said Sinatra was lying, and all hell broke loose. Sinatra and the Gaming Board went to

181

war. Investigations were begun. Obscene phone calls were exchanged. Threats were veiled. The mix of big-time entertainer, major mob figures, and the state's Gaming Control Board was juicy, and the battle inspired headlines in newspapers everywhere. When the smoke cleared, Sinatra was publicly spanked. Forced to get out of gaming, he sold his interests in the hotels.

The Board's standing up to the powerful Sinatra, a major entertainer who sometimes ate lunch with the President, told the public that Vegas was serious about running a clean shop.

But, Leon Mandel notes in *William Fiske Harrah,* "It wasn't the extirpation of the evil Sinatra influence that marked a turn toward respectability for Nevada in the public eye; rather it was the appearance of a legend of a different stripe."

The legend was Howard Hughes, the reclusive and somewhat nutty billionaire. In 1966 Hughes arrived in Las Vegas secretly by private train, and within a year he bought three casino properties off the rack, properties which reputedly had been owned by organized crime. Hughes might not have been playing with a full deck, but he also was not playing with a marked deck. He smelled not of gangsterism but of big business, and his debut in town is regarded by many as the point at which the gaming industry began to enter the mainstream of American business. (There's something to this, but Glenn Schaeffer points out that Hughes was not exactly a Bill Bennett when it came to running casinos. In the late 1970s Hughes's Summa Corporation was the biggest gaming corporation in Nevada, with the Frontier, the Landmark, the Silver Slipper, the Sands, and the Desert Inn, and now all of those properties are dead or at least running a very high temperature.)

The push for purity in gaming reached its rinse cycle in the mid-1970s. We can get a good view of it from Emmett Michaels, a man who spent part of his career protecting the goose and today is a major protector of golden eggs. Michaels is director of corporate security for Circus Circus Enterprises. But in the mid-1960s he was chief of the FBI's organized crime task force in Las Vegas. His mission: to run the last of the gangsters out of town.

In 1977 the FBI felt it necessary to bring a team of twenty-five agents into Las Vegas to investigate hidden mob interests in casinos. Michaels, then an FBI special agent in New Haven, Connecticut, had been keeping an eye on the five New York mob families. Now he was brought into Vegas as the supervisory agent for the organized crime squad. He was to be the "out in the street guy," he says, in charge of the technical surveillance squad, and his assignment was clear: put together a case against the Chicago, Kansas City, and Milwaukee mobs that had influence in casinos.

"Part of the problem when I first came to Las Vegas," he says, "was that people here took the attitude of denial that there even was a problem. They pretended that organized crime didn't exist in Las Vegas, even though everybody knew it did. They sort of protected it. When we started to plant microphones and record people talking about how to skim at a casino, that began to change."

The casinos were for the most part being run by respectable businessmen. "Probably pillars of the community," Michaels says without irony. "But some hotels were built with money from the Teamsters Union pension fund, and the Teamsters Union was controlled by the Chicago mob.

According to Michaels, there has never been a Las Vegas mob "family." The casinos that were mob-controlled were always controlled by out-of-town mobs.

He says, "Las Vegas was an open city, with the Chicago LCN [La Cosa Nostra] having most of the influence, basically through the Teamsters Union. But it wasn't like New York, where you had the five families controlling everything. In Las Vegas you had Detroit mob members, St. Louis mob members, Milwaukee, and so forth, but the Chicago family was the most prominent, even though you had families right next door in Phoenix and Los Angeles."

Michaels says the boys from the Windy City had the most control because through the moneylending process they had acquired influence in the Tropicana, the Stardust, the Fremont, and the Hacienda. The Stardust was the flagship. These places, by the way, are all clean now, run by guys who pack electronic organizers, not pistols.

"So let's say you're a businessman back then," Michaels says, "and you want to start a casino. If a businessman wanted to build and he couldn't get the money from the bank or other legitimate sources, because he didn't have the assets or whatever, he would either borrow the money from the Teamsters Union pension fund, or he might be 'blessed' with a gift. And all of a sudden these people that blessed him are saying 'Okay, we loaned you money, and in addition to paying back the Teamsters fund, you owe us a finder's fee, and that is going to cost you, say, five thousand dollars a week for the rest of your life.'

"So in order to pay back the money without the Gaming Commission knowing about it, the casino owner had to skim the money off the top, and pay in cash."

When he got to Las Vegas, Michaels found that there were as many ways of skimming casino profits as there are to skin a cat.

"One way," he says, "would be to write up phony fills. That's when you deliver chips to a table. Let's say a baccarat table. A fill slip for two hundred thousand in chips would be written up, and the proper people would sign it, but the chips would not be delivered, and the two hundred thousand would go out the back door. Another way of skimming would be to bring in some extra slot machines or blackjack tables. By law, each casino is supposed to have just so many tables, and you would tell the Gaming Commission, I've got forty-five black-jack tables, or whatever. But these guys were always changing the configurations of the casino, and sometimes on the weekend these guys would sneak in twenty extra tables, and all the money from those tables would be skimmed. On the paperwork it would be as if the tables never existed. Of course, to do all this, you had to have your people in the key places. A lot of floormen would know what was going on. These days the casinos are full of accountants, career people, and well-trained casino people who went to college. But then, you had pit bosses and casino managers who had grown up on the streets, guys who had gone to jail, not college.

"None of this would be possible today. You couldn't possibly hide a table. With the corporations today everything is run so systematically, the way we have our drop boxes, and our table counter, and surveillance and the counting room."

The strategy of Michaels's task force was to try to trace the skimmed money. How was it being taken out? How was it being transported back to Chicago? Their tools were tape recorders, cameras, lots of man-hours and, in one case, an expert lip-reader who told them everything one crook was saying to another. Working in twelve-hour shifts, seven days a week, Michaels and his men watched the suspects. The work was a bit more tedious and less glamorous than it is on TV.

"Chicago would sent out a courier," he says, "a low individual in the mob. He would fly into Los Angeles or San Diego, rent a car, and drive to Las Vegas and contact another low man.

"There was an enormous amount of work in even figuring out which guy to watch. We ended up following this one guy who worked at the Stardust. He was a low man named Buster. He was an old guy who didn't seem to do anything, but it turned out he was a member of the Chicago mob. We had this guy under surveillance for weeks, twelve-hour shifts, day and night, seven days a week.

"On a Thursday or Friday Buster would leave the casino and get in his little car. He would drive twenty miles an hour and he would stop at maybe fifteen different parking lots, supermarkets, whatever. Then at some point he'd be in a parking lot, and all of a sudden another car would pull up, and in it would be some guy from the same casino, someone that Buster had just talked to an hour earlier. The guy would hand Buster a big brown bag and drive off. We were videotaping all of this.

"Buster would drive home and take the bag of money upstairs to his apartment. We had a camera on his house, too.

Then on Sunday morning Buster would come down, and if he moved his car across the street and parked it on the other side, that was a signal to somebody that today was going to be a payoff day. If he didn't move the car, there would be no payoff that day.

"After he moved the car, Buster would go back upstairs and come down again with the bag of money. He would put the bag in the trunk. The bag probably contained between two hundred thousand and two hundred fifty thousand dollars in skimmed money from several casinos. Then Buster would go to Mass at St. Christopher's church.

"Then he would come out of Mass and drive around town for about an hour, with the money still in the trunk. Then the guy from Chicago, with the rental car, would pull up and they'd make the transfer of the bag, and the guy in the rental would drive back to the airport and fly home to Chicago. For a while they were coming from Chicago once a month, but then they got greedy and started coming twice a month."

All the hours of surveillance paid off. For months Michaels and his men compiled evidence against dozens of shady characters. In 1977 the Stardust, the last mob-controlled hotel, was stripped of its license, and by the mid-1980s the FBI's evidence was used to get convictions against Vegas mobsters in Chicago, Kansas City, and Milwaukee, bringing the era of the Las Vegas gangster to an end.

(It's irrelevant, but interesting, that in September 1992, the Stardust, under its new management, became the victim of a more blatant form of skimming, when a sports book employee walked off one night with $500,000 in cash.)

Michaels says there are no mob-influenced hotels in Las Vegas today.

"There are some criminals in the city," he says, "just as there are in any city. But mostly they are low men who come here looking to get into something. They are into street crime, drugs and the like."

In November 1986 *Fortune* published a list of the fifty wealthiest, most powerful, and most influential organized crime leaders in America and their territories, based on information from FBI agents, federal prosecutors, and local law enforcement officials. None of the fifty had a Las Vegas address.

Speaking for the FBI, in March of 1993, Special Agent Burk Smith of the FBI's Las Vegas Bureau said, "We are not aware of any organized crime involvement in the Nevada Gaming Industry. With the various agencies having an investigative or administrative interest in the industry, that is, the Federal Bureau of Investigation, the Nevada Gaming Commission and Control Board, the Las Vegas Metropolitan Police Department and others, sharing information and working together, it would seem improbable that a significant organized crime presence could exist and we not know about it. Of course any such allegations would be, and are, checked out thoroughly."

Michaels left the FBI to take a job with Howard Hughes's Summa Corporation, and he is one industry observer who believes Hughes's entrance into gaming was pivotal for the industry's image.

"Hughes," he says, "was the first legitimate guy that brought in the accountants, and the really first-class operators that were all honest people. He installed the proper control and reporting procedures."

The main protectors of the Las Vegas goose today are the five part-time members of the Gaming Commission and the three full-time members of the Gaming Board, all appointed by the governor. For the most part their duties are segregated, and the Commission has no authority over the Board, except that it can approve or disapprove a Board recommendation for a gaming license.

The Commission makes policy and collects taxes. The Board investigates existing, or would-be, license holders, and enforces the rules. While Commission members come from a variety of backgrounds, the makeup of the Gaming Board is specific: one member with an accounting background, one with a legal or administrative background, and one with a law enforcement background. In practice the Gaming Board is the authority that is involved with casinos from day to day.

"The Board has three divisions," says member Tom Roche. "There's Auditing, Electronic Services, and Investigation and Intelligence Gathering.

"Through its auditing division the Board prescribes minimum standards for internal control. That covers things like the proper way for a dealer or boxman to put money in the drop box, who will sign fill slips, and so forth."

The electronic services division includes the mechanics and computer whizzes who make sure that the slot machines are not truly the one-armed bandits they've always been called. "We have to make sure there are no cheating devices in slot machines and video poker machines," Roche says. "The intelligence of each machine has to be approved."

The main job of the investigative arm of the Board is to check out license applicants.

There are two kinds of gaming licenses in Nevada, mainly because gaming is not confined to casinos. You can find slot machines in bars, restaurants, Laundromats, even the most godforsaken gas stations on the road to Reno. So if you run a bait shop in the desert and you think you need to raise your revenues a bit, you can install a few slots, no more than fifteen of them, by getting a restricted license. The state won't take any of your drop, it'll just sock you for an annual tax of $250 per machine, plus a quarterly tax of $90 per slot for the first five machines and $45 per machine for the next ten.

But a big operation needs a nonrestricted license, which allows it to have slots galore and table games. The process of getting such a license can be as long and tedious as a twi-nighter in Seattle. If the applicant has extensive holdings out of state, the investigation could take a year and easily cost $1 million, which would be paid by the applicant. "On the other hand," says Roche, "if you've lived in Nevada all your life, and are known to the Board, it could be a lot shorter and a lot less expensive."

The license continues to be expensive after you've got it. With a nonrestricted license you pay a fee for each slot and table, as well as a graduated tax based on gross revenues. The tax starts at 3 percent for the first $50,000, goes to 4 percent for the next $84,000, and tops out at 6.25 percent for everything over $134,000 a year. Roche says the State of Nevada gets about $390 million a year from all these taxes and fees. All these taxes and fees, by the way, are bargain-basement prices when compared to charges made by other states for gambling activities.

During the licensing process the burden is on you to prove you are fit to have a casino license. If you've been running with a bad crowd, or if your picture is on a poster in the post office, you're going to get turned down, and all the whining in the world won't make you a casino operator.

"On the other hand," says Roche, "once the license is issued, it is our burden to prove you are doing something wrong, such as associating with a known gangster. We are different from New Jersey. We feel that if you have survived the licensing process you have earned our trust."

In Nevada the Gaming Board also tends to be a lot less meddlesome than in New Jersey. For example, the Board has no specific regulations about how a casino markets itself.

"But we do keep an eye on things," Roche says. "If someone is advertising that their slot machines have a ninety-eight percent return, it had better be so. If not, we will ask them to bring their advertising in line with what's really happening on their machines. We try to give each license holder enough latitude to distinguish himself from other gaming operations. But we do have an all-encompassing rule that says that if you do anything in your marketing or advertising that reflects poorly on the state of Nevada or the gaming industry, we can take disciplinary action, such as revoking, suspending, or restricting your gaming license."

The casinos are also on their own if they want to introduce a new game or make minor changes in the rules of an existing game.

"If they want to offer ten times odds on craps, or let players double down on three cards, that's okay, as long as they don't change the basic generic game," Roche says. "If they want to offer a new game, it has to be field-tested by us. We test for integrity, for the possibilities of cheating, for the hold percentage, and so forth. Then we will make a recommendation to the Commission."

The Gaming Board also has its own cops.

Roche says, "On a twenty-four-hour basis we have investigators on covert operations at casinos, watching for procedures, maybe picking up dice or checking a roulette wheel for balance. And we have our electronics guys opening slot machines to look at the E-Prong, which is the intelligence of the machine, to make sure it matches the one we have on file at the office, and that the paybacks are what they say they are."

While these measures are taken to protect the customer from casino cheating, Roche says occasional customer and employee cheating still goes on.

"I think people underestimate the perseverance and work necessary to try to maintain the integrity of this industry. We have set up a system of checks and balances to try to mitigate this, but cheating does occur. However, we are different from New Jersey, in that we work in cooperation with the industry, exchanging intelligence information with them."

Roche says the Board tries to weed out bad employees in advance.

"We don't believe we should have thousands of agents trying to police an industry full of disreputable employees. So we go through the extensive licensing process, and there is a work permit process for every employee in the industry.

He must have a work card, which he gets from the local police department, and we have ninety days to object, and say why that person should not have a card, and we can go to his place of work and yank his work card."

(Some casinos go the Board one better. CCE, for example, because of the high number of kids in the hotel, fingerprints employees and runs additional background checks to make sure nobody with a history of sexual offenses gets a job at one of its hotels.)

While the criminals may have departed Las Vegas, the mythology has not, and the fear of mobsterism still inhibits the growth of the casino business. In the spring of 1992, for example, Glenn Schaeffer was flying frequently to Chicago to discuss with the governor, mayor, and state legislators and various minority organizations the merits of building, in cooperation with Caesars and Hilton, a huge new casino and entertainment complex in downtown Chicago. He found, he says, that a frequent complaint among the naysayers was that Vegas gaming would bring organized crime. "It was incredible, some of the absurd things I had to listen to," he says. "And the press would occasionally repeat it, *The Chicago Sun Times* particularly. Reporters sometimes don't care dearly enough about facts; they will write whatever makes a good story. For example, there was this group called the Chicago Crime Commission, a kind of self-appointed moral guardian, made up mainly of ex-cops who have opposed our proposal.

"So one day this group announces that they've received this letter, allegedly written by some capo in hiding, in the witness protection program. And he says our project is a terrible idea, because the mob controls every form of gambling in the country. This is so silly. Well, I saw the letter and the spelling is perfect, there's a nice turn of phrase here and there, the grammar's correct, even the use of metaphor and some nice alliteration. This letter was not written by some street criminal. Someone on this commission wrote it, or, more likely, someone had it written and sent to them. It was so transparent. A number of reporters who saw it were laughing at it.

"*The Chicago Tribune* knew enough not to publish it, but the *Sun Times* published it. And that, of course, gave the TV news a story. So I'm coming out of the Chicago Rotary Club one day, where I've given my stump speech for the project, and I'm besieged by reporters. 'What about this letter?' they want to know. 'Let me ask you something,' I said, 'if next week I come up with a letter from some anonymous saint, asserting that our proposal is the essence of moral perfection, are you going to treat that as a news story?' Of course not."

(The *Sun Times,* like the *Tribune,* eventually endorsed the casino proposal. But by early 1993 the Chicago casino proposal appeared to be dead, mainly because opponents feared it would bring mobsters, an amusing irony, inasmuch as the gangsters that Las Vegas *did* have were imported from Chicago.)

13

Guarding the Golden Eggs

The Gaming Board is in the business of protecting the goose, the industry itself. The individual casinos have to guard the golden eggs, the money generated by gambling. They do this through casino security and casino surveillance, two separate but closely related operations.

Emmett Michaels, in his role as CCE's director of corporate security, is in charge of all the individual hotel security departments, those people who make sure the hallways aren't on fire and also send guys up to tell the kids in room 907 to pipe down. And he is also in charge of security surveillance, the uniformed security people in the casinos. Casino surveillance, however, the so-called "eye in the sky," reports directly to the comptroller's office.

Despite this technical difference, the hundreds of people who make up security surveillance and casino surveillance are, in practice, a team whose job it is to catch cheaters.

The eye in the sky is another Las Vegas innovation for which Bill Harrah is generally given credit. Originally it was just a crawl space with a one-way mirror looking down on the casino. Today's eye in the sky, at every casino in Las Vegas, is an extremely sophisticated electronic marvel, a room with more glowing lights and fancy switches than the cockpit of a 747. Dozens of television monitors display pictures being delivered from cameras placed above every gaming table, as well as near exits, over slot sections, in the cashier's cage, and in the counting room.

(Hotel security, at least at Circus Circus, has its own eye in the sky, with its own bank of monitors that show what's going on in the corridors and the parking lot.)

While an eye in the sky might have 40 screens, the casino could have 100 or more cameras. But each screen is like a television that gets every channel, so the security officer on duty can tune in to any table at any time, from different angles, and in close-ups so extreme that he could tell the time on a player's wristwatch.

At high-rolling hotels like Caesars Palace, eye in the sky employees keep logs on certain big players, particularly those who have hefty lines of credit and are playing with money borrowed from the casino. The log might tell a supervisor what time a customer started playing at a particular table, the size of the bets, and how much he or she won or lost.

Here, for example, is a log entry which was reprinted in

No Limit, the Gary Ross book about compulsive gambler Brian Moloney:

> *March 13, 1982. Caesars Atlantic City. Frank Hines.*
>
> *10 p.m. Brian Maloney* [sic] *on game. Received two markers for total of $45,000. Bets up to $10,000. Lost $30,000 while I observed game.*
>
> *3:30 a.m. Baccarat 1. Maloney* [sic] *still playing. Bets up to $20,000.*

At Circus Circus, because there is almost no credit and the minimums are low, such logs are not kept.

The main job of the eye in the sky and the people who man it is to spot cheaters. In Las Vegas there are two kinds of cheaters: employees and customers.

"The Gaming Board screens everybody who comes to work for us," Emmett Michaels says, "but you still end up with a certain number of dishonest employees. Some employees are always thinking of new ways to steal casino money, and some of them get very good at it. We had one recently, a blackjack dealer who was taking a couple of hundred a day out of the casino. We got a tip from a reliable source that this guy was stealing. That's how we find out a lot, through tips. So we watched this dealer, and we watched him and watched him, but we couldn't spot anything. We went back to the source and said, 'Are you sure this is the guy?' The source said, 'Yes, somehow this guy is stealing from you.' Well, it turned out that whenever a customer at the table would finish with a cup of coffee, this dealer would move the empty cup

197

over to the side, which is what he is supposed to do. Only, before he moved it, he would pass his hand over the hundred-dollar chips and palm one; then as he moved the cup he would let the chip fall into it. Then the cocktail waitress, who was in cahoots with him, would come around and take the cup away on her tray, dump out the chip, and split with him later."

The gaming tables are not the only place where employees give themselves bonuses. Though casinos always keep teams of people at work in the cashier's cage and counting room, to watch each other, cheating is still accomplished there.

A security director at another hotel, who would rather not be identified, tells this story:

"We had one woman who worked part of the time in the counting room. She was a very bright, very attractive young woman, well educated, great personality, sharp, the kind of employee you'd like to keep. Whenever she had to work in the soft count room, she would know which crap tables had taken in the most money and she would make sure she counted the drop boxes from those tables. [The soft count at a casino is paper money. Coins are tracked separately, and they are the hard count.]

"Included with the cash in those boxes were promotional coupons, which customers can put down as a free bet. Along with the counting, this woman's job was to sort out those coupons. So she would do her counting room stint and leave the counting room, clean as can be. But in her other job she was the person who received the paperwork from the counting room. Those promotional coupons were considered paperwork. They had to be tallied and so forth. So they would be sent to her as part of the paperwork.

"Well, it turns out that when she was counting, she was slipping hundred-dollar bills between those coupons that she was stacking up. Of course, when the coupons got back to her, she would take out the hundreds and she'd be home free. Now if this woman had taken just a few hundred bucks each time, she could have gotten away with this forever. But she got greedy. She was taking thousands. We have a system of checks and balances, so we know pretty much how much should be in a drop box, and when there's a sudden shortage like that, we know something is wrong. So we kept an eye on her and we caught her. We had her arrested, of course. Whenever something like this happens we learn something and we are able to guard another gate."

At CCE hotels customer cheating is almost nonexistent, simply because nobody is going to risk jail for small bets, and big bets are more likely to draw attention at casinos like Circus Circus, where Mr. and Mrs. Middle America are often playing for two or three dollars. Perhaps for that reason, security directors at other casinos are less anxious to be identified when talking about customer cheating. Nobody wants to leave the impression that his store is vulnerable.

But security people in Las Vegas will talk about customer cheating. They say that the most common form of customer cheating is past-posting, and it ranges from the pathetically clumsy to the impressively smooth. Past-posting means placing a bet after a decision has occurred, whether it is the rolling of the dice, the falling of a roulette ball, or the showing of a blackjack's hole card.

The security directors have videotapes of past-posting schemes, many of which are run by gangs of three or four cheaters who will spend months, even years, holed up in apartments with casino equipment, practicing their technique.

One videotape shows a past-posting operation at roulette, a game in which each player has his or her own color of chips. This three-man dodge requires that a cheater play at each end of the roulette table. A third cheater bumps up against player A, who slips, let us say, red chips into his hand. Then those red chips are secretly passed into the hand of player B. When the ball lands on a number that is near player B, player A distracts the dealer. Meanwhile, player B puts red chips on the winning number and walks away. The dealer then sees red chips on the winning number and pays off player A, who, of course, could not possibly have placed them late, because he's at the end of the table farthest from the number.

The degree of expertise and ingenuity among the cheaters is admirable. One form of cheating occurs when a player hands the dealer a stack of twenty $5 chips for a $100 chip, then cashes the $100 chip back in for the stack of fives before he leaves. Seems innocent enough, except that the stack of fives is really a spring-loaded canister into which his partner, the dealer, has popped a dozen or so $100 chips, or checks, as they are called by casino personnel.

The punishment for these crimes is not always what casino operators might hope. Arrests are made and cases are prosecuted, of course, but sometimes the cheaters merely have their wrists slapped.

In 1991 security men at one major Strip hotel spotted members of a blackjack gang casing the casino. Knowing that the gang's modus operandi was to find an inexperienced dealer in the morning and sit at his table in the afternoon, the security team notified the Gaming Board and the local police, and a trap was set.

The gang returned later and began its operation. In this particular scheme, one low-betting cheater sits at third base, just to the dealer's right, with a tiny mirror concealed under his left hand. The combination of his expertise and the dealer's inexperience results in his being able to lift his hand and, in the mirror, read the dealer's hole card in that split second when it is laid down, or flashed. He then signals his heavy-betting cohort at first base, and money is made.

On this particular afternoon, once the security people were sure that a mirror was in play, they moved in. The bad guys did not go gently. Cards went flying, tables were tipped over, gang members were wrestled to the floor of the casino. On the videotape it looks like a scene out of a Chuck Norris movie.

The men were arrested, tried, found guilty. Even though it was well known among Vegas security people that this gang had been operating for seven years without getting caught, the offenders were put on probation, a shockingly light sentence in a city that is so dependent on these particular golden eggs.

Though there is no way to keep an accurate count, some

Las Vegas security people say that one baccarat racket raked in more than $7 million at a high-roller casino before the crooks were caught.

One man who claims to be familiar with the case says, "They had a guy who could memorize two or three decks of cards. The dealer was in on this, and she would leave one section of the deck unshuffled. So when that section came up, the guy knew what every card was going to be. I once sat down with this guy, after he was caught, and watched him. He named every card in a deck. Just like Dustin Hoffman in *Rain Man*."

High tech has also come to the casino-cheating business. In one operation a blackjack player wears a transmitter in his boot and taps a code for each played card. The signal is sent to a partner sitting at a computer in a van in the parking lot. The partner enters all the cards into the computer, and the computer figures the probabilities for remaining cards. In other words, it is the ultimate card counting system.

Slot machines are not immune from crooks, either. There are people who will buy pounds of lead and mint their own counterfeit one-dollar tokens.

One hotel security officer recently grabbed two grandmothers in their fifties who had very carefully designed a piece of steel. It was tooled to fit exactly into the coin receptacle to simulate the insertion of a coin, but it had a hook on it so that it could be yanked out and used over and over.

Emmett Michaels at CCE says that in the casino security game all you can do is all you can do. He doesn't see a day when there will be no cheating.

"But overall, cheating is pretty rare," he says. "Most of my workdays have nothing to do with cheating. Every industry has pilferage, of course, and we probably have less than most industries, but because our inventory is cash, it makes for more interesting reading. Let's face it, stealing cash is a lot more exciting than stealing widgets."

14

The Wizard

In 1971 Bill Harrah sold 13 percent of his northern Nevada gambling empire to the public for $4 million.

"It was," says Leon Mandel in his biography of Harrah, "a breakthrough of enormous proportions." Gaming, according to Mandel, had been "dragged by its hair to respectability." And Bill Harrah had done the dragging.

"The SEC and the great national money exchanges had conferred the respectability. Well, at least the diploma," Mandel writes. "It had been Harrah who had qualified the business for its ascendancy into decent society."

Mandel notes that Harrah was followed onto Wall Street by many gaming companies. "Yet," he adds, "it is critical to understand that was possible only because in the stiff, staid atmosphere of Wall Street, Harrah's, its reputation and its people, overcame 'the industry's image in the east.' "

Mandel says that the sale of Harrah stock changed the financial community's perception of the company and, by extension, its perception of gaming companies.

"If the company was traded over the counter, and then on the American, and finally the New York Stock Exchange, it must be as clean and hearty as General Foods."

It would be closer to the truth to say not that Harrah's sale changed Wall Street's perception, but that it *began* to change Wall Street's perception. Willard Brown, a vice president with Dean Witter, says that as recently as 1988, "fully half of the institutional investors I talked to were prevented from buying gaming stocks, for two reasons. One was 'All gaming companies are controlled by the Mafia.' The other was 'It's immoral.' "

While institutions are enthusiastic investors now, Brown says that at the time, the boycotting of gaming companies probably depressed gaming stocks and made the good ones, like CCE, an even better buy for those who were more sophisticated about Las Vegas.

Today almost a dozen publicly owned gaming companies are being traded on Wall Street. Some of them have familiar names, like Caesars and Hilton. Others are not so well known, like Promus and Aztar. Some are big, like Mirage, others small, like Rio. Some are in related industries, like United Gaming, which runs slot routes, and IGT, which makes slot machines. But there is only one legendary gaming stock on Wall Street, and that is CCE.

In 1983, with a company that had reached even beyond

his dreams, Bennett had loftier visions. He believed that even though he had mined the middle market more effectively than anyone in gaming history, the vein remained rich. There were far more customers to be reached, there was far more money to be made. But reaching those customers and earning that money would require CCE to expand, not just by adding to the existing properties, but by building new properties. Big properties. And bank money with which to build was not only expensive, it was scarce. Bennett and Pennington decided that Circus Circus would go to the public for the money. Like Bill Harrah, they would issue stock.

Mel Larsen recalls, "When we went public there was some concern, because we were new to that business. We knew this would allow us to make major expansions. We knew if we wanted to grow, and compete with the big boys, we would have to go outside for funds. But we worried. 'Is the stock going to sell?' we wondered. Glenn was not here yet. He came in shortly afterward, and it scares me now to think how inexperienced we were. I knew nothing about Wall Street or stock. I had never even bought any stock, and all of a sudden here I am going off with Mr. Bennett to Wall Street, and making up kits to give to analysts. I had no idea of what they wanted. I just winged it."

On October 25, 1983, with Drexel Burnham as underwriter and Michael Milken's people doing the selling, CCE became a public company, raising $66 million by selling more than 4 million shares to preferred buyers at $15 a share. Many of those preferred buyers turned around immediately and sold the stock on the open market at $16.50, which is common with new issues. On that first day the CCE stock hit a high of $16.87, closing at $16.25, and for a short time it was the most actively traded stock on the New York Stock Exchange, finishing third for the day behind Hewlett-Packard and AT&T. It was the first time a Nevada corporation had ever led the pack. The stock, in fact, was oversold, and Bennett and Pennington added some of their own stock to the sale. Estimates at the time were that Bennett and Pennington had made $27 million, impressive at the time but chickenfeed compared to what was coming.

Bennett and Pennington were not the only members of the CCE family to make money from the stock. The CCE people who bought it new and held it are today millionaires.

Mel Larsen recalls, "I had bought a commercial lot in Phoenix for twenty-six hundred dollars. When we went public I sold the lot for forty-three thousand dollars cash and I bought Circus Circus stock. It was the first stock I ever owned. Also, I had a house in Phoenix that I'd gotten for twenty-six thousand dollars. I sold that for a hundred thirteen thousand dollars and I bought some more Circus Circus stock."

Larsen is a helicopter pilot who does the flying for a lot of those opening shots of golf courses that you see on televised golf tournaments. Today, thanks largely to his CCE stock, he owns three pink helicopters and the space to park them, at a huge spread he has built just a few miles down the road from the big pink Circus Circus tent.

Now CCE was in the stock market. But neither Bennett nor the men under him knew much about dealing with investors. Bennett let it be known that CCE was shopping for someone who knew the market, the banks, the investors, and the gaming industry.

Dan Lee, a Drexel Burnham analyst who specialized in gaming stocks, and Michael Milken, each provided a name. The name was the same: Glenn Schaeffer.

Lee knew Schaeffer as an executive at Ramada Inns and believed that Schaeffer's efforts had been pivotal in Ramada's recent sale of 7 million shares of stock, a sale which, Lee says, had put Ramada back on its feet.

Schaeffer, barely thirty at the time, had grown up in Pomona, California, in reasonable comfort. His father was a manager in industrial research for Union Oil. His mother, a homemaker, was a trained biologist. So Schaeffer had smart genes. The older Schaeffer, who had a Ph.D. in organic chemistry, was big on academic achievement, which had been his ticket off the farm, and Glenn knew from an early age that Dad would prefer his son to become a scientist.

Which young Glenn could certainly have done. He was an early whiz at math and science and a straight-A student. But as each generation places itself in opposition to the one before it, Glenn gravitated not to science, but to the arts. He wanted to write.

At the University of California, Irvine, Glenn kept his distance from the Bunsen burners. He majored in English literature, minored in economics, got all As, and ended up with an A.B., *summa cum laude,* before he was old enough to vote, a master's in literature at age twenty-one, and the knowledge that a life of scholarship was not for him.

But he still loved writing, mostly plays and stories. One play led to a UC fellowship, and from that came a novella called *Kicks* which helped Schaeffer get into the prestigious Iowa Writers' Workshop. The workshop is to young literary novelists what Lakers training camp is to schoolyard basketball players. Schaeffer, one of 25 selected from an applicant pool of 500, went to Iowa during the mid-1970s, an era in which the workshop produced Tracy Kidder (*The Soul of a New Machine*), Allan Gurganus (*Oldest Living Confederate Widow Tells All*), Jayne Ann Phillips (*Machine Dreams*), and W. P. Kinsella, whose book *Shoeless Joe* became the film *Field of Dreams.*

However, few graduates of any writing program achieve fame, and fewer still get rich, a point brought painfully home to Schaeffer by the noted novelist Vance Bourjaily, who was his adviser and mentor at Iowa.

"I remember a day at Bourjaily's farmhouse, located in a dell on the outskirts of Iowa City," Schaeffer says, "when he told me that his novels . . . a couple of which I considered to be the real thing . . . had never generated enough income for him to live on. The competition among dedicated artists in the scant market for literature was fierce and the economic stakes, for most of us, were awfully low. I took this lesson to heart right away."

Schaeffer knew that the life of a literary novelist was not for him. He just wasn't the type to live in a garret, or even a farmhouse in a dell. By the end of his stay at Iowa, Schaeffer had, he says, "figured out that I was geared to upward aspiration." He adds, "I lacked a certain hardiness for the writer's life."

Still in his early twenties, Schaeffer got his Master of Fine Arts degree, and while his Iowa classmates headed for the New York literary scene, he went in more lucrative directions.

Schaeffer, who had boxed in college, went off to do battle in the business world. "I discovered that stockbrokers, at the top rung, were America's highest-paid salespeople, and more important, they were engaged with the instruments of finance, which was the language of big business," he says.

So Schaeffer ended up at Dean Witter in Westwood, California, where he was trained in securities, insurance, commodities, and options. His fine mathematical mind got a chance to romp that it never had in Iowa, and he could quickly compute finances, margin-account calculations, option straddles, and the like. Schaeffer loved the numbers and "that language of big business." However, he didn't care for cold calling any more than the Charlie Sheen character did in *Wall Street*.

"In those days cold calling was the prescribed method for building a clientele," Schaeffer says. "The drudgery of placing a hundred phone calls a day to total strangers in order to find ten who listen to you, three who deign to meet you, and one who will trade with you was oppressive to me."

So Schaeffer took a different approach. Walk-in cold calls. "I'd prowl the hallways of downtown Los Angeles skyscrapers, barging into offices of possible clients, preferably attorneys."

This approach worked, and Schaeffer began to make money. But the businessmen and -women Schaeffer dropped in on were more than prospective clients. They were also prospective employers, and at advertising and public relations firms, Schaeffer would answer questions about interest rates or stock ideas and then would grill the would-be client about his or her own business. Through this networking he met a creative director who taught him copywriting. One person led to another, and Schaeffer got a job as an account executive in the financial relations division of the famous Hill and Knowlton public relations firm.

There Schaeffer was, in his own way, a writer again. He certainly wasn't going to be Joyce Carol Oates, but at least he was making better than a scratch living. "I specialized in writing corporate annual reports, corporate fact books, and executive speeches to groups of securities analysts," he says.

At Hill and Knowlton Schaeffer also did financial research and worked on proxy fights and tender offers. "Our job in proxy fights and tender offers involved writing advocacy advertising and devising publicity strategy."

Schaeffer quickly caught on at Hill and Knowlton. In his middle twenties, he was a top account executive, jetting all over the West and regularly meeting with CFOs and CEOs of publicly traded corporations. He knew he was grooming himself for something, but not being a gambler, he probably never imagined that his mark would be made in the gaming industry.

"During my second year at Hill and Knowlton I was assigned to an account that had simply walked in the door. Caesars World. They had just expanded into Atlantic City and the founders, the Perlman brothers, were getting flak from the New Jersey Casino Control Commission. Caesars wanted a corporate public relations campaign that would tell its side of the story as a leader of a legitimate industry."

At the time Caesars also was trying to solidify its presence on Wall Street. For a brief time in 1978 Caesars stock had been a high flyer in the wake of Resorts International's rocketing. (Resorts was the first company to open an A.C. casino, and it had a year's head start on everybody else.)

For the next year Schaeffer worked closely with Caesars' top management, learning the gaming business. Though his main job was to guide the company's corporate relations with the business press and Wall Street, he inevitably got involved with marketing and employee relations.

One afternoon he was eating lunch in his office when he got a call that would pull him deeper into this fascinating industry. The call was from a vice president at Ramada Inns, Inc., who wanted to know who at Hill and Knowlton was doing the great work for Caesars. Me, Schaeffer said.

Ramada had recently bought the Tropicana in Las Vegas and was building the Tropicana in Atlantic City (now called Trop World). The company was looking for an investor relations executive who could explain the gaming industry to the banks, Wall Street investors, and the business press. So Schaeffer, who, a year earlier, had known a lot more about mixed metaphors than he did about high rollers, was soon on a jet for Phoenix, where Ramada was headquartered. There he interviewed for, and accepted, the job of director of corporate affairs. When Caesars heard about the Ramada offer, it immediately offered Schaeffer $10,000 more. But it was too late. Hands had been shaken at Ramada, and Schaeffer honored his commitment. He had just turned twenty-seven years old. Though it was a painful time in his personal life—he had just gotten divorced after a five-year marriage—his future looked bright, and the source of light seemed to be the gaming industry.

Shortly after Schaeffer signed on, everything at Ramada went to hell. The A.C. Tropicana was way over budget and the banks were bolting. The company was flirting with insolvency. Not surprisingly, heads rolled. Bill Isbell, chairman and son of the founder, resigned, and he was replaced by a Phoenix securities lawyer named Richard Snell. Snell's mandate was simple, if not easy: assess the damage, rate the managers, and come up with a recovery plan.

Part of Snell's strategy was to interrogate the corporate management team. When Schaeffer got the microphone he didn't sugarcoat it. He criticized the company's performance and told Snell that Ramada's low reputation with investors was well deserved. Then he told Snell what he thought had to be done to get back the company's credibility with Wall Street and the banks.

"Then do it," Snell said.

When the corporate staff did its year-end dance of promotions, demotions, reassignments, and terminations, Glenn Schaeffer ended up as vice president for public and financial affairs, acting as assistant to Snell.

During the next two years Schaeffer helped Ramada climb up from the mat. He called on mutual fund managers and nervous creditors. He convinced the former that the company would prosper and the latter that the company was sound. Briefly he locked horns with Michael Milken who in 1978 had shepherded Ramada's $100-million issue of subordinated debentures. That issue had been Drexel Burnham's first major underwriting of original, high-yield debt and had arguably been the beginning of the junk bond era.

(One irony here is worth noting. One of the reasons that gaming companies had not expanded greatly in the past was that getting bank loans had always been much harder for gaming companies than for other businesses. The reason was that banks saw gaming as the "sin industry" and wanted nothing to do with it. When the growth explosion finally came in the industry it was thanks to Milken and the sale of junk bonds. Milken, of course, would become as infamous in his sphere of dishonesty as Bugsy Siegel was in his, and the junk bond business which Milken created would in many minds replace gaming as the new "sin industry.")

Milken was understandably somewhat territorial about Ramada debt, since his clients owned a lot of it.

Schaeffer recalls, "Milken's first response to my missionary work on Wall Street was to order me to butt out. He and his traders were, in his view, the supreme spokespeople for Ramada. Eventually he backed down and I ran my own program."

Though Milken held his tongue, he and his people were never far away. They would check in with Schaeffer from time to time to get health reports on Ramada and the gaming industry in general. Milken himself would drop in at Phoenix headquarters when the spirit moved him.

This was the early 1980s, and it would not be until later in the decade that investors started making money from Las Vegas gaming stocks. At this time Atlantic City was where the action was, and Schaeffer soon became the expert in Atlantic City gaming stocks, regulations, and prospects.

Because Ramada's stock and its bonds had plummeted to prices that reflected its proximity to bankruptcy, investors who participated in the recovery made money. Within two years the Ramada stock went from $4 to $12 and the bonds from $50 to $90.

Schaeffer was off to a great start in the corporate world, and it seemed that he had enough. Still in his twenties, he was making nearly six figures. He was a corporate officer of a big international company. But still he felt that he was missing out on something. There was an adrenaline flow that just wasn't there with Ramada. What Schaeffer wanted, he realized, was something more adventurous. When you feel that way at a crap table you play "the hard ways," you take a bigger risk for a bigger payoff. But Schaeffer wasn't a crapshooter, he was a young financial hotshot. He started looking for something daring. He wanted to be part of an ambitious growth company whose value could rapidly multiply.

He knew there was a know-how to managing for fast growth, and he was interested in the practice, not the theory. He needed to be apprenticed to the right place. In 1983, through his contacts with venture capitalists, he had looked into how "hot" new high-tech companies went public with initial offerings, and thought there might be a place for him in that realm. "I wanted a spot among an inner circle of movers," he says. "I wanted to be where youth and energy and creativity would pay off."

Opportunity came when Dan Lee and Milken recommended Schaeffer to Bill Bennett. Schaeffer and Bennett met in Bennett's office in December 1983, only a few months after Circus Circus had gone public.

Schaeffer was impressed both by Bennett and by the company. Circus Circus was in the midst of a vivid growth run. "Its chart for nearly a decade had sloped due north," is the way Schaeffer puts it. And Bennett struck Schaeffer as the classic get-up-and-go entrepreneur. He knew from the start that Bennett was no pussycat, but he didn't care; he wanted to work hard and he wanted to get rich. Bennett's executives had little experience with professional investors and knew little about the financial reporting of public companies, something at which Schaeffer was expert, so he knew he would be needed. But he wouldn't be needed only for what he was already good at. "I don't hire just position players," Bennett told him. "I'm not looking to draft a tight end or a wide receiver. I hire good all-around athletes. It's the team with the best overall athletes that wins in the long run. I'm looking for someone who can play the game.

"You need a title," Bennett told him. "You're going to be senior vice president, but we have to figure out of what. Not just investor relations. I want general managers. We'll figure out what you're good at when you get here. We'll start you with financial relations and planning, but we may stick you in a property and you may run it. We'll determine what your greatest value is to the corporation once you are here."

This was fine with Schaeffer. It meant he wouldn't be simply the numbers man, or the public relations man, at CCE. He would learn new skills and grow with the company.

While Bennett might have had little Wall Street experience, it was not lost on him that Schaeffer had made a lot of people richer through his work at Ramada, and that many of those investors would follow him over to CCE.

Schaeffer joined CCE in early 1984, several months after the company went public, and his first title was senior vice president for corporate development. He was in charge of financial planning and corporate communications. Within six months he was named chief financial officer of the company and elected to the board of directors. At thirty, he was the youngest CFO of any company listed on the New York Stock Exchange.

During the next decade, with lots of cash, a huge line of credit, satisfied stockholders, and Schaeffer in place, William Bennett pushed his company forward in ways that had never been seen in the industry.

With cash in hand and a promise of growth to stockholders, CCE began looking for places to build.

For some time Bennett had had his eye on Laughlin, a small town on the southeast tip of Nevada, along the Colorado River. Twenty-five years ago Laughlin, which has been called everything from "a neon Oz rising out of the sand" (*Venture* magazine) to "the hottest, most Godforsaken River Valley in the United States" (*St. Paul Press*), was no more than an eight-room motel and bait shop. Don Laughlin bought the hotel, the Riverside, eventually turned it into a successful fourteen-story casino hotel, and gave the town his name. Today Laughlin, Nevada, is a mini–Las Vegas with a waterfront view. It is a hugely successful operation with ten casinos and almost $400 million in revenues, most of it from Southern California, Phoenix, and Albuquerque. If Don Laughlin is the man most responsible for this, then Bill Bennett gets the silver medal.

CCE was the first company to pour major bucks into

Laughlin. In 1983 CCE bought the Edgewater, an ill-conceived 150-room, nearly bankrupt hotel, and added 450 rooms.

"Place didn't even have a connected casino," Bennett says. "You had to walk outside of it to gamble."

CCE renovated the Edgewater, and the place rolled so many sevens that right away Bennett and his colleagues looked for new ways to capitalize on Laughlin.

"We realized we needed more rooms," he says. "The Edgewater had been a good investment, and we thought we could expand in that market."

Three years later CCE opened the Colorado Belle next door to the Edgewater. The Belle, on the banks of the Colorado, was a 608-foot authentic replica of a three-deck paddle wheeler attached to a six-story hotel with 1,238 rooms. The combination of the Laughlin location and the riverboat motif drew a crowd whose income would put them in the high end of the middle market.

Bill Paulos, who has been general manager of both Laughlin hotels, says, "At the Colorado Belle our customers were largely older people, fairly well off. They came from Chicago or the Midwest, but they had second homes in the sunbelt, Arizona and California."

The Colorado Belle, perhaps the most successful hotel launch in history, not only made big money immediately, it did so without draining bucks from the Edgewater, whose profits increased. In 1991, another 970 rooms were added to the Edgewater.

The success of the two CCE properties in Laughlin did

not go unnoticed by the competition in Las Vegas. Harrah's, Ramada, Golden Nugget, and Hilton all headed for the river.

By 1992, the Colorado Belle and the Edgewater were one and two in Laughlin profits, and the combined CCE properties were raking in 40 percent of all Laughlin gaming profit.

Then, in 1990, came the Excalibur, with more rooms, more games, more customers, and more profit than all the previous CCE projects.

In fact, during the decade after the public offering, CCE built the most rooms, added the most casino space, and built the most new properties in the history of the industry, and every expansion went immediately into black ink.

The growth of the company was mirrored by the stock. As investors, particularly institutional investors, became more sophisticated about the industry, they began adding CCE shares to portfolios that included McDonald's, Disney, and Wal-Mart.

Dean Witter's Willard Brown says, "The company was desirable because it had the ability to duplicate its own success. It was number one in cash flow, it had the best management, and it knew how to develop properties. Success in the casino business is basically the ability to develop properties, that's what you look for. When Mr. Bennett came to Las Vegas in the nineteen-seventies he looked around and saw that there was a vast middle-income market that had not been cracked. I'm sure he knew that he would make money, but I bet that even he had no idea he would make this much."

Just how much money that is, depends, of course, on what day it is. But the CCE stock has been the greatest performer in the history of the industry, and one of the great stock stories of any industry, and Bennett's wealth was estimated at $550 million in 1992, when he finished about in the middle of the *Forbes* list of the richest 400 Americans. Since 1983 the company's earnings multiplied more than fivefold at a compound annual rate of 30 percent, and the company led the industry in profit growth, profit margins, rate of return on investment, rate of return on equity, and the creation of new jobs. (In fact, in 1993, Circus Circus would become Nevada's biggest employer, surpassing even the state government.) By 1992 CCE was second to the Mirage in total revenue, but led in every other key category. By October 1992 the stock that had debuted at $15 was trading, on an equivalent base, at $216. (Counting two-for-one splits in the meantime, the $54 price of CCE shares would be $216, which means that for his or her original $15, the holder of one share now had $216, or a $201 profit on a $15 investment in ten years.) Bennett, of course, had more than one share, enough in fact to keep him in wieners for quite a long time. In late 1992, after selling off some of his equity over the years, he still had 4 million shares, or 7 percent of the company.

Throughout the eighties, with Schaeffer as financial strategist, the company was like a boxer who seemed to get stronger as his opponent got weaker. CCE, for example, acquired an enormous line of low-priced bank credit, more than $500 million, that would be the envy of any company, especially those gaming competitors that were burdened, sometimes crippled, by high debt from junk bond financing. CCE's bank credit, in fact, was one of the largest lines in the Western United States, and may well have equaled the total credit lines of all other pure gaming companies combined.

The low cost of debt, of course, only made it easier for CCE to build properties while the competition was scrambling just to make the mortgage payments. In 1988, CCE became the first pure gaming company to achieve an investment-grade rating on its public debt. (Hilton, which has both gaming and hotel properties, is also investment-grade.)

By the late 1980s CCE had come to exemplify for Wall Street what a gaming company could be, and, in fact, there were a number of gaming and gaming-related stocks that made people rich. When Schaeffer engineered the company's buyback of 30 percent of its own stock, right after drastically reducing its cost of debt, he received rave reviews for financial wizardry. By 1990, he was featured on the cover of *Institutional Investor* magazine as one of America's outstanding corporate financiers. His annual reports were winning awards. Soon he became the industry's leading spokesman. And when he spoke it was usually not of "gambling" or even of "gaming." He talked about "entertainment megastores." He talked about a "new product," the combination of a casino theme park, shopping mall, and theater under a single roof. And in 1992, when Luxor was announced, he promised that it would be "the most outstanding example yet."

Phil Hevener, the dean of Las Vegas gaming industry writers, says, "To Wall Street, Glenn Schaeffer, not Steve Wynn, is the face of the gaming industry."

Though Schaeffer was first in the minds of Wall Street during this period, at the end of the decade he was only third in the CCE hierarchy, behind Bennett and Richard Banis, who was president.

Banis, who had joined the company in 1978 as controller and later served as a general manager and as chief operating officer, had become CCE president in 1988 when Bill Pennington retired. Banis had already been on the board of directors for five years. However, by 1990 Schaeffer had risen quickly in Bennett's esteem, and a conflict was developing, at least in Bennett's mind, over the progression of power.

When Bennett announced in February 1991 that he would be retiring, the normal line of succession would have put Banis, forty-seven, in the chairman's throne and Schaeffer in the presidency. But in his heart, perhaps, this was not the way Bennett wanted it.

By July 1991 Bennett had reconsidered and had retracted his retirement announcement. Whether he was more concerned about what he would do at home or about forcing Banis's hand is a matter of conjecture. But the effect was that Banis gave Bennett an ultimatum: Either retire as promised, or I leave. Bennett stayed. Banis left. (Not empty-handed, however. In July 1991 he sold 175,000 shares of CCE stock for more than $13 million, and that was less than half his stake.)

This was as close as CCE would come to generating juicy gossip, and Bennett told a *USA Today* reporter at the time, "Mr. Banis and I had some philosophical differences in the way this business should be run."

One philosophical difference was that Bennett had always given his managers the authority to manage at the different properties, and they were rewarded or chastised accordingly. Banis preferred to centralize power. Of course, the bigger philosophical difference was that Banis thought Banis should take over the company, and Bennett apparently thought Schaeffer should.

A CCE executive puts this spin on the whole affair:

"Rick Banis is a talented executive. I think Bennett was genuine when he announced his retirement, but sometime later, perhaps, he felt as if he had jumped off a cliff. After a couple of months, it didn't feel right to him. He was increasingly displeased with Banis's actions and style. I think Rick sensed that he didn't have the support he needed, so he went to Bennett and said, 'You leave and let me succeed you, or I'll be unhappy here.' And Bennett said, 'Then you had better leave.' "

As of February 1993, Bennett had not put a date on his retirement, but it seemed clear that he would stay on through the opening of Luxor, and that you could safely bet your bankroll on Schaeffer to replace him.

15

The Genie

By 1999 you and your cousin Maureen will probably live within driving distance of a casino. So to really understand the gaming industry and the forces that will shape Circus Circus and its competitors as we move deeper into the 1990s, we need to look at the wave of legalized gambling that is sweeping across North America. This wave is moving so fast that by the time you read this chapter some of it may be outdated.

Certainly Nevada has never had a monopoly on legalized gambling. Over the decades legal games of chance have sprung up in American cities from San Francisco to Steubenville, Ohio. Casinos came and went in many places, depending on the mood of the public and who was in office at the time.

But by 1976 casino gamblers were too sophisticated for back-room games, and going into business was too expensive to be subject to the whims of every new mayor. That year is as good a place as any to mark the beginning of a new age of casino gambling, an era in which gaming became rooted and tenacious. In this era individual casinos may come and go, but casino gaming is here to stay.

In 1976 the State of New Jersey was strapped for cash. The once lively beach trade in Atlantic City was declining rapidly. (And this was even before medical waste started washing up on the New Jersey shore.) So folks started thinking, "Well, maybe gambling isn't such an evil after all," and registered their approval of Atlantic City gambling by a state-wide referendum and an Atlantic City vote. Casino gambling became legal in that coastal town, which until then had been most famous for its Miss America contest, and the fact that its streets were known to every kid with a Monopoly set. Soon Atlantic City's gaming industry became to casino gambling what the Boston Red Sox are to baseball: a good team that will never win the World Series and doesn't even play up to its potential.

When the gambling towers began to rise on the beach at A.C. there was much optimistic talk about how games of chance would boost the local economy and lift the huddled masses out of poverty. Money was made, but not by the masses. And almost from the day that the first Atlantic City casino, Resorts International, opened, most of the publicity about A.C. gambling has focused on the fact that the new industry didn't put a chicken in every Atlantic City pot. Dirk Johnson, writing in *The New York Times* (Oct. 6, 1991), notes, "Atlantic City's struggling neighborhoods are testi-mony that gambling's rising tide does not lift all boats."

Arguably, the problem here is not that gaming has underperformed, but that it was oversold by Resorts International and some New Jersey politicians as a cure for many social ills. The fact is that jobs were created by the casinos, and the unemployment rate in the region went from 20 percent to less than ten percent. In addition, tax revenues have surpassed anyone's published expectations, but the benefits of casino gambling go to only one group of people, the elderly of New Jersey, whose medical costs are partially defrayed by casino taxes.

Atlantic City today is a study in contrasts, reminiscent of those intercuts that often begin films about European revolutions, in which we see shots of the few rich and then shots of the many peasants. In Atlantic City the row of casino hotels glitters like a necklace along the beach, but the city blocks west of the gambling halls are dismal and gray, so that the "charming city on the Jersey shore" is today less charming than a discarded beer bottle. Gambling has worked no miracles in Atlantic City. But then, why should it? Nobody asks a new chain of frozen yogurt franchises to save the local economy all by itself.

Lost in the reams of negative publicity is the fact that overall the casino business in Atlantic City has been good. If there are big hotels gasping for money, and there are, it's because they're six miles in debt—not because wily gamblers are taking home huge sacks full of money, but because casino financing did not come cheaply in the 1980s. When casino gambling came to Atlantic City the cost of building there was about three times per square foot what it was in Nevada. Furthermore, the money to build was financed for the most part by high-yield bonds. As a result, the majority of investors in Atlantic City gaming operations could have done as well by investing in U.S. treasury bonds. Considering all of this, plus the high cost of regulation and the higher taxes, it's amazing that New Jersey gaming has produced any winners at all, notably Caesars and Harrah's.

So sure, Las Vegas was chewing its lip for a while. But as it turned out, there was nothing to worry about. Though billions of dollars have crossed the betting tables in New Jersey, there is no evidence that the money leaked from the pockets of Las Vegas casino operators. Atlantic City probably cut into Las Vegas's table game business, mainly craps, but it was a minor nick at most. Overall, the two markets have both grown, independent of each other, since gaming arrived on the Jersey shore.

There are many reasons that the success of Atlantic City gaming has done no serious damage to Las Vegas gaming, and most of them contain clues to Las Vegas's success. Here are seven:

1. Atlantic City is not as much fun. In Las Vegas, it is said, gambling is fun. In Atlantic City gambling is gambling. Nobody goes to A.C. for a vacation, anymore. Or, as one A.C. casino manager put it to a *Newsweek* reporter, "We still have to answer the question, Why would anybody want to come here?"

2. Atlantic City can't bring in as many high rollers. Can you imagine Mario Puzo saying to George Burns, "Screw Las Vegas, George, let's take a bus to A.C.?" No. That's because

Atlantic City is widely regarded as an armpit, while Las Vegas is generally viewed as a glamorous playground for the rich and famous. Also, Atlantic City does not have a full-fledged jetport, so it can't lure the mega-rollers from Japan, Indonesia, and Hong Kong.

3. Atlantic City attracts different players. Atlantic City's customers are not people who decided to go to Jersey instead of Vegas. They are people who would stay home or visit an OTB parlor if there were no Atlantic City. One-fourth of all U.S. residents live within 300 miles of Atlantic City. Forty million adults live less than a gas tank away. They can drive into town for a few hours or a day, without having to pay for a hotel room.

A typical Atlantic City player would be Walter Eiland, who is from just outside Philly, where he runs a country-club restaurant that is dark on Mondays.

"Every Monday morning I'm up at six," he says. "I drive down and I'm at the tables when they open at ten. [Note: since the interview with Eiland, A.C. has gone to twenty-four-hour play.] I shoot craps. Fours and tens, that's all I play. I got a system. I make about a thousand bucks every Monday and drive home."

Eiland, of course, is lying. Anybody who could make a thousand dollars at craps every Monday would almost surely show up on Tuesday. But he's typical in that he goes to Atlantic City once a week and goes home the same day. There are a lot of Eilands on the East Coast, and thousands of them don't even drive home. More than 40 percent of A.C.'s customers are driven home on the bus, which is how they came into town. Every morning on the New Jersey Turnpike and the Garden State Parkway you can see busloads of gamblers—senior citizens and mostly slot players—heading toward Atlantic City. And every evening you can see the buses going back, moving, one would think, a little faster because the weight of so much cash has been removed.

Depending on what the competition is doing, the New Jersey casinos lure these small bettors into their stores with a variety of incentives: free bus rides, lunch vouchers, rolls of quarters, whatever it takes. In recent years the A.C. casinos have been reducing the number of freebies. It seems that too many passengers were just coming to town for the free lunch and a chance to feed the pigeons in front of Bally's. Cutting back on bus passengers has increased profits for most casinos.

One reason that Atlantic City has not hurt Vegas much is also the reason Vegas is not threatened by some of the other new gaming venues. It is that even though Las Vegas is known around the world, gambling to a large extent is regional. According to a visitor profile study done by the Las Vegas Convention and Visitors Authority, 50 percent of the 20 million people who come annually to Las Vegas are from the West, and 35 percent of them are from California. Less than 10 percent are from the East. It's easy to see a New Yorker going to Atlantic City or Las Vegas. But for a Californian to fly across the country so he could gamble in Atlantic City would border on the irrational.

4. Atlantic City is not a good place to bring kids. Which is ironic, because for years Atlantic City had been a family vacation spot, and Las Vegas has been, well, Las Vegas.

One reason that Atlantic City can't compete with Vegas

for the family market is that land is too precious and building costs too high. In A.C. you've got to build high and then fill every bed in every room with bettors, preferably high rollers. You can't waste space on kiddie pools, magic shows, or video arcades for little people who don't pour money into slot machines.

5. *Las Vegas is cheaper.* In Las Vegas you can find two-dollar crap tables, one-dollar blackjack, even low-stakes baccarat. In Las Vegas you can find a room for $29, a buffet meal for $2.98, a show for $10, and at every casino you can park for free. In A.C. the minimums are higher, the rooms and meals are more expensive, the video poker payoffs are smaller, and in 1993 the state passed a law requiring casinos to charge a two-dollar parking fee in their garages. The money would go to the state, not the hotels, and is in fact a tax.

None of this means that Atlantic City casino operators are greedier or less efficient than their counterparts in Las Vegas. It means that the cost of operating is much higher in New Jersey, and it means that the State of New Jersey rakes in more taxes and is not very good at overseeing a gaming industry. Which brings us to reason number six.

6. *Hemorrhoidal regulators.*

Gaming is much more important to the economy of Nevada than it is to the economy of New Jersey. That fact is reflected in the relationship between the state and the gaming industry. In Nevada the regulators, in the form of the Gaming Commission and the Gaming Control Board, are viewed as a necessary restraint on a volatile industry. In New Jersey the regulators, the Casino Control Commission, are seen as a pain in the ass.

Even though every third cabdriver in New Jersey has twenty bucks on the Knicks to cover the spread, in Atlantic City casinos you'll find no sports book, and horse track simulcasts were not even allowed until May 1993. And even though there's a poker game in every neighborhood from Tenafly to Tuckerton, you couldn't find one in an Atlantic City casino until the summer of 1993. And it wasn't until recently that the New Jersey casinos were allowed to run twenty-four hours a day.

The business press has certainly taken notice of the profit-inhibiting effects of the New Jersey Casino Control Commission.

Daniel Seligman writes in *Fortune* magazine in March 1987:

One reason that players cannot expect a price break in Atlantic City is New Jersey's heavy-handed regulation. Take slot machines, regarding which the Casino Control Commission has an abundance of regulations. They specify that the machines cannot take up more than 30 percent of casino floor space, that you cannot increase the number of machines without filing papers in Trenton, that a certain number of the machines must offer nickel play, that no more than half the machines can be made by one manufacturer, and that the payout on all machines must be at least 83 percent. In fact, the average payout in town is now about 88 percent. But

*a casino wishing to compete for handle-puller busi-
ness by raising that proportion would run into still
another regulation, which is that you are not allowed to make advertising claims about payouts.
The rationale for this extraordinary rule is that
the gullible public might be misled; the result of the
rule is that the gullible public loses more in the
slots. Peter Boynton, who runs Caesars Atlantic
City, recalls that his casino experimented briefly
with a 95 percent payout in 1982, but the commission would not allow him to say "Our Slots Pay
More." Says Boynton: "We would never do it again.
Nobody would know, so what would be the point?"*

*It is hard to believe that regulation must be as
burdensome as it is. The regulators, consisting of
the commission and a separate Division of Gaming
Enforcement, are paid for by the industry itself. In
Nevada, by contrast, the cost of state regulation
comes out of general revenues. The self-financing
feature in New Jersey means that the apparatus has
every incentive to continue building its staff and to
expand the reach of regulation. Indeed, the head
counts at both the commission and the division go
up almost every year.*

What Seligman seems to be saying, politely, is that if
your brother-in-law is out of work, you make a rule that says
all blackjack tables have to be forty-nine inches high, then
you hire your brother-in-law to measure the height of blackjack tables.

Tight regulations discourage players from coming to the city. They also discourage casinos from setting up shop. Circus Circus Enterprises has been asked many times to take up residence on the boardwalk, but has always declined.

"The main reason for that," says Glenn Schaeffer, "is that there are too many rules and regulations that inhibit a company's ability to show the customer how it is different from other companies. Over the years we have developed a competitive edge through our marketing strategy and our way of doing business. What would be the point, and profit, of setting up shop someplace where everybody has to do business the same way?"

This tight regulation may represent the principal difference between Nevada and New Jersey gaming. Nevada is a customer's market. There the customer's attitude and behavior, likes and dislikes, determine what changes will be made in the product. New Jersey is a regulator's market, where the bureaucrats determine the product and its price.

7. The Climate. So is Las Vegas worried about Atlantic City? Not really. It's true that some Las Vegas hotels have sevened out in recent years, and more will follow. It's true that in the late 1980s one out of three Las Vegas casinos lost money. But all that has more to do with the realities of the new Las Vegas than it has to do with East Coast competition. In fact, you could argue that Atlantic City has helped Las Vegas.

"Atlantic City has bred a whole new generation of gamblers," says security analyst Mark Manson. And according to Rob Powers, a spokesman for the Las Vegas Convention and Visitors Authority, "Atlantic City has created more opportunity for people to gamble. Now when people on the East Coast want to see something more than a few casinos and a boardwalk, they come to Las Vegas."

Despite all these negatives, Atlantic City is still a great place to buy chips if you like casino gambling. Atlantic City is not Las Vegas, but it sure as hell isn't Pawtucket, Rhode Island, either. It is the second-best place in America to gamble. (By the summer of 1993 there were many signs that Atlantic City was responding to the challenge of new gaming arenas around the country. Horse betting and poker had finally arrived in the casinos. A new "corridor project" had been announced, that would link the Boardwalk with a new convention center, and plans were at least on the drawing board for three new hotels, a lagoon, new shopping areas, an elevated Boardwalk across town, and a new visitors' center.)

However, up to now the really big game in this wave of legalized gambling has not been casino gambling in Atlantic City or anywhere else. The big money has been in the state lotteries. In 1992 thirty-six states had lotteries.

Nelson Rose, writing in the April 1992 issue of *WIN,* the gambling magazine which used to be known as *Gambling Times,* puts things in perspective.

"The largest form of legal gambling in the country is the state lottery," Rose writes. The latest generation of state-run lotteries began with the New Hampshire state lottery in 1964; today, Rose says, "Government-run lotteries in the United States net about $8 billion a year. By comparison, last year the casino industry in Atlantic City had a net loss of over $250 million, while all the casinos in Nevada combined were able to make less than $700 million."

He goes on to say, "State lotteries are bigger than privately owned casinos in ways other than the bottom line. More people play a single big state lottery each year than visit all of the casinos in Nevada or Atlantic City."

The trigger for all this second-looking at legal gambling is simply that the states are broke. In 1991, stock analyst Tom Hantges says, "twenty-six states had to raise taxes a record ten billion dollars in order to maintain existing programs."

Rose says, "A wave of legalized gambling is sweeping the nation. Like dominoes, state after state is turning to legal gambling as a source of revenue."

Even with, or perhaps because of, the state's outrageous hold percentage, by 1992 the lottery was starting to lose its allure, and a quarter of the states that had lotteries were watching profits plummet. Many had turned to new lottery products, such as video terminals that offer blackjack, poker, or keno. Many states, such as Arizona and Massachusetts, have considered putting slot machines at horse and dog race tracks.

Once a week in most states you can find a news story about a little old lady who found a winning lottery ticket at the Laundromat, or a group of workers at an umbrella factory who bought a batch of lottery tickets together and made $17 million. From such stories are dreams created, and they tend to obscure the fact that the state lottery is the ultimate sucker bet.

Playing the state lotteries is cheap, it doesn't take any time, and the payoff can set you up for life. There are dozens of reasons that a state lottery would make a lot more money than a casino, but being a bargain is not one of them. In fact, compared to the state lotteries, Las Vegas casinos are Santa Claus. In Las Vegas for example, if you play craps you can get the house advantage down to 0.6 percent, and the worst bet you can make at a crap table gives the house an advantage of just under 17 percent. Compare that to the state lotteries, which overall give the state a house advantage in the range of 49 percent.

The biggest reason for the discrepancy between lottery payoffs and casino payoffs is, of course, the fact that the states have given themselves a monopoly on the lottery business. If there were two competing lotteries in a state, the payoffs would be much higher. Another reason that state lotteries are such a poor bet is that they are run by the state, an organization not known for its efficiency. You might argue that the money is used to improve society and lower taxes. But since the lotteries came in, a lot of people haven't noticed the improvement.

Generally speaking, the state lotteries are not competition for Las Vegas. They are two different things, and it is difficult to imagine a person buying a two-dollar lottery ticket instead of flying to Las Vegas. Casinos are in the entertainment business; they sell an experience, not the hope of sudden riches. State lotteries, on the other hand, don't have an experience to sell. Nobody actually enjoys waiting in line at the 7-Eleven. The states are selling the promise of "Get rich quick," and have lately become shameless in producing television ads that portray cleaning ladies taking over corporations and the like. All of which puts the states on shaky ethical ground, to say the least, when they oppose casino proposals. The real importance of the state lotteries to the casino industry is not that they gave people a new way to gamble, but that they gave people a new way to look at gambling. Instead of getting on your knees and shooting craps behind the candy store, now you walk into the candy story and place a bet with, of all people, the state. The states put the imprimatur of respectability on gambling. Bill Thompson, professor of gaming at the University of Nevada, Las Vegas, says, "The nation's inhibitions toward gambling have been completely broken down, and why not? If your own state approves of gambling in the form of the lottery, then it must be all right."

By making gambling mainstream, middle-class, and ordinary, the states have let the genie out of the bottle.

Among the places where the genie had shown up by early 1992 were riverboats on the Mississippi River. Just as many states turned to lotteries for help in paying the bills in the 1970s and 1980s, several riverfront states turned to literally floating crap games in the early 1990s. Iowa legalized riverboat gambling on the Mississippi River. Illinois did the same thing. Wisconsin, Missouri, Pennsylvania, and Indiana all had casino debates burning up the state legislatures. In Kansas, Steve Wynn had proposed a $300 million casino hotel and entertainment complex.

(The riverboat customers, it seems, are just as zealous as those in Las Vegas. Just how zealous was made clear in September 1992 when Sandra Sanchez wrote in *USA Today,* "Gamblers on Mississippi River waters take betting seriously. Seriously enough for many to stay on casino riverboats until they were physically forced off waters directly in Hurricane Andrew's path.")

The big gaming companies did not rush to join in the

riverboat action. For one thing, the riverboat states are taking a lot more money off the top than the Vegas casinos are used to giving up. Illinois and Iowa take 20 percent of the gross, compared with 6.25 percent in Nevada and 8 percent in Atlantic City.

Riverboat gambling, like the lotteries, seems to pose no threat to Las Vegas. One reason is the low limits. Iowa, for example, limits losses to $200 a trip. And you have to buy a ticket to get on the boat. Places like Davenport and Bettencourt, Iowa, are not competition for Las Vegas any more than the Las Vegas Stars are competition for their parent team, the San Diego Padres. They are farm teams, preparing new players for the big leagues of Nevada.

Another venue of the new gambling can be found in western towns. In 1989 Deadwood, South Dakota, a historic Old West town, voted to legalize slot machines, blackjack, and poker, and raised millions for historic preservation in its first year.

(It was in Deadwood, incidentally, that Wild Bill Hickok was shot playing poker. Legend has it that he was holding aces and eights at the time, which is why that combination is called a Dead Man's Hand.)

Apparently folks in Colorado thought Deadwood had a fine idea, and soon Cripple Creek, Black Rock, and Central City, all in Colorado, voted in casino gambling.

By 1992 the protect the border mentality had taken root. Louisiana had elected a high-rolling, high-living crapshooter by the name of Edwin Edwards governor, and the City of New Orleans approved a contract for one casino on the Mississippi River. The State of Mississippi had approved riverboats, but the riverboats weren't required to leave the shore. Washington and Montana had joined California in allowing poker clubs. South Carolina had legalized video poker, as had South Dakota, West Virginia, and Oregon. Oregon also had blackjack in certain counties. Slots were permitted in the ocean counties of Maryland. Vermont was considering legalizing video poker. Almost every day brought news of a new gaming prospect.

And then, of course, there are the Indians. Casinos are being built on Indian reservations all over America. In the 1990s casino gambling has done more for Native Americans than Kevin Costner. The Indians in turn have added inexorable momentum to a great wave of legalized gambling that began sweeping across the U.S.A. twenty years ago.

The Indian Gaming Regulatory Act of 1988 says that Indians can operate any kind of gambling that is allowed in the state where their reservation is located, and can set their own betting limits and rules. While there aren't many states with casinos, there are a lot of states that "allow" casino games on a short-license basis, the "Las Vegas nights" popular at churches and fraternal halls. That is the loophole through which Indian tribes in several states have slipped their casinos. Minnesota, for example, has a dozen Indian reservation casinos. Michigan and South Dakota have Indian gaming. By the end of 1992 twenty-two states had Indian gaming operations, and by some estimates Indian gaming had already become a billion-dollar business.

So this Indian gaming industry is not small-time and neither are the individual casinos. In 1991, for example, the Mashantucket Pequot Indians opened the $60-million

Foxwood Casino and high-stakes bingo hall in Ledyard, Connecticut. Foxwood had 128 table games in 240,000 square feet of gaming area, 45 poker games, $4 million in chips, an indoor waterfall, and appearances by Kenny Rogers. Foxwood, with windows and more subdued atmosphere, does not look like a Vegas casino. However, the numbers are the kind that Las Vegas understands. The Ledyard casino, which had no slots but is closer to Boston and New York than Atlantic City is, was taking in $.5 million a day and getting 10,000 to 20,000 visitors when it first opened. By the fall of 1993 a high-rise hotel was almost complete at Foxwood and a second casino had been opened. Foxwood had become the largest casino in the western hemisphere.

Many people see Indian gaming as a boon to a people who haven't had too many boons lately. The University of Nevada's Thompson says, "Firecrackers, wrestling with alligators, selling beads . . . I can't think of anything that gives as much hope for general social development, employment, economic development, health, and education as gaming operations."

Indian gaming also has its detractors. Many in the industry, for example, are afraid that the unregulated Indian casinos will eventually give birth to a cheating scandal that will hurt the entire industry. And the success of Indian gaming breeds resentment among state officials because it is tax-free and siphons off revenues. The implications of this are great. There are Indian reservations all over the country, and none of the money that goes into them comes out in the form of state tax revenue. How long are antigambling states going to sit back and watch millions of untaxed dollars pass through local casinos before they legalize casinos and take their cut?

Donald Trump, for one, was not happy about Indian gaming. In May 1993, Trump called for a "level playing field," and filed suit against the U.S. Interior Department to stop the agency from giving Indians preferential treatment when it comes to gaming. Some gaming observers saw that as a move directed at New York governor Mario Cuomo, who had recently signed a contract with two New York tribes allowing them to open tables-only casinos dangerously close to Trump's Atlantic City locations.

Anti-Indian gaming sentiment will continue to grow in the industry. One Las Vegas executive, who prefers not to be named, puts it this way, "The black people in this country were slaves for years and have been held down in a variety of ways, but nobody is suggesting we give them a tax-free monopoly on gaming casinos. During World War Two we interned thousands of Japanese-Americans unfairly, but nobody says give them a gaming monopoly. So, why the Indians?"

Thompson says, "The Indians only have a five-year window of opportunity before there is competition designed to head it off." John Peters, executive director of the Massachusetts Commission on Indian Affairs, says, "The federal government has problems when Indians begin to get into the money market. They talk about wanting to establish economic diversity but they don't really want it."

While the market for casino gambling is nowhere near saturated, it is, like any market, limited. And sooner or later the marketing range of one casino is going to overlap the market of another. Atlantic City and some of the riverboat states are likely to suffer more than Las Vegas, because Las Vegas is a total entertainment destination where people go for conventions, vacations, shows, and glamour. The riverboats and A.C. make their money off the day visitor who comes just to gamble, the same person who is drawn to the reservation.

This gambling wave tends to be self-perpetuating, and there is no end in sight. When a state legalizes gambling, the state next door sees money going out the window. Iowa legalized it, which meant that people from Illinois could spend their money in Iowa. So Illinois legalized it. In Connecticut the Pequot Indians had barely opened the doors on their hugely successful and non–tax-paying casino when the state started discussions with Steve Wynn about the possibility of building two $350 million casino resorts in Hartford and Bridgeport, and Harrah was putting together a plan for a 1,000-room Connecticut casino hotel.

In January 1993, however, the Pequot Indians cut an extraordinary deal with the State of Connecticut, aimed at stifling competition and maintaining the Foxwood monopoly in gaming in the state. Until that time Foxwood had no slot machines, and would have none until and unless the casino won a lawsuit against the state, which claimed it had the right to forbid slots. Under the new deal, worked out with Connecticut governor Lowell Weicker, who was dead set against the expansion of gaming in Connecticut, the state would allow slot machines at Foxwood, and the casino in turn would pay the state a $100-million-per-year tax for as long as Foxwood had a gaming monopoly in the state. The deal was, in effect, a poison pill. If the state wanted to bring in Wynn or

Harrah's, they had to first swallow the loss of $100 million in yearly revenues, a fact which is significant ammunition for the antigaming forces. (A few months later the Indians raised the guarantee to $113 million, citing better-than-expected slot revenues.)

Foxwood's CEO, Michael Brown, says, "The deal self-destructs if the state allows slot machines in any form. We're saying the state can do whatever it wants, but if they legalize casinos or slot machines we're on our own again."

Atlantic City's reaction to this deal was, predictably, mixed. The bad news for A.C.: Connecticut now has slot machines. The good news: there probably won't be any casinos in Hartford or Bridgeport, which could draw away a lot of A.C.'s New York customers.

The spread of casino gambling is not slowing down the growth of Las Vegas, or of its gaming industry. Las Vegas is still one of the fastest-growing cities in the country, and Vegas casino owners see the riverboats, the small-town casinos, and the reservations as prep schools for Las Vegas.

"One thing we in the industry understand," says Glenn Schaeffer, "is that a major social phenomenon of the nineteen-eighties was the legitimization of gambling. Its spread will be one of the key social themes of the nineteen-nineties for a number of reasons. Local and state governments, facing fiscal strain, like the idea of voluntary taxation, and they will experiment with gambling."

If there is one aspect of all this that worries Las Vegas, it is the possible spread of gambling in California, where 35 percent of Las Vegas's business comes from.

"When they did try to get casinos in California," Phil

Hevener says, "the gaming industry got in bed with the Christian right. Now there's a strange alliance." Hevener says the Las Vegas industry found ways to fund some of the Christian right's efforts to head off casino gambling in the Golden State.

In November 1992 the Agua Caliente Band of the Cahuilla Indians announced that they had made a deal with Caesars World Inc. to bring a casino onto their reservation near Palm Springs, California. However, unless a court rules otherwise, the Indians will be limited to the games already allowed in the state: bingo, horse racing, lotteries, and card games.

"The thing that has hurt us the most," says Bill Paulos, "is the card clubs in Southern California. That has really hurt poker in Las Vegas."

Glenn Schaeffer says, "I think state-sanctioned casinos in California are unlikely. In a diverse, huge economy like California's, casino gambling is not the boon it would be elsewhere. And a Native American reservation casino cannot yet come close to offering the variety of entertainment experience that Las Vegas offers. In fact, it will be decades, if ever, before anybody can come close to what the Las Vegas Trip offers. And if it does happen someplace else, Circus will be there."

The fact is that it probably will happen someplace else.

Gaming on a small scale has its problems, and some of the people who voted for it in small jurisdictions are now wondering out loud if a little bit of gambling is as impossible as being a little bit pregnant. Deadwood, for example, found that casinos couldn't simply bring in revenue and leave everything else alone. Business brings people. People are customers. Customers lure businesses. Businesses buy property. Buyers push up prices. Customers also mean traffic. Traffic means air pollution, accidents, a new stop light on the corner, etc.

It seems that casinos need their own space. They can't be just one feature of a small area. In a small, populated area they become, inevitably, the dominant attraction. And so they are most compatible with their area when they are isolated, as is often the case with Indian reservation casinos, or when they are in an area that is a gaming destination.

Lyle Berman, president of Grand Casinos Inc., which runs casinos in Minnesota and Mississippi, says that Mississippi's Gulf Coast, for one, will become a destination resort and might have as many as ten casinos. And in September 1992 Henry Gluck, CEO of Caesars World, told Roger Gros of *Casino Player* magazine, "Gaming will move forward at a predictable rate, but I feel that it will slow down somewhat in the smaller areas. Some of the experiments aren't working very well; places like Iowa and Colorado. Iowa isn't profitable, and Colorado has too much saturation and little in the way of marketing skills."

Gluck sees the future of gaming in the bigger towns that can compete with Las Vegas in a broader way. He told Gros, "New Orleans is a major tourist attraction with many attributes. It has a football team, a large convention center, and many built-in features. It is a major international hub and a world attraction. It will be a major competitor."

Ironically, the new Las Vegas has probably contributed to the new attitude toward gambling and the creation of so much competition. Who can say how many city politicos and state legislators stayed or played at Circus Circus and flew home with a sanitized view of the city which allowed them to support legalized gambling? And now, for the first time in its history, Las Vegas must meet the challenge of outside competition.

Phil Hevener is probably the most knowledgeable person writing about the gaming industry, and he says that Las Vegas has been anticipating this competition for years and preparing for the challenge by changing the nature of the product. In a 1991 editorial in *Casino Journal,* he writes:

> *Gaming grew up. It hired some image enhancement specialists, put on some new clothes, learned about makeup, and people elsewhere began to see that they might as well give gaming a chance in their communities.*
>
> *But now, the most creative people associated with the Las Vegas gaming industry were already adding a lot of bells and whistles and glow-in-the-dark racing stripes to their respective products. They were still living off gaming and they were still giving away a lot of food and hotel rooms, but they were filtering it all through the allure of special events.*
>
> *You were not going to Las Vegas just to shoot craps for three days, you were going to see the finals in the All-American Something-or-Other. And did it ever work like a dream. People came here to*

watch the National Gizmo Tossing Finals and they also spent some time at the tables.

Las Vegas was evolving, but not all of the most important people were sure what this meant. A number of the analysts and those who make important things happen in money centers around the world could not see the difference in gaming in Las Vegas and gaming anywhere else . . . on a riverboat in Iowa, an Indian reservation in California, or a small town in South Dakota.

The point is—what all those places offer is pure and simple gambling. What Las Vegas offers is gaming and a lot more. You hear more people these days talking about selling entertainment, not merely gaming. It is in the direction of more entertainment that Las Vegas is evolving. Places and institutions such as Las Vegas have to redefine themselves every once in a while and that's what's happening.

Hevener is writing about the things Las Vegas has already done to set itself apart from the minor-league gaming experiences. But if plans for future growth are any indication, the job has hardly begun. The city and the industry are moving quickly into another new age of casino gambling. And the way is being led not by Mafia dons or Frank Sinatra, but by the Wizard of Oz, tales of treasure, and an ancient Egyptian pyramid.

16

The New Jewel in the Crown

"For a while Luxor will be the most important building in the United States, in terms of signature architecture," Glenn Schaeffer says. "Possibly no major comparable building will be built in any U.S. city for years."

Schaeffer is sitting in a stuffy makeshift conference room at the Trumbull Company, in the western part of Massachusetts, in Lenox, a bucolic New England town best known for Boston Symphony Orchestra concerts at Tanglewood. He is talking about the pyramid-shaped hotel which CCE plans to open in the fall of 1993. Now it is the fall of 1992. Along Massachusetts' famous Mohawk Trail the leaves are streaked with fiery reds and golds, colors more spectacular than even the glittering bulbs of the Las Vegas

Strip. In this unlikely setting, Glenn Schaeffer is discussing the cutting edge of high-tech entertainment with a former Hollywood wonderboy.

Schaeffer has joined a team of executives and creative people for a day of recapping and brainstorming in this somewhat cramped former supply room. They are in this room because Douglas Trumbull and his crew have filled every inch of the building with high-tech equipment. The room contains a conference table, bulletin boards, a telephone, a VCR, and one narrow window. Coffee has been consumed, pencils have been sharpened, sleeves have been rolled up. To an extent, these men today will both describe and dictate the future of Las Vegas.

Sitting next to Schaeffer in this onetime storage building, now one of the busiest special-effects movie studios in the country, is Douglas Trumbull. Trumbull will be describing the program of the three "participatory adventures" that will make up the four-acre theme park in the center of Luxor, now about one year away from opening.

Trumbull, fifty, knows a thing or two about special effects. His mother was an artist, and his father was a movie special-effects man, though he left the business when Doug was two years old. But Trumbull, who grew up in California, had the FX bug. When he was twenty-two he became a background illustrator for Graphic Films, a Los Angeles animation studio, and the work he did for *To the Moon and Beyond,* a short film created for the 1964–65 New York World's Fair, caught the attention of renowned director Stanley Kubrick.

Kubrick asked Trumbull to do some preliminary drawings for a film he wanted to make, and the result was that

Trumbull became one of four special photographic effects supervisors for *2001: A Space Odyssey*. Trumbull's most significant contribution to the film was probably his development of slit-scan photography, which made possible the famous Stargate corridor sequence. His experience with *2001* solidified in him a belief that a movie audience is entitled to a technically first-rate production and established his allegiance to the technological aspect of filmmaking.

Trumbull went on to create special effects for *The Andromeda Strain* and such milestone movies as *Close Encounters of the Third Kind* and *Blade Runner*. But like everybody else in Hollywood, Trumbull wanted to direct. And he did. In 1970 he wrote and directed *Silent Running*. In 1983 he produced and directed Natalie Wood's last film, *Brainstorm*.

Hollywood, however, can be a vast wasteland for a man like Trumbull, whose interest lies in technology, and he left Tinseltown both figuratively and literally.

"I feel that the feature motion picture industry peaked out in the nineteen-fifties," he says. "The motion picture industry consists of about 4,000 flat-screen multiplexes, and is involved almost entirely with how do you get a certain director together with a certain actor or actress with a certain story and get it on two thousand screens in one day. The business is totally incapable of changing in any technological way. The feature movie industry hasn't even been able to get digital stereo sound going in theaters yet. There is no big-screen stereo or three-D or anything else of quality."

The thrust of Trumbull's career had always been artistic and technological, long on visual impact and short on power lunches. He wanted to be part of the new entertainment tech-

251

nologies. And those technologies, he says, are emerging not in the film industry, but in theme parks.

In 1987 Trumbull set up a special-effects company called Berkshire Motion Picture Corporation. After what he calls "a couple of minor jobs," Trumbull and his company moved to the front of the line when he was called on to create the *Back to the Future* ride at Universal's theme park in Orlando, Florida. Filmed in Omnimax and projected onto an eighty-foot dome, the ride gives passengers the experience of time travel in eight-seat DeLorean cars through landscapes and adventures from the past to the future. The *Future* ride employs filmic special effects with a dynamic motion simulator in a theater setting. Its 7 million riders in 1992 established it as the world's top theme park attraction. After *Future* the company became Berkshire Ridefilm, and if you wanted to see the state of the art in simulator technology you had to go to Massachusetts. Ridefilm was spun off into a subsidiary company that now creates special simulator rides, and Trumbull has gone on to form the Trumbull Company Inc. (TCI), which for the moment is mainly in the business of creating attractions for Circus Circus's Luxor Hotel, scheduled to open in October 1993.

It was the *Back to the Future* ride that drew Glenn Schaeffer to Trumbull. In 1991 Schaeffer traveled extensively in search of entertainment ideas that would enhance the theme of the Luxor building. The *Future* ride had achieved the kind of success that CCE liked to associate with.

"Glenn knew that he wanted three attractions," Trumbull says. "He knew he wanted one to represent the past, one the present, and one the future. I came up with three ideas and we went with them."

In the fall of 1992, the three attractions were the most ambitious new projects under way for an American theme park, and Circus's assignment for Trumbull, says Schaeffer, "is to outdo *Future.*" Just as Bugsy Siegel turned to Las Vegas because he didn't have what Hollywood wanted, Trumbull has turned to Las Vegas because Hollywood doesn't want what he has. The involvement of Douglas Trumbull, and people like him, in the Luxor project suggests that the new Las Vegas, not Hollywood or Orlando, will be the laboratory for new forms of entertainment. Innovation by nature is expensive and risky, but that is what Las Vegas is all about.

Trumbull says, "In Las Vegas you will see things happening that are far in advance of anything in Orlando or Hollywood." What's going on there, he says, gives us a glimpse of what we will see everywhere.

"I think we are moving toward the urban entertainment center," he says, "where the entertainment center will be the third anchor in a shopping mall, along with a Macy's or a Bullock's. But it will be there on its own merits, not to draw people to the mall stores. It will be a very diverse center, with simulation rides, theaters using special photographic processes. You'll have interactive video games and virtual-reality-type experiences."

Trumbull, who is developing his own version of virtual reality, says, "You hear a lot about lasers and holograms and it is all bullshit. None of it works. The real technology is in computers and digital imagery and film."

The Trumbull Company occupies 60,000 square feet of industrial space which houses a complete movie studio. Only a small area is used as production office space. The rest is the art department, machine shops, electronic shops, model-building workshops, a simulation theater, a film laboratory, editing facilities, a commissary, and four stages. On two of the stages, sophisticated new computerized motion-control systems photograph miniatures and various special effects. On the other two, actors will perform stories of adventure that in the autumn of 1993 will entertain visitors to the new jewel in the CCE crown, the Luxor Hotel in Las Vegas.

The Trumbull studio has a fully integrated filmmaking facility with state-of-the-art computer technology for all phases of project development, including computer-aided design (CAD) for visual imaging, models and miniatures, computer-aided manufacturing (CAM), computerized motion-control photography, computer-generated imagery (CGI), high-resolution digital-image compositing, and digital audio. This is definitely not a part of the old Las Vegas.

Though the Luxor project is enormous, it is not one that has been on the drawing board for years. CCE tends to move quickly on new properties. Bill Paulos describes the incubation of Luxor this way:

"Glenn says, 'Our stockholders want us to expand. We need some more growth, and the market is right. What should we do?' So we get Veldon Simpson, our architect, and all our creative people together, and we say, 'Okay, we need some concepts of what we want to do.' Obviously we need some themed entertainment. Obviously we believe in stretching the envelope the way we did with the Colorado Belle, the largest boat built in the desert since Noah, and the Excalibur, the largest hotel in the world. So we come up with Luxor, probably the most complete entertainment resort in the world.

"The architect came up with the pyramid idea. Mr. Bennett and Glenn said, 'Yeah, that's a winner. Then we can do this and that, and put this here and that there.' Then we ask our engineers, 'Is it possible to do this, is it possible to do that?' And they say, 'Yeah, it's possible.' It's going to be an engineering achievement, this Luxor. It's a marvel building. People were skeptical. They said, 'You know, you can't do that, it's too hard,' or 'You can't do it for that price, it won't be cost-effective.' "

Veldon Simpson, the architect who is given credit for the pyramid idea, says, "The pyramid was an evolution. First we had this conventional building that was stepped back, like plateaus. Every three rooms, we stepped back two rooms. It had an adventure theme. In back of the main hotel, which was in the shape of a U, we had a five-story hotel, and over it there was a pyramid-shaped glass atrium.

"Once we designed that atrium we kept seeing the advantages of an enclosed environment and it kept getting bigger and bigger in our design. I thought, 'Why don't we use all the money we are spending on the rooms and on this glass atrium, and use the rooms to actually make the shape of the atrium?'

"When you think about it, it's quite cost-effective. In the average hotel casino you have a tower and a very elaborate facade. What we did is took the rooms and made that the skin of the building, in the shape of the atrium. We didn't get to the Egyptian theme until then, but we knew we needed it to carry along the whole pyramid thing."

Schaeffer, taken with the idea of a pyramid, hit the books. The pyramid, he read, is the strongest form known to man. Its geometry, four sides converging to a single point in space, is said to be the purest structural shape. Since the dawn of mankind the pyramid has been a symbol of power and strength. This pyramid would rise from the desert 6,000 years after the first pyramid was constructed in Egypt.

Glenn and his colleagues began to see the Luxor project as a mysterious form containing lost micro-cities in the state of discovery by archaeological excavation. The past, the present, and the future would coexist in a single environment, frozen in time.

In November 1991, when the hotel was still called Project X, CCE announced plans for the building. William Bennett said at the time, "This is a collaborative production of imaginative architects, cutting-edge movie producers, science-fiction writers, special-effects designers, and experienced casino operators who are determined to bring an ultimate fantasy environment to our customers. Visitors who enter the pyramid will find themselves engaged in a world that's found nowhere else. We intend to create one of this country's most amazing places."

It's a telling quote. If you subtracted the four words "and experienced casino operators," you wouldn't even know that Bennett was talking about a gaming establishment. His words would sound for all the world like a description of a new Disney project.

Bennett went on to say that the CCE pyramid would

have an exterior of bronze reflective glass and a thirty-story interior atrium. The theme would be exploration. It would be, said Bennett, "a vehicle that transports its visitors to extraordinary and mysterious places of times past and future."

Along with Douglas Trumbull's high-tech interactive movie attractions, Project X, Bennett promised, would let customers move through the hotel by spaceship or watercraft and elevators set at a thirty-nine-degree angle. The hotel would have 2,500 rooms and 90,000 square feet of casino, all kinds of state-of-the-art technology, exotic scenery and artifacts, a full-scale replica of King Tut's tomb, and the "River Nile" running through the interior.

In December 1991 Schaeffer told *The Las Vegas Business Press* that the pyramid wasn't a conscious idea. "It just appeared one day," he said. In the same interview he said that Project X would have "a secret place, a place where you can stand and see an image of the pyramid up in the atrium, just as the vision came to us." Pyramids, Schaeffer reminded readers, "are full of mysteries." When asked how CCE would come up with a name for the hotel, he said, "It may come to one of us in a dream." All of this suggests that CCE wants to make the most of the pyramid's alleged magical qualities. After all, if you want to mold a casino into a shape that people think will bring them luck, a pyramid is a lot more exciting than a horseshoe.

The name, which Schaeffer plucked from a list submitted by Joyce Gordon, came only after CCE had paid thousands of dollars to a consulting firm that came up with "Pyramid Pyramid" and "a lot of names that sounded like automobiles." It is amazingly apt. Besides being the name of the Egyptian city where the famous temple and tombs are located and more than half of all Egyptian antiquities have been discovered, Luxor sounds like "Luxury," has an X like Excalibur, and also contains the sound of "luck."

Luxor means "The Palaces." The ancient temple was built by two kings, Amenhotep (or Amenophis) III and Ramses II. One of its two obelisks remains standing today, and its inscription reads, "As long as there is a heaven my name shall be known."

If the design of Luxor is impressive, just as impressive is the way CCE will finance the project.

Bennett says, "We can fund this entire project from our internal cash flow, with substantial free cash left over."

And if things get tight CCE can always tap its line of credit. As of October 1992, the company had $375 million still left on its credit card.

The price tag leads laypeople to ask how Luxor can be more spectacular than the Mirage, which cost more than twice as much.

"I think at the Mirage they waste money," says Veldon Simpson. "They do everything two or three times. I don't know how they managed to spend that much money. Of course, MGM is going to be a billion dollars, but I think it is worth it, it's such an enormous project."

Simpson says it is unlikely we will ever see spectacular projects like this in Atlantic City. "In New Jersey," he says, "everybody has got his hand in three pockets, and that is just reality."

Now, in Lenox, Massachusetts, Schaeffer is trying to make sure Luxor doesn't cost much more than that $300 million, and that all the promises to the public are kept. Among the cadre of CCE executives and consultants is Veldon Simpson. Simpson, who came to Las Vegas from Arizona in the early 1980s, has done so much work for CCE that he feels like a part of the family. Simpson was the architect on the Colorado Belle, the CCE Las Vegas expansions, and the Excalibur, for which he roamed all over Europe with Bill Paulos looking at castles. Even in the midst of the Luxor project Simpson is architect for the new MGM Grand, across the street from Luxor, as well as Grand Slam Canyon, the water-theme park being built at Circus Circus Las Vegas.

Also present is Bill Paulos. Presently general manager of CC Las Vegas, Paulos is the company's go-to man when opening day of a new hotel arrives. It was Paulos who ran the Colorado Belle during its first years, and it was Paulos who headed Excalibur during its extraordinarily profitable start. Now Bennett has tapped Paulos to be general manager of Luxor. But more than that, Paulos is an integral part of the planning team.

Along with Paulos, Schaeffer, Trumbull, and Simpson are Charles Silverman, the gaming industry's leading decorator; R. C. White, CCE's director of construction; Peter Jackson, a well-known choreographer and producer of Excalibur's King Arthur's Tournament, the best-attended production show in Las Vegas; and Cary Rich, a principal with Insight, Inc., a firm that builds environments for rides, most recently for Disney at EuroDisneyland.

This day's exercise is to chart the entire experience of a Luxor customer, from ticket line to doorway to preshow to show to exit, on each of Trumbull's three extravaganzas.

Blueprints are spread across the table. Charts and elevations are pinned to the corkboard walls of the room. The object is to make sure that no seams will appear in the final product. A month earlier, Bill Bennett presided over a similar skull session in this studio, specifically to examine the ride dynamics.

As a warm-up, Trumbull leads the group through the working studio. First the model room, where local sculptors are assembling cityscapes from laser-cut model pieces for the film; then on to the computer graphics lab, where artistic wonks are "texturing" spaceships and creating realistic finishes for various effects in the films, devising animated sequences that can be inserted into the film by digital computer.

"In fact," says Schaeffer, "the Luxor project benefits in no small measure from computer-imaging developments wrung from the big-budget *Terminator 2* movie starring Arnold Schwarzenegger. You know that fabulous indestructible recombinant molten man? The molten man exists only on computer disk."

Finally the group moves through the shooting sets, where sophisticated miniature cameras are mounted on high-tech gantries poised above a glittering Lilliputian city, circa A.D. 2500. This city will be "discovered" on one of the participatory adventures.

Schaeffer is intrigued by this sort of thing. In the months ahead he plans to sit through casting calls in Los Angeles, observe rehearsals on a Hollywood soundstage, help to shape movie scripts, critique dailies from the films, and serve as guinea pig while Trumbull tries out variations of body sonics

for seats in the theaters and motion control for the simulator
ride. Already, Schaeffer has run a constant shuttle back and
forth from Las Vegas to the Berkshires as the studio has
ramped up into full film production. Schaeffer's assignment
from Bennett: find a centerpiece for the Luxor pyramid that's
innovative by all standards of the gaming industry—and of
the whole entertainment industry.

So Schaeffer and Paulos spent a couple of weeks early
in the predevelopment of Luxor scouring theme parks in
Florida, California, and even Japan. Acutely vulnerable to
motion sickness, Schaeffer nonetheless swallowed Drama-
mine tablets and climbed on and off everything that was
drawing crowds anywhere. He careened through the *Back to
the Future* ride one day, and within a week he'd contacted
Trumbull. Trumbull, it turned out, was going through a
breakup with his partner; Circus subsequently set up
Trumbull in his own company, and gave him his charter: create three fresh attractions involving technology, theatrical environments, and story lines that outstrip any other themed
attractions of their type in the country. Bennett told Trumbull
that the attractions must in essence create a mythology about
the Luxor pyramid, and that they must deliver that mythology
on a preset budget. If he succeeded, Trumbull would share a
slice of their revenue; if he failed, he would cover the over-
ages.

Trumbull went to work.

After breakfast and the studio tour, the group moves
back into the conference room. The discussions and critiques
cover the whole Luxor building.

Paulos begins speaking to the gathering. He's telling

most of them things they already know, but this is a day for making sure everybody has the big picture.

"When you drive in from the airport," Paulos says, "you will see this three-hundred-fifty-foot-tall pyramid. As you drive up you see the porte cochere, which is a replica of the Sphinx that is one hundred fifty feet tall. You will see an obelisk out front. That is a major symbol of Luxor. The pyramid, of course, is the icon, and that is what will appear, for example, on the chips. You will also see a major decorative pool, right in front of the Sphinx, when you drive up. During the day it will be a water show, with dancing waters, right in front of the Sphinx. At night there will be a spray of water shooting fifty-five feet in the air. That will create a water screen, and we will project onto that screen various famous Egyptian artifacts, such as the death mask of King Tut. It will look almost holographic.

"When you walk in the front door you will be looking down into the casino. Everything is in Egyptian style. You will notice that nothing is actually ancient. It is all built as if this was the first day the temple opened. This is not a bunch of ruins. It is alive with vibrant Egyptian colors and light. You will be standing on a bridge under which the Nile River flows. This is real water; it is a river that is anywhere from eight to twenty feet wide at various places. There are real boats on it.

"You will see people in these boats, twenty to a boat. Some of them will be hotel guests, going to the elevators to their rooms. Others will be taking the full boat trip around the circumference of the inside of the building. The entire decor of that trip will take them from thirty B.C. to four-thousand B.C.

"The bell captains, the front desk staff, everybody, will be wearing Egyptian garb. These will be more like costumes than uniforms. Some will look ancient, others will have a more modern look to them.

"The overall feel that you will have is that you have entered a luxury hotel. But the rooms will be between fifty-five dollars and seventy dollars. The approximate average daily rate will be sixty dollars. There will be some luxury suites and there will be two hundred seventy-five mini-suites. Each of the mini-suites will have a bedroom and a side room that has a Jacuzzi tub with a view.

"When you walk out of your room and look over your balcony, you see the full atrium. The largest atrium in the world. That's a lot of air-conditioning.

"From that balcony you will be able to look down on the attraction floor. There you will see the three major attractions Doug is preparing, and they will be housed in buildings representing past, present, and future. We have an eighty-five-foot replica of the Chrysler Building, for example.

"When you go to the casino you will come back down through the thirty-nine-degree-angle elevator. We didn't enclose it in glass. We were afraid of scaring somebody. The stakes in the casino will still be aimed at the middle-market customer, but this is definitely a step up economically. You probably won't find fifty-cent roulette, the way you will at Circus Circus. Instead of a one-dollar blackjack table you might find a three-dollar table, but most of them will be five dollars and twenty-five dollars. You will be able to bet more money than at Circus Circus.

"This is the first time ever that the upper-middle-class guy gets value. Normally, value is directed toward the middle class or the lower middle class. This time the guy that normally stays at the Hyatts around the country, the guy that normally pays one hundred fifty to two hundred fifty dollars a night, is going to come in and get that level of service and he's only going to pay seventy dollars or eighty dollars for a room and maybe not even that much.

"There will be seven restaurants. You will have a delicatessen right on the Nile River. On the mezzanine level there is the Nile Fish House and a gourmet museum restaurant. For entertainment we will have an arena show with a very Egyptian theme. On the casino level there will be a lounge. Downstairs, across from the showroom, we are going to build an eighty-thousand-square-foot replica of King Tut's tomb."

Veldon Simpson is up next.

Simpson, a fiftyish Mormon with a medium build and bright white hair, has been doing work for CCE for seven years now. Simpson eats, breathes, and sleeps architecture, and at a time when most architects can't find work in the United States he is doing two of the most important buildings in the country, MGM and Luxor.

"To call Veldon a firm is too strong," Glenn Schaeffer says. "He is more of a one-man army. Veldon is always there when we do brainstorming sessions about Luxor. He is one of the most imaginative people."

Simpson came to Las Vegas in the mid-1980s from Scottsdale, Arizona, where he worked on a variety of buildings, but mostly hotels. For the past seven years his work has been exclusively on casino hotels. Among his non-CCE projects were the remodeling work at the Frontier and the finishing work at the Riviera, the kinds of jobs which will come again, but after Excalibur and Luxor will probably seem boring.

Simpson is certain, however, that nobody will build new hotels that are boring. "The bottom line for Las Vegas," he says, "is that a lot of states are going to have gaming, and we have to come up with a product that is so spectacular and get out so far ahead of everybody else that nobody, no matter what they do, will ever be able to catch us. What we have going for us is the high-tech tools to do it. I have forty people in my operation, and they are mostly architects and computer people. With all this high tech it is unbelievable, but we can build these huge properties in less time than it took us to build the hundred-and-fifty-room properties in the old days."

In Lenox, Simpson begins by telling the team a bit more about the front of Luxor.

"The Great Sphinx," he says dramatically, "is a crouching beast with the face of King Khafre. It rises at the base of the great Luxor pyramid. The front legs extend out into the front water feature, the Sacred Lake of Karnak, where the holographic-type images appear on the water screen between the Great Sphinx and the Great Sign, which is an obelisk over one hundred eighty-five feet high. The obelisk, with its hieroglyphic cartouches, will spell out the secrets of the inner space of the pyramid and communicate via laser lights to the eyes of the Great Sphinx. The Sphinx will cause the water in the Sacred Lake of Karnak to gather into a giant water screen, and from the base of the screen will rise an Egyptian image which will appear as a water holograph, part water, part light, and part film."

During his spiel, he speaks often as though the building already exists in reality and not just in his mind. "Building the pyramid," he says, "is not nearly so complicated as everyone seems to think. I believe the Egyptians built a few that have held up well. It is fairly straightforward in terms of engineering, even though there is really nothing like it. In San Francisco there is the Transamerica Building, which has a pyramid on top, but it is not like this. In fact, there is probably nothing like this in the world. There is a pyramid in Memphis, but it is a steel-frame structure, a sports facility. This is the largest atrium in the world and there is nothing to compare to it. Some of the people who think it can't be done suffer from envy and jealousy. The engineering on it is pretty straightforward. It is mostly low-bearing masonry construction. We kept cantilevering the floors in. We have a twelve-foot cantilever that makes up the thirty-nine-degree angle of the pyramid. Once we reached a certain point we had to build a way so that we could get inside to do the construction. We couldn't keep moving to shore up the building so we had to keep building it. We went as far as we could with cantilevers. On the twelfth floor we stressed the pyramid to the corners so that it was like building off the ground again. We could have gone to the fourteenth but we wanted the safety factor of the twelfth. In effect, we were back to zero grade. We did that at twelve, fourteen, and sixteen.

"The only real complication was for exhaust for kitchens. Since we have no roof, we have to send the exhaust down and under the hotel. And we had to give special attention to bathroom exhaust. In a normal straight-up building the bathroom exhaust typically is vented to a shaft that goes all the way through the building. We could have done the same, but it would have been costly and difficult, so we vented the bathrooms out through the skin of the building. Probably the first ones to do that. It's a good solution and it's inexpensive.

"Then there's the elevator," Simpson says. "The elevator will travel seven hundred feet per minute, at a thirty-nine-degree angle. MGM's will also be seven hundred feet per minute but that will be straight up."

As an aside, Simpson says, "You know, one of the things that's been great about this project is that everybody involved gets excited about their piece of it. When we brought the idea to Otis Elevator they brought in their top engineering people from all over the world. They were all so excited just to be associated with Luxor. Everybody is like that. The builder just can't wait to do it. It is so exciting just to be around the damn thing.

"This angled elevator will be an innovation. It hasn't been done before. The Eiffel Tower goes at an angle for a while, but then it is vertical. Luxor's elevator is at an angle all the way. Now, normally an elevator has a trailing cable. It is the spinal cord of the thing with all the sensors and controls that go along with you. With this angle you can't do that, because the cable would drag, so everything has to be controlled with microwaves. We have a microwave station, where computers run the elevator. It's like running a toy car across the living room floor.

"We close off the pyramid at the twenty-eighth floor. Floors twenty-eight, twenty-nine, and thirty have suites. At the twentieth floor we close off the atrium. From your room you can look down at the atrium. You've seen the atrium at the Hyatt in San Francisco? Well that's less than a million cubic feet and ours is twenty-nine million cubic feet. This will be the largest hotel atrium in the world. It compares to the Astrodome. We're talking huge. Just the sheer size of this space will humble you.

"The second floor is, of course, the experience floor. Overall, the concept is that we have discovered a pyramid in Las Vegas and when we went inside and started to excavate we discovered past, present, and future. The past is like ancient Egypt. We have, of course, the Nile River, sixteen hundred and ninety feet long, flowing around the base of the pyramid. The present is like New York City, almost a *Dick Tracy* or Gotham City atmosphere. The future is filled with very futuristic buildings. After you go from thirty B.C. to four thousand B.C. on the river barge you come back out and go through a fog bank like a time warp, back to a very futuristic city that existed before Egypt.

"What I like about this building," Simpson continues, "is that it is architecture that does something, that you can actually experience. You can cause it to do things. The obelisk in the center of the pyramid is known as one twenty-five, forty, the latitude and longitude at the center point of the pyramid. One twenty-five, forty is the heartbeat of Luxor, standing dormant until sundown, when it transforms its static form into a dynamic instrument. At sundown the obelisk will come

268

alive and its hieroglyphics will light up from inside and spell the word 'Luxor.' Once the obelisk goes through its calculations and finds the coordinates, a laser beam shines through the obelisk and goes out, right through the top of the pyramid, where it hits a photo cell on a control panel, and that activates a beam of light that you can see from Los Angeles. We call this Re, the Sun God. The light, lasting a fraction of a second, goes off in a series of twelve. If you are flying over Los Angeles or Phoenix you will see it. If you are orbiting the earth in a space shuttle you will see it. Re is three hundred billion footcandles in power, and it is the greatest single light beam in the world."

Simpson talks a bit longer about what he calls "dynamic architecture." He says, "For the first time the individual will be able to experience dynamic architecture. It is where engineering and imagination coexist."

The idea clearly excites Simpson. In his press material on Luxor he has written:

Dynamic architecture will have evolved as we bridge over the idea that architecture is no longer static and three dimensional. The concept of dynamic architecture will be realized for the first time in history when three dimensional structures incorporate real time fourth dimensional aspects of space, time, motion, and beyond to emotion. Since the beginning of time architecture has been the gauge by which man has been measured, understood, and judged. The pyramid, Luxor, by virtue of its simplicity, is the essence of dynamic architecture.

Next up is Trumbull, the host.

"The experience floor is directly above the casino floor," he says, "and it is open to the atrium. There are acres of indoor space divided into three zones, which represent the past, the present, and the future. Each ride is distinctive, but there is a common story line running through all three. However, you don't have to see them in order, and you don't have to see them all to get the experience. The first one, representing the past, is an action adventure that extrapolates from everything we learned on the *Back to the Future* ride. It's the most sophisticated adaptation of flight-simulation technology for entertainment purposes. We have a very powerful motion base.

"A flight simulator," Trumbull explains, "is a device for simulating an illusion of realism for a pilot in an airplane. But it doesn't have to be an airplane. It could be a Conestoga wagon or a spaceship or a submarine, or anything you could imagine. You can use simulator technology and a very powerful film technique, to complete a one-hundred-eighty-degree wraparound movie experience, combined with motion to confuse and stimulate you to where you feel like you are really there, participating in some activity.

"Each of the three attractions has a distinctly different philosophy. This past attraction represents what you might call the naïveté of the past, or the innocence I suppose, the less technical world of swashbuckling action and adventure such as you find in the Indiana Jones movies, where the hero and heroine behave in more simplistic ways and bravery and heroism play an important role."

The story line related to the pyramid story that Trumbull and his writers have concocted, he says, follows an archaeologist who has found a hieroglyphic tablet, sort of like the Rosetta stone, and a woman from somewhere else who has an occult experience as a result of an eclipse of the sun while she is on vacation in Mexico. For unknown reasons she is able to read the hieroglyphics, and they turn out to be directions to a buried city which happens to be directly below Las Vegas. They dig this city and find two miles underground a highly advanced civilization that predates the Egyptians. The whole is an action-adventure story with bad guys who want to steal the treasure in the hidden tomb and so forth, while the hero and heroine want to use it for good.

"This experience," Trumbull says, "uses film and optical simulation technology. Just imagine a flight simulator built for fifteen people, and you'll have an idea. This ride will last about four minutes."

At this point Schaeffer steps in to blow Trumbull's horn for him.

"Doug," he tells the group, "is a master of this stuff, and he's at the top of his form. The stars of this show are his special effects. There are two components. You will enter the preshow area, and you will be brought into this fantasy adventure step by step while you are waiting in line to board the simulator. The story is fed to you gradually and you become part of it as you go into the simulator."

271

"The present show is completely different," Trumbull says. "It takes place in a three-hundred-fifty-person theater that is a live broadcast studio. You will see a live broadcast of a television talk show called *Luxor Live*. It is a pretty amazing show about the occult, which is topped off by spectacular three-D movies in the theater and a series of very sophisticated illusions. By the time you leave the show you will not be sure what is reality and what is illusion. This uses various kinds of film and video projection, and also Showscan, which is a film process that I developed a few years ago.

"The present ride is about today in transition. It is a representation of the world in transition philosophically, politically, and economically. It is a very sophisticated utilization of high technology done in the form of a live television talk show. The audience will be invited to participate. The show will be a hybrid of a lot of the crap we are seeing today on television, with an exploitation moderator like Geraldo Rivera. It will be a very funny show because the moderator has invited guests of diametrically opposing views as to spirituality and philosophy, science and technology. Nothing has ever been done like this.

"What happens is that through the illusion of film and video projection, and three-dimensional photography, it will be revealed that the entire show you are participating in is an illusion and that there are no people there. It is quite a mind-blowing experience. The audience will think we are using holography, but we are not. It is an illusion technique using film, screen, mirrors, three-D. I think it's going to be not only exciting and funny, but I think that there is a positive human values aspect of these kinds of entertainment. You would be happy to take your kids to any of these three shows.

"One of the guests on the show is the owner of the Luxor Hotel, who is the hero in the past story. There will be a feed from Egypt, featuring the woman who is the heroine in the past story. She is in Egypt waiting for an eclipse of the sun so that she will have another vision. There is also a visit from a villain who has kidnapped the girl in the past ride. He breaks into the TV transmission raving about how he owns the temple. Running through the story is a crystal sphere that has hieroglyphs all over it. It is discovered that the sphere is actually a time machine that the Egyptians used to come forward in time to see what is going to happen in the future. However, that sphere cannot be used for time travel until the mysterious crystal obelisk is found.

"In the future show the obelisk has been found, and that sphere, that time capsule, has been expanded into a three-hundred-fifty-person theater. You are in the time capsule. That is the whole theme and decor of the theater. This show, like the present show, is about sixteen minutes long and it has a curved screen that is about seventy feet tall and thirty-five feet wide."

After Trumbull talks, the others speak. By the end of the long day everybody in the room not only knows how big the atrium will be and the themes of the rides, but also the color of the drapes, the size of the parking lot, the number of actors in the live show. Each creator influences all the others. Decorator Silverman comes up with a couple of new touches for the guest rooms, based on the detailed story lines from Trumbull's attractions; ride designer Rich decides to thematically spruce up an episode on the Nile River Ride. Architect Simpson opts to redesign the outside skin of the first theater so it fits more strikingly with the attraction inside the theater. Schaeffer gives the green light for an expanded preshow for the last attraction. Paulos solves a queuing problem with respect to the middle attraction; and so forth. Trumbull narrates and fields questions, his assistant director taking notes during the discussions. Set designers, motion-control engineers, sound and light experts, production managers are summoned on occasion to explain fine points. There are numerous sidebars—talks about other theme parks, the powers of emerging film technology. A profitable brainstorming session takes place near the end of the day regarding another simulator-film attraction at Grand Slam Canyon, which has just commenced construction.

When it's dark the CCE team heads out to the Pittsfield airstrip and boards the company jet back to Las Vegas. During the flight the team further edits the "dinosaur walk" at Grand Slam Canyon. Peter Jackson, sketching on a yellow legal pad, lays out the program for a matinee production show.

The business isn't about old-time gambling anymore. It's about that new Las Vegas of the mind. It's about, says Schaeffer, "a search to entertain within environments that the customer isn't used to seeing. We don't tell our consultants and our own executives what exactly to come up with.

First we let them stretch, then we edit, partly with dollars, partly with pragmatic sense. I think creativity comes mainly from legwork. We get out there and look around, set the benchmarks, and then aim high."

17

The New Kingdom

The gaming industry for many years was thought of as recession-proof. However, 1991 proved otherwise. Revenues sank all through that recessionary year. Two-thirds of the casinos in Las Vegas lost money. And in October 1991, compared to October 1990, the industry's win figure took its biggest one-month plunge ever. The falling revenues were especially troubling to the State of Nevada, which had expected a 7.5 percent increase.

In December two big casinos, Main Street Station and the Riviera, declared bankruptcy. The industry's troubles, of course, trickled down. Unemployment rose in Las Vegas, housing sales declined, and the experts who had predicted that Las Vegas would continue to lead the nation in growth now said, "Well, maybe . . ." At one point the Las Vegas Hilton was offering rooms at twenty dollars a night to get gamblers in the door.

Surprisingly, during the first nine months of the year the number of visitors to Las Vegas actually went up. But the visitors were bringing smaller bankrolls. Then in October, normally the best tourism month, came the Comdex Computer convention, whose 120,000 participants are, says *The New York Times,* "notorious nongamblers."

Paul Lowden, president of Sahara Resorts, told *The Times,* "Business is awful. The win is off, and the pie is sliced up more."

What was going on here, however, was more than recession. The economy may come back, but some Las Vegas hotels will not. Robert Reinhold, writing in *The Times,* says:

> *The recession appears to be accelerating a significant shakeout in Las Vegas that has been building with the opening of major theme hotels like the upscale 3,049-room Mirage, and the downscale 4,032-room Excalibur in the last two years. Moreover, three huge new projects on the drawing boards will add 10,000 rooms to the Strip by 1994, meaning more competition than ever for the gambling dollar.*

While most gaming operators see a rosy picture for the future of Las Vegas, they see also a massive reshuffling of the economic deck. Recent years have shown a gradual redis-

tribution of the Las Vegas wealth from the hands of the many
to the hands of the few, and the gap between first world and
third world gaming establishments is growing wider.

The birth of the "Orlando of the West" means that there
will be exciting new theme hotels and an expansion of the
market. But there will also be bankruptcies and the passing
of some old familiar names.

Early in 1993 one of those old familiar names, the
Dunes, closed for good. Built for $4 million, the Dunes had
opened May 23, 1955, on what was then the southernmost tip
of the Strip. It featured 200 rooms, dancer Vera-Ellen in the
"Magic Carpet Revue," and a thirty-foot fiberglass sultan on
the roof. Built by people with no gaming background, un-
thinkable in today's market, the Dunes faltered coming out of
the gate. But in 1957 new management came in and began
making money. By 1965 the Dunes had grown to 24 stories
and 1,000 rooms, and Vera-Ellen had been replaced by the
big hit "Minsky's Follies," which featured the bare breasts
that had become a Las Vegas trademark.

The Dunes became one of Vegas's hot spots in what
many people consider the town's heyday. Lionel Hampton's
band paraded through the casino, playing Dixieland jazz.
Frank Sinatra rode a camel to the front door. Billie Holiday
made the Dunes her only Las Vegas hotel. But the Dunes was
never far from scandal. The feds had so much business with
the Dunes over the years they should have rented office
space. The last decade at the Dunes was not a pretty sight.
Lawsuits, countersuits, labor problems, bankruptcy, IRS investigations, changing ownership all proved the point that

you can't make money just by opening the doors to a casino. By June 1992 the Dunes was losing $2 million a month, and its newest owner, Masao Nangaku, had to unload it for $75 million, less than half of what he had paid for it in 1987. The buyer? Steve Wynn, who planned to close it down and turn it into a training center for his Treasure Island people, and eventually to blow it up and build another theme resort on the site.

The Desert Inn, the Riviera, and Bally's might avoid the fate of the Dunes, but they are just some of the hotels that have to be brought in for repairs. And most of downtown is in trouble. The causes of the breakdowns are debt, geography, and obsolescence. The Riviera and Bally's, for example, were Milken clients, and both are overfinanced. Bally's debt became too heavy to haul when the Excalibur opened and Bally's revenues dropped. Bally's has also been hurt by the shifting center of Las Vegas gravity. For many years the "four corners" has meant the intersection of Flamingo and the Strip, and that was the place to be. You had Bally's on one corner, Caesars on another, the Dunes on a third, and the Barbary Coast, right next to the Flamingo Hilton, on the fourth. Three of them are still there, but a lot of the money isn't. The flow of bucks is being diverted uptown to the Excalibur at the intersection of Tropicana and the Strip, which will be the new "four corners." There, by the early part of 1994, you will find the Excalibur, the MGM Grand, Luxor, and the enduring Tropicana, which has the good fortune to be in the right place at the right time. On that one intersection you will find more hotel rooms than exist in the city of San Francisco.

But high debt and a shifting population of gamblers is only part of the problem with these ailing hotels.

"The fact is," says Glenn Schaeffer, "that a lot of these places were poorly managed even when they had a competitive product, and now comes obsolescence. Nobody thought there was obsolescence in Las Vegas, but there is, and we have been seeing it since the nineteen-eighties. You can't take a nineteen-fifties box or a nineteen-sixties box and transform it into a thirty-story glass pyramid with an atrium, like Luxor; you can't transform it into an Excalibur, or an MGM Grand. When Circus opened in 1968 it was a tent, so we were able to build onto it and expand around it on our big piece of property. We had the real estate to grow on and the money and ideas to make it happen. Many of these places don't."

"Most bankrupt hotels don't close," says Tom Hantges, the Las Vegas stock analyst. "They just reorganize to get rid of debt."

That may save a few, according to Schaeffer, but it will just delay the day of reckoning for others.

Schaeffer doesn't think we are going to see empty buildings on Las Vegas Boulevard. "I certainly hope not," he says. "Like any mall, you don't want any dark, empty stores." But the sad fact is that some hotels are simply not going to come back. Reorganizing won't be enough for many of them.

"These older places have to figure out how to keep customers. Unless you have a well-defined market niche in this industry, and do something well, you're in trouble. It's no longer enough to be just a big building that offers gaming.

That's not competitive. This is the age of the total entertainment environment. MGM, Excalibur, Luxor, and Treasure Island are the new product."

There is one saving grace. The three major stores that are going up will help the others. Many of the older places will become bedrooms for some of the big themed hotels. Not everybody can stay at MGM, Luxor, or the Excalibur.

None of this talk about big themed hotels and the family market and Disney World, by the way, should discourage the gambler who still wants the taint of immorality in his or her gaming holiday. Las Vegas will not become a playpen for tots. There will still be plenty of ways to get sophisticated gaming action. The Hilton hotels, while not noted for innovation, are very solid and well run. They are not for kids. Neither is Caesars, or even the Mirage, or the Golden Nugget, or any of the other casinos downtown. In fact, even after the new casinos are built, three-quarters of the gaming houses will be gloriously unsuitable for children. The Rio, for example, is famous for the skimpy outfits on its cocktail waitresses, and anybody with a good eye can see that a breast man does the hiring at the Imperial Palace.

Sex, after all, has been a major ingredient in Las Vegas's success. Trip Gabriel, in his *Times Magazine* piece, writes:

> *It was Siegel's business masterstroke to link the thrill of gaming with the anticipation and payoff of sex. Suggestively clad cigarette girls, cocktail waitresses, and showgirls were everywhere. Inevitably, some worked as call girls for the house eliminating the infelicitous appearance of open solicitation.*

*That formula—sex, luxury, and the mob's hand in
the till—built and powered Las Vegas for 20 years.*

Perhaps Las Vegas is no longer "Sin Town USA," but
neither is it a Baptist convention. (Actually, there has been at
least one Baptist convention in Las Vegas, and it was Bill
Bennett who said, "They came with the Ten Commandments
in one hand, and a ten-dollar bill in the other, and they didn't
break either one.") There are still, for example, plenty of
hookers in town. They are perhaps a better-dressed and more
refined group than they once were, no longer so obvious that
a deacon's wife from Arkansas could spot one. But they are
there in sufficient numbers, and always will be, discreetly
working the hotel lounges or advertising in local entertainment magazines. When Las Vegas is courting the family
trade, it certainly doesn't want prostitutes to look like prostitutes, but on the other hand, if the widget convention has to
announce, "Oh by the way, boys, the last hooker left Vegas
yesterday," there will be a lot fewer widget-makers flying into
McCarran.

And if there's a little less flesh bared in revues these
days, it's because there are fewer revues. But plenty of risqué
entertainment is still available. A lot of guys figure, If you
can't drink booze and watch women dance naked, then what's
the point in going? Boys, after all, will be boys, and one of
their favorite places to be boys is Las Vegas.

One sinful casualty of the times, however, will probably
be the so-called "sex tease" clubs. The cops are out to close
these clubs, not because they provide sex, but because they
don't. A sex tease club, and there are several in Las Vegas,

is a small, very dark barroom where nearly naked girls lure male tourists in with undisguised promises of sex. The customer is then given a price list, usually from a burly male bartender, for various "bottles of champagne," and told that he can take his champagne into the back room with the girl and do whatever he likes. It is made clear, from the winking of eyes and the toning of voices, that the prices correspond to various sexual thrills.

There are only two problems with the transaction. One is that the prices are sometimes incredible. There are $300 bottles of champagne, $500 bottles, $1,000 bottles. One poor soul from Tennessee reported dropping $8,000 in such a place in January 1993. The other problem with the transaction is that for all this money you're spending you don't get any sex. What the customer gets is a chance to drink his champagne with a beautiful young lady, but as soon as the customer gets frisky, he is invited to leave by a man twice his size.

When people in Las Vegas talk about the future these days they talk primarily about three projects which will add 10,000 rooms to the town's inventory, 2,000 rooms more than all of Atlantic City. The biggest of the three is the MGM Grand Hotel and Theme Park, which with 5,000 rooms will be the biggest hotel in the world. The controlling hand of this project belongs to Kirk Kerkorian who as of October 1992 controlled 73 percent of the company. Kerkorian is no stranger to Las Vegas. He developed the International, which is now the Las Vegas Hilton, and the original MGM Grand, which is now the financially troubled Bally's. Both were the largest hotels in Las Vegas when they were built.

The MGM Grand, which *The New York Times* describes as "the boldest statement yet that children and gambling really can go together," will have a Hollywood theme. Visitors will enter the resort through the paws of a nine-story golden lion and go on to a 15,000-square-foot "Emerald City" attraction. The MGM will have 171,500 square feet of casino space, 3,500 slots, 150 tables, and a 33-acre theme park with 12 rides, dozens of other attractions, and a perfunctory selection of restaurants and shops. It will also have a sports arena bigger than Madison Square Garden, and a child care center.

Veldon Simpson, the architect for Luxor, is also the architect for the MGM Grand's hotel and casino, though not the theme park.

"It will be the largest hotel in the world," he says. "This project is so huge that they had to buy the Tropicana's golf course and part of another existing property. It will be a large cross-shaped building that is all in emerald-green glass. In the center part of the whole thing you walk in through the lion, which is eighty-eight feet tall. That's a lot smaller than the sphinx at Luxor, but still pretty phenomenal. Then you will be confronted with Emerald City, under a huge crystal dome. And you'll be surrounded by huge green glass crystals. There's a yellow brick road that runs right through the entrance."

The *Wizard of Oz* theme, says Simpson, is only part of the MGM story. "There will be different themes throughout," he says. "Basically, it is overall a motion picture theme, with the theme park being the back lot of a large movie studio."

MGM is being built in the belief, says the company's chief executive, Robert R. Maxey, "that we can turn this place from being a gambling town into *the* great American vacation spot."

Industry watchers, like Hantges at USA Capital Management, have projected that more than 10 million people will visit the MGM extravaganza in its first year, and he, for one, believes that MGM will have total revenues of $500 million in its first year, and about 12 percent of the Las Vegas gaming revenue pie.

"The three major projects currently under development," he says, "will catapult Las Vegas into the family travel segment of the tourist market, an area in which it has never truly competed." In other words, he's saying that Orlando had better watch out for its backside.

Competitors like CCE and the Mirage don't seem to be worried that the big new hotel will make their stores look like last year's product. In fact, the guiding belief behind all of this building is not "Our building will be better than your building, so people will come here instead." The belief is that the combined buildings will elevate Las Vegas to new heights of attractiveness as a destination, and the entire market will expand. Instead of drawing 21 million, the city can draw 25 million or 30 million. These companies are not simply interested in getting a bigger slice of the pie but are also keen to expand the pie.

"The competition between CCE and the Mirage is not the battle of the titans," Schaeffer told a reporter for *The Las Vegas Business Press*. "The thing that's important is to grow Las Vegas. We can do that together." He also says, "What Steve Wynn and Bill Bennett do is put product on the Strip that the whole world has to see, and they come, and we help sell everybody else."

Wynn has said that he expects a Las Vegas synergy like that of Orlando, where Disney World draws people to town and other attractions benefit. Quoted in the *Times Magazine* article, Wynn said:

Kerkorian's going to hire a sales force to fill those 5,000 rooms. And they'll reach out further to sell the family aspect of this town. And where are they going to come? To the Mirage. They're coming for the midway, we benefit. This is what's going to protect Las Vegas in its next generation ... the fact that we're not building little dumps with casinos anymore, we're building fantasy resorts. Kirk Kerkorian is going to be successful just like I was, and then there will be nobody spending $60 million on little twerp joints anymore. We spend a billion, two, and the game gets richer, the game gets more exciting.

At Hilton, the only big player in town that is not building a theme park, the view is also positive. Michael Stirling, whose job is to pull in international players, says, "The Orientals absolutely love theme parks. Disneyland and the other parks on the West Coast are extremely popular with them. If you're trying to convince your wife to go to Las Vegas, it's a lot easier with a theme park. That's like saying, 'Dear, they have a big Gucci store.' They just can't sell the trip to their wives by saying, 'Oh, and I may lose thousands of dollars.' That's just not the way to approach your wife and family."

A second major project is the Mirage's Treasure Island. Dan Lee, the same individual who helped take Circus Circus public when he was at Drexel, is now senior vice president for finance and development at the Mirage. He says the new project will be a 3,000-room sister facility to the Mirage, built right next door on the Mirage property. The price tag will run about $430 million.

"We're going to have three thousand more rooms," Lee says, "and we will be more oriented toward the middle market. There will be family shows with a pirate theme, big action spectaculars with an outdoor theater that will reproduce a village out of Stevenson's *Treasure Island.* Every hour there will be a free live reenactment of a battle between pirate ships."

The third big project will, of course, be CCE's pyramid-shaped Luxor.

Veldon Simpson says the effect of all this building is "making the rest of the Las Vegas skyline look tired and dated."

"I think," he says, "that it will force everybody else to come up with something spectacular to stay in the hunt. Hilton, I think, will be forced to do something spectacular in order to survive."

However, Simpson says that being spectacular doesn't necessarily mean you have to spend $1 billion, or even $600 million.

"You don't have to spend a lot of money to do unique things," he says. "There is nothing more comfortable than staying at a little boutique hotel, and there are creative things you can do to make such a place an attraction. You just can't be dull anymore."

If Luxor, MGM, and Treasure Island are the brides of the new Las Vegas, there are also a few bridesmaids primping for the big 1993–94 unveilings.

At the beginning of 1993 Bob Stupak, at Vegas World, was erecting a 119-story, 1,012-foot supertower called the Stratosphere, said to be the world's tallest tower and ninth-tallest structure. If the project is completed, and some say it will not be, the top of the tower will be a fifteen-story glass pod containing a revolving restaurant, indoor and outdoor observation decks, and a thrill ride of some sort.

By October of 1992 Caesars had already added to its allure by installing animatronics as well as the Forum Shops at Caesars Palace, a Vegas version of Rodeo Drive, made to look like a Roman village.

The financially troubled Bally's also was in the game. In 1993 Bally's agreed to construct a monorail that would link it to the MGM Grand. Two days later Bally's announced a $12-million expansion, which would include a series of moving sidewalks, gardens, fountains, and a new plaza with an eight-foot orb that will seem to magically hover over cascading waters.

A few entertainers joined the game. In December 1992 the Jackson family, led by Jermaine and Tito, announced plans for an $87-million, 400-room resort on Tropicana Road. A few months later Debbie Reynolds and her husband, Richard Hamlett, bought an old casino off the Strip and began renovations to turn it into the Hollywood Hotel Casino and Motion Picture Museum.

The original Circus Circus hotel is also in the expansion game. In August 1993 Circus Circus Las Vegas opened Grand Slam Canyon, a five-acre water-themed attraction built above the hotel's west parking lot. The park features 140-foot peaks, a 90-foot waterfall, and a coursing river, roller coaster, and flume ride along with creeks, water slides, and gondolas. The entire park is covered by a vented pink space-frame, like a biosphere, to make it usable in any weather. There is an admission fee for use of the canyon, but, another sign of creeping Disneyism, CCE has announced a "master ticket" that will let a visitor experience Grand Slam Canyon, the Showscan theaters at the Excalibur, and the high-tech rides at Luxor for one price.

Meanwhile, back at Glitter Gulch, plans were being discussed for something called "the Fremont Street Experience." This was a proposal for a giant awning to be stretched over Fremont Street from Main Street to Fourth. All sorts of special events and celebrations could be staged under the $70-million awning. There also would be something described as "an amazing Disney-like light parade," possibly a redundancy downtown, where the biggest tourist attraction is the flashing colored lights that make midnight look like noon. Nonetheless, downtown desperately needs such a transfusion, even more so with the arrival of the three new casinos out on the Strip. Or, as one downtown casino owner put it, "If we don't get the awning, you can have the keys to my place."

(By the end of 1993 the awning project had become more urgent with the cancellation of another planned downtown project. Church Street Station was to be a $170-million downtown retail and entertainment complex under the Park Hotel, developed by Bob Snow, who built the First Church Street Station in—guess where—Orlando.)

The Sahara, the Stardust, Palace Station, the Desert Inn, and the Rio were also in the midst of major expansion projects. And there were other signs that Las Vegas is busting out all over. Silver Canyon, a $600-million destination resort on 1,300 acres in the foothills of the Black Mountains, was at least on the drawing board. This development was to include a hotel and a 350-room resort without gambling, to be managed by Caesars World. Steve Wynn, of course, had bought the troubled Dunes. And at McCarran Airport they were getting ready to spend $300 million for a new runway and the resurfacing of old runways. Perhaps most significant in the long run, by the middle of 1992 it was becoming clear that much of the "new Las Vegas" won't even be in Las Vegas. New Orleans had opted for a huge new casino, Hartford was talking to Steve Wynn, and Glenn Schaeffer was racking up frequent flyer miles with trips to Chicago.

The Chicago plan, while not breathing well by the fall of 1992, was also not dead. Under the proposal CCE, Hilton, and Caesars World would build a $2-billion casino and entertainment complex; that's about twice the cost of the MGM Grand. The resort, which would house four or five casinos, would make Chicago "the most exciting destination in the world," according to Giovenco at the Hilton.

(By the beginning of 1993 Giovenco had moved on to ITT-Sheraton, which had decided to get seriously into the gaming business. In June 1993 ITT-Sheraton bought the Desert Inn for $160 million. Shortly after that, Giovenco resigned.)

Billed as a family entertainment center, the project was to consist of a 100-acre complex with a performing arts center, and a high-tech theme park with computer and movie-simulation rides like the ones Trumbull has developed for Luxor.

While the project had its supporters, like Chicago's Mayor Daley, it also had its detractors, like Illinois governor Jim Edgar, who says, "I really think we have enough gambling in Illinois now."

The arguments for and against the center were the same ones that were being heard in New Orleans and Hartford, Connecticut. A casino will provide jobs, attract tourists, pour money into the economy and the treasury, and bring conventions to town, said some. A casino will bring crime, compulsive gambling, and the kind of reputation that will drive conventions away, said others.

By October 1992, however, Schaeffer made it clear that if the project didn't go in Chicago, something like it would be offered elsewhere in the Midwest. The choices were certainly not infinite, or, as one executive associated with the project said, "Let's face it, you can't put a two-billion-dollar entertainment complex in downtown Detroit and turn Detroit into a tourist attraction." However, given the country's growing acceptance of gambling, the high rate of unemployment, and the nearly empty vaults of most state and city governments, it seemed likely that the Chicago project would find a home somewhere.

The idea that the "Las Vegas of the mind" might open branch offices in Chicago, New Orleans, or Hartford is probably good news for the CCE's and Hiltons of this world which have the cash and the wherewithal to enter the new markets. But most of the people who benefit from Nevada gaming won't benefit from Connecticut gaming or Illinois gaming, and that is why the state is trying to stay one step ahead.

"Burying my head in the sand won't change what is happening," Nevada governor Bob Miller told a 1992 summit meeting of the state's top gaming executives.

Stock analyst Tom Hantges estimates that Las Vegas now has enough advantages to keep it at least five to seven years ahead of everybody else.

While the idea of five-year leads and seven-year leads seems to imply a pie-slice philosophy, Glenn Schaeffer, when he articulates the future of his city and his industry, seems less concerned about slices and more attuned to the expanding pie theory.

In his "How Does Nevada Compete?" paper, Schaeffer writes of the "Super Southwest," and says it is "the most economically dynamic and fastest-growing region in the United States over the coming decade."

Southern California, Schaeffer says, is the center of this activity, and it will grow as the role of the Pacific Rim in global economics grows. "Los Angeles is already an international city," he writes, "and, a surprise to many, already stands, in its suburban sprawl, as the largest manufacturing location in this country."

Schaeffer envisions a Los Angeles–Las Vegas nexus,

and compares Las Vegas to the Coney Island of years ago, a park to "amuse the millions," while nearby New York grew into the world's most prosperous city. He writes:

> *The consumer's appetite for entertainment as their relative affluence increases will be dramatic. Certainly, relative income growth in the Super Southwest will lead the U.S. in coming years. The futurist Herman Kahn believed leisure and recreation would be the great industry in the U.S. by the early 21st century. It's striking that, in 1990, the fastest-rising category of spending in American households was entertainment, which moved up to third place in the American consumer's overall budget, right behind housing and food, but surpassing clothing.*
>
> *Entertainment is a dynamic consumer category, for its sells, ultimately, to the imagination and the consumer's desire for new experiences, which are defining human traits, and nearly infinite in their demand potential. You don't run out of closet space for fun.*

Schaeffer sees in the future of Las Vegas a critical massing of entertainment product that will have no equal except in Orlando, Florida. He sees mainstream travelers taking an "obligatory" vacation in Las Vegas for an experience that "you won't get on Indian reservations or riverboats."

While the popular press has been smitten recently with the novel idea of children in Las Vegas, Schaeffer sees the two most important consumer groups, in terms of spending power, as "the ever-present baby boomers and, increasingly, the golden grays." The fastest-growing consumer segment, he says, "is the long-lived American generation, fifty-five-plus, consumers who own houses, possess pensions, and receive social security." These people, he notes, don't have bulging house payments, don't buy so much food now that the kids are gone, and don't dress up much.

"But they do buy entertainment," he says. And he's hoping they will buy it from him.

Obligatory trips? Dynamic consumer categories? Defining human traits? It is difficult, even amusing, to imagine such phrases passing through the lips of Bugsy Siegel. Clearly something new is going on here. Just as Bugsy had a dream that he wanted to build in the desert, a new dream is being built. This one is being built with stockholders' money, under the watchful eyes of accountants. Certainly, as in any business, pencils are being pushed, micromanagers are gumming up the works, and cost effectiveness is being measured down to the penny. But in the glowing eruption of Steve Wynn's volcano, in the literary allusions of Glenn Schaeffer's prose, and in the sheer brassiness of Bob Stupak's tower, there is ample evidence that Las Vegas has not lost its dreamers. There are still Bill Bennetts. And even Jay Sarnos. And they are out there in the desert building the strangest sorts of places for the person who likes "the flip of the card, the roll of the dice, the sound of guys shouting 'Yo' at the crap table, and the way young women shriek for joy when they drain a hundred silver dollars out of a slot machine."

And they are gambling some very serious money in the hope that Glenn Schaeffer's fellow Iowa Writers' Workshop graduate, W. P. Kinsella, was right when he wrote, "If you build it, he will come."

Epilogue: The Banishment

They have a saying in Las Vegas: "That's why they call it gambling."

Let's say you're sitting at a blackjack table. You've got a big bet on the table. The dealer has a six showing and you have eleven on your first two cards. (If you don't know anything about blackjack, trust me, that's a good situation.) So you double your bet. You get a two, and the dealer ends up with twenty-one. You were looking like a big winner, and now you are a big loser. As the dealer rakes your chips over to his side of the table, the guy next to you says, "That's why they call it gambling."

In other words, at the gaming table, nothing is a lock, nothing is for sure.

By February 1993 I had completed this book and delivered it to my publisher. Under the terms of my agree-
ment with CCE, Glenn Schaeffer was allowed to read the
manuscript and offer corrections of fact. When I got the
manuscript back from him I began to make changes, as well
as additions that the publisher had asked for.

On the night of February 17, 1993, I was scheduled to
conduct my final telephone interview with Schaeffer, to discuss the additions. I called him at the appointed time.
"Glenn's in a meeting," his secretary, Carole Parker, said.
"Can you call back later?"

I called back later. I sensed commotion. Finally, Glenn
came on the phone. "Gary, I can't do the interview," he said.
While I found him gregarious in person, Schaeffer had always been a man of few words on the telephone, and this was
no exception. I said I'd get back to him.

The next day Glenn Schaeffer resigned as president of
Circus Circus Enterprises, Inc.

Gary, I thought, you've got great timing. Here you have
managed to complete a book which says, among other things,
that Glenn Schaeffer is the future of gaming, on the very day
that he quits his job in the gaming industry.

Right from the beginning I had told Glenn Schaeffer that
I was not looking to "get" the company. I was not looking for
scandal or controversy. I just wanted to write fairly about an industry that was not always treated fairly in print. Controversy,
it turned out, was merely waiting for me to finish the book.
Glenn's resignation, said *The Wall Street Journal,* "sent a chill
through Wall Street." Industry analysts, according to *The New*

York Times, "were stunned by the news." Everybody was taken by surprise.

Suddenly, investors and the business press had doubts about Circus Circus. The company which I had chosen as my model of excellence now had people worried.

The Glenn Schaeffer story was quickly placed into a larger context. Three months before Schaeffer's departure, Mel Larsen had been obliged to leave when Bennett eliminated his job. A month after Schaeffer left, James Muir, CCE's chief operating officer, resigned. A Circus Circus insider and an outside expert on the industry both told me, "More heads will roll." One stock analyst told *Business Week,* "You have to wonder why that much management leaves at the same time." Rumors began leaking out of Las Vegas. Two workers had been killed in separate accidents during the construction of Luxor. (True.) Giant cranes were trapped inside the pyramid and nobody knew how to get them out. (Not true.) Luxor was recklessly overbudget and behind schedule. (Not true.) Glenn Schaeffer had plotted a palace coup. (Not true.) Circus Circus, it seemed, had finally had a losing season in public relations if not in revenue. (In fact, in terms of profit, things were more than rosy. For the year ending January 31, 1993, Circus Circus had a record $117 million in net income on revenues of $843 million, sustaining its position as the nation's most profitable gaming company.)

My first instinct after learning about Glenn's resignation was to a) Find out what the hell was going on, and b) Rewrite. Perhaps I had been a bit hasty in saying that Glenn Schaeffer was the heir apparent at Circus Circus. Perhaps I was unwise in telling my readers that they could probably bet their bankroll on Schaeffer to take over CCE. It is, after all, hard to be the most important person in an industry when you don't even have a job in that industry.

But no, I decided. I would not rewrite. For one thing, there was little time if we were to meet an October 1993 publishing date to coincide with the opening of Luxor. But, beyond that, everything I wrote was true in the context in which it was written. Schaeffer really had been the heir apparent, with emphasis on "apparent." And even Phil Hevener, a guy who knows a thousand times more about the gaming industry than I do, said that Glenn Schaeffer was "the face of gaming on Wall Street."

Besides, this didn't really change anything. Circus Circus would continue to make money, and somebody else would just have to be the most important person in gaming in the 1990s. For all I knew, it could be Schaeffer in some other role.

As for the part about what the hell was going on, I got on the phone. Schaeffer was a good soldier. He didn't bad-mouth Bennett or Circus Circus. He was still a "consultant" to CCE, a polite arrangement under which he was not allowed to take employment elsewhere in the gaming industry for the rest of the year. There many reasons for Schaeffer not to say anything unpleasant, not the least of which was that he probably still owned a bushel of stock in the company.

"It's better if you call Circus Circus," he said.

"They'll give me the straight story?" I asked.

"I didn't say that," he said.

I already had a pretty good idea of what had happened.

Bennett had once said to me, "I'm going to stay here until I'm sure this fellow"—meaning Schaeffer—"can run the place right. After all, I still own a few shares of stock."

I thought at the time he was joking. Now I knew he wasn't.

As Bill Bennett describes Glenn Schaeffer's resignation, Schaeffer was catching hell over the Chicago project, and he didn't take the criticism well. Bennett thought Schaeffer had spent too much money pursuing the joint project with Hilton and Caesars. Bennett says it was not spent wisely, too much was spent on public relations.

"It was all done in a sloppy manner," Bennett says. "I don't think they set it up right."

In fairness to Schaeffer, equal amounts were spent by CEO's Barron Hilton (Hilton) and Henry Gluck (Caesars).

All of which reminds me of something Schaeffer said when we were discussing Bennett's rules of business.

"Sometimes you'll explain to him what you want to do, in your department, or with a contract or policy. Then he'll lean back and think it over, and he'll say, 'Well, that's not the way I would do it. But we're going to do it your way.' This means that you now own it, you've just acquired equity in this thing, and you'd better see that it turns out well. 'And,' he will remind you, 'I reserve bitching rights.'"

But there was more to this than bitching rights over the Chicago debacle.

"We got into a beef," Bennett allegedly told *The New York Times,* though Bennett tells me he didn't say that.

In any case the beef, or whatever you want to call it, was the same beef that Rick Banis had had with Bennett a year earlier. What it amounts to is "You said you were going to retire, but you don't seem to be doing it."

Banis, also highly regarded by Wall Street, had resigned when it was made clear to him that Bennett was not going to step down soon and turn over the reins. Now here it was all over again. Bennett had decided that after Luxor was built, he would not go to his $11-million, seven-acre estate in La Jolla, California, and play with his speedboats and biplane. He was going to stick around a while, which, at least to Schaeffer's ears, was a way of saying he lacked confidence in the younger man. Before Schaeffer's seat had even cooled off, Bennett had moved 55-year-old Clyde Turner, former CFO at the Mirage, into Schaeffer's office.

While the business press took the slant that Bennett simply didn't want to step down, Bennett tells it differently. He says yes, he wants to quit, but his replacements keep disappointing him. They spend too much money, they are not as tight-fisted as he is, and that is not in keeping with the philosophy that has made Circus Circus great.

While I can't say that I expected Schaeffer's resignation, I can say that I perceived differences in the men's styles, which, as it turned out, played a part in things. It had always seemed to me that Bill Bennett was the kind of guy who would go into a guest room with a plunger to unblock a toilet if there was no one else to do it and it would save a customer. Schaeffer, I thought, would arrange to get the customer another room, and if the hotel was full he would get the customer a room at a more expensive place. Still, it seemed to me, style was style, and results were results, and nobody could deny that the company had done well with Schaeffer as

CFO and president. "Glenn," Mel Larsen had said, "has made millionaires out of a lot of people." But that apparently was not enough.

After Schaeffer resigned, Bennett said, "I told him that he needed to learn the operations side of the business. He knew I was upset that he hadn't gotten involved in operations. He thought casinos were like oil wells; you turn them on and they pour out money."

The stock market did not take Schaeffer's departure well. The CCE stock, which had recently been at 50, fell as low as 43. Wall Street was concerned, of course, that CCE no longer had Schaeffer, but even more, the Street was concerned for the first time about Bennett. Would he drive out every smart cookie who came along? Would he be threatened by the very men whom Wall Street trusted? Would the company develop morale problems? Would Bennett ever actually retire? Wall Street hates questions. The money goes where there are answers.

In the end, all of this is more about egos than business. Nobody wants to settle for the silver medal.

"Glenn Schaeffer could have stayed," Phil Hevener says. "He could have taken his bawling out from the board of directors and stayed on as president, and he probably would have become chairman. But his ego wouldn't let him do that. He and Rick Banis made the same mistake. They thought Bill Bennett would lose interest in running the company his way. They were wrong."

No matter which side you took, everybody agreed that Bill Bennett was in control. Though by this time he only owned seven percent of the company's stock, he could claim the allegiance of at least 90 percent of the board of directors, and the weight of history was on his side. He was, after all, the man who had built the company. And the company was still the best in the business.

As for putting a date on Bennett's retirement, you'd have a better chance at picking six winning keno numbers. When he hired Clyde Turner, Bennett told *Business Week,* "I've wanted that rascal for years. I can see him running this company." But he also said, "I don't imagine I'll be around here in seven or eight years. I'd rather be on my boat."

Of course, these recent events caused repercussions for me and my book. Glenn Schaeffer had been my main source, and even though I am an independent journalist I was, in the corporate mentality, a "Schaeffer man." If I had worked for Circus Circus, I might have lost my job. But I wasn't an employee, so all I lost were my lines of communication. A book that should have been a public relations dream for the company was suddenly problematic. I had praised the company, sure, but I also had praised Schaeffer, and the company had let him go. What were stockholders to think?

Was this book a good thing or a bad thing for Circus Circus? The folks at the top were divided. The result was several months of silence during which time a number of loose ends could not be tied up, and the October publishing date was lost.

To make a very long story short, Bill Bennett in the end was gracious, as always. He accepted the fact that Glenn Schaeffer would remain prominent in the book even though he was gone from the corporation. Bennett invited me back to Las Vegas and set me up with tours of the latest projects: Grand Slam Canyon and Luxor.

It was there that I returned to Glenn Schaeffer's office not to speak with Schaeffer, but with its new occupant, Clyde Turner.

At the time of Glenn Schaeffer's resignation Turner had recently retired after almost fourteen years with Steve Wynn, first at the Golden Nugget and later at the Mirage. Turner had run the Golden Nugget hotels in downtown Las Vegas and Atlantic City.

"At one point," Turner says, "when there was a Golden Nugget in Atlantic City, I would commute to New Jersey from Nevada every Monday and fly home on Thursday or Friday."

Like Bennett, Turner had another career before gaming. He had had an accounting business which he built into a statewide firm, the largest in Nevada. In 1970 the governor appointed him to the Gaming Commission. During his three years there he authored the first revisions to the accounting regulations for gaming in Nevada—called the internal controls—regulating everything from the way money is counted to the way dice are handled. When Turner left the Mirage, it was to start yet another business.

"Most of my accounting business had been related to construction," he says, "and after the Mirage I wanted to go into the construction business. I'd always wanted to start a family business so I could get my sons involved in it. But during my years at the Mirage and the Golden Nugget, I had always considered Bill Bennett a friend, and I've always had enormous respect for the man. So when he called, I agreed to

305

talk to him about coming to Circus Circus. And, frankly, the conversation was so positive that I agreed to come out of retirement."

Turner was quick to add that he doesn't see this as an interim move. "I'm here to stay," he says. "If and when Mr. Bennett chooses to leave I hope I'll be one of the people considered to take over. But I'm not pushing him out. I like the man and I like working with him."

Sixteen years older than Glenn Schaeffer, Turner possesses a style very different from that of his predecessor. He is more homespun, more relaxed, more inclined to digress into non-business talk. He had just gotten back from Australia on CCE business, but he talked first about how nice the people were and how clean they kept the city of Sydney.

By this time the seas beneath the Circus Circus ship had calmed and things were, in many ways, better than ever. The stock had found its true level once more, and the summer stockholders meeting had voted a three-for-two split. By August a CCE share was selling for almost $40, the equivalent of $60 in the pre-split arithmetic.

Like Schaeffer, Turner had found that much of his day was spent comforting stockholders and counting, depositing, spending, or borrowing large amounts of money.

"My first job was to go to the investors and re-instill confidence that the company was still going somewhere," he says. "The stock price is related to whether or not we are a growth company, and we are. I had to go and spread the message that I was going to support Bill Bennett and his vision. Now we are growing faster than ever. The second significant thing I did was, I went out and raised three hundred million dollars at the lowest rate in nineteen years to make sure we had a capital base underneath our footing. Next on the agenda was to go to a group of sixty banks to expand our credit line to six hundred fifty million, or possibly eight hundred fifty million."

All this low-cost money will be available to support a variety of new projects, including the Sydney, Australia, project.

"It's still in the proposal stage," Turner says. "We've got a plan and we've got three local architects working on it as part of a special urban planning team. It will be a beautiful building that has to live up to the standards of the Sydney Opera House. The people of Sydney are very sensitive about what is put there. All they have now are slot clubs, and those are in the suburbs. If we win the bid for this casino we will have a twelve-year monopoly."

Australia is not the only possible international location for a Circus Circus hotel. The company has put together a joint venture with Caesars Palace and Hilton for a casino in Windsor, Ontario, Canada.

Meanwhile, back in the United States CCE has climbed aboard the riverboat craze in Mississippi.

"We have a site in Tunica, Mississippi, the nearest site to Memphis. We hope to open by next May. It's on the river, of course. All Mississippi casinos have to be on the river, but they don't have to be floating boats out in the water. They were wise enough down there to see that that would create traffic problems on the river, and increase the chances of someone being hurt," says Turner.

Even closer to home, Circus Circus is building again in Reno, which seems to be experiencing a resurgence.

"The Reno project is not as big as Luxor, but we think it is really very high style for Reno. It will be quite significant. It's a hotel with the theme of a Spanish seaport on the island of Atlantis. There will be some neat stuff inside. We'll have fifteen hundred to two thousand rooms and a one-hundred-thousand-square-foot casino. The architecture will be quite modern, with a big bubble dome."

The Reno project, being built between the existing Circus Circus, Reno, and the Eldorado, will be a joint project of Circus Circus and the Eldorado. Turner says we are going to see a lot more joint projects in the future.

"But not the type of joint projects we brought to Chicago," he explains. "As gaming spreads to new locations we are going to see a lot of joint ventures between local people and established gaming companies."

With the stewardship of all this growth, it is not surprising that Turner, like Wynn and Kerkorian, is solidly committed to the expanding pie theory of the new Las Vegas. He says, "The only way anybody can get hurt with all these new projects coming on is if these companies with the big new projects don't expand the market by their entry. I believe the market will expand dramatically. If there is any risk to be evaluated it is the risk Kerkorian is taking with MGM. Circus Circus has always targeted a family market, but it's not a theme park market. Kerkorian is really coming at the theme park market—the theme park is the whole guts of it—and that's the risk, though I'm sure his prices will be competitive. In fact, Grand Slam Canyon is really our competitive move in response to Kerkorian. What we have done with Grand Slam Canyon is to say there is no way that we can lose, because the theme park customer who goes to MGM will want to visit Grand Slam Canyon. We are going to get whatever market he reaches, that's part of our whole strategy. Grand Slam Canyon is designed to make a profit, it is not a giveaway.

"One way to look at all of this is like Disneyworld when they have a new attraction. People come back for another look. But what is also true of Disney, and is true of Las Vegas, is that people never see the whole thing on one visit. I know when I go to Disneyland I either get tired before I see the whole thing, or the kids I'm with get tired. It's the same in Las Vegas. You can't see it all. You have to come back."

If Turner believes in expanding pies, he also believes in the middle market as Bennett does, and neither man has illusions about the kind of person who will sleep in the high-roller suites at Luxor.

"Steve Wynn spent three million dollars a suite for some villas that he has for high rollers, and in retrospect I'm not sure that he would do it again," Turner says. "We won't have anything like that. Luxor is aimed at what you might call the upper middle-market, people who will play craps and twenty-one at a fairly high level. We will have suites, sure, but this is Circus Circus. We're not talking about sheiks and high rollers from Hong Kong."

One thing Turner does have in common with Schaeffer is a keen mind and an ability to articulate the changes in the gaming industry with reference to literature, history, and popular culture.

"We have," he says, "the icon of the riverboat, which has

allowed people to consider passing laws that allow gaming to be conducted on riverboats. I think we've all been scripted from childhood through movies like *Showboat,* with Howard Keel, and *Mark Twain* to see some romance attached to the riverboat. Gambling has always been a part of that scenario. It convinced us that riverboats were not formidable. That is different from the icon of Damon Runyon's *Guys and Dolls* with New York crap shooters and garment district guys playing in alleys.

"So we saw the riverboats come in, first in Iowa, and then in other states. They made gaming palatable. But what is now happening is that this change in people's beliefs about gaming has allowed new conversations to take place. Circus Circus is leading a concept that is geared to convincing politicians, governors, mayors, legislatures that to just do riverboats is not a significant social contribution.

"What we are doing is bringing urban planners into our equation. We have hired our own urban planner and we don't go to any meeting with any political body without him as part of our team. His job is to pick up the sensitivity of the community, to understand their needs, and what we can do that will integrate our project into the community. That, of course, was the whole controversy in Illinois. Chicago is a city with a great deal of pride, and there was concern about how the joint project would fit into the total environment."

The openings of Luxor, MGM, and Treasure Island should not be seen as Las Vegas reaching its peak, Turner says.

"There will be more new projects," he says. "Steve Wynn is going to build on the site of the Dunes. That's one hundred sixty-five acres. Wynn has been one-upped and he doesn't take that lightly. He is going to do everything he can, artistically, to come up with something that is even more than Luxor.

"Many of the marginal properties will make comebacks. Marginal properties tend to change ownership. And people with money often go where angels fear to tread. And there will be other new projects. There will be some dynamic things over the next five or ten years that will surprise people. It will all work if we continue to do a good job with the people who come to town. The whole issue is making sure we treat guests right. We have to make sure there is enough for them to see, enough to make them happy while they are here, so that they will go home and tell other people, and they will come.

"At the end of the day, Las Vegas is the place. Despite all the new locations and the growth in gaming, Las Vegas is the place that has the infrastructure and the weather. What you have in Las Vegas will not be created anywhere else in our lifetime."

Turner is right, of course. There will not be another Las Vegas soon, maybe never. But the one that exists, the New Las Vegas, will continue to evolve, and it will do so without Glenn Schaeffer at the helm of Circus Circus. Turner will watch the company grow, just as all his predecessors did. And Bill Bennett will retire, sooner or later. And I and my friend Strunk, like millions of others, will continue to fly into McCarran and work on our betting systems, and sometimes we will win and sometimes we won't. And Glenn Schaeffer, the Iowa Writers' Workshop graduate, will remain unemployed for a while, and maybe he'll even write a book. And maybe he'll say that what he learned from all of this was that Bill Bennett was the house and he was just a player. And maybe he'll say that a player is supposed to have a good time, but lose in the long run, and that he did have a good time and he did lose. And when he drives by the stunning new pyramid on Las Vegas Boulevard, and sees all those families from Iowa gaping at a make-believe sphinx that is bigger than the real one, maybe he'll say that he thought he had a sure bet, but that somehow the dealer's hand reached out across the table and pulled away his chips.

I guess that's why they call it gambling.

Acknowledgments

There are dozens of people I want to thank for their help in the creation of this book. Among them are the Rev. Frank Strunk, Herb Winstead, Harry Fritts, Arnold Levine, Marge Levine, Allan Feldman, Billy Weinberger, Victor Rogers, Carole Parker, the staff of the Las Vegas Public Library, the staff of the UNLV library, Susan Jarvis, Joyce Gordon, Adam Fine and the staff of *Casino Journal* magazine, Phil Hevener, Tom Tomlinson, Mel Larsen, Gary O'Keefe, Dave Hardy, Bob Leightenheimer, Bill Paulos, Doug Trumbull, Drew Zellman, Gail Provost, Veldon Simpson, Charlie Parsons, John Giovenco, Dan Lee, Mike Hartzell, Tom Roche, Jay Sevigny, Mike Sloan, Bob Prince, Nancy Sturmer, Sid Diamond, Burke Smith, and Barbara Perris.

313

I want to thank my agent, Russ Galen.

I want to thank Truman Talley for having faith in the book when nobody else did.

I want to give a special thanks to Emmett Michaels, who was particularly gracious, friendly, and helpful.

I want to thank William Bennett for taking the time to share his memories and his wisdom.

And most of all, I want to thank Glenn Schaeffer, who got me the green light, filled in all the blanks, and pointed me in all the right directions.

INDEX

315

325